Thrift

Thrift

Samuel Smiles

Waking Lion Press

The views expressed in this book are the responsibility of the author and do not necessarily represent the position of the publisher. The reader alone is responsible for the use of any ideas or information provided by this book.

ISBN 978-1-4341-0264-5

Published by Waking Lion Press, an imprint of The Editorium

Any additions to original text (publisher's preface, editor's notes, etc.) © 2009 by The Editorium. All rights reserved. Printed in the United States of America.

Waking Lion Press™, the Waking Lion Press logo, and The Editorium™ are trademarks of The Editorium, LLC

The Editorium, LLC
West Valley City, UT 84128-3917
wakinglionpress.com
wakinglion@editorium.com

"Be thrifty, but not covetous; therefore give
Thy need, thine honour, and thy friend his due,
Never was scraper brave man. Get to *live,*
Then live, and use it; else it is not true
That thou hast gotten. Surely use alone
Makes money not a contemptible stone."

—George Herbert.

"To catch Dame Fortune's golden smile,
Assiduous wait upon her;
And gather gear by ev'ry wile
That's justify'd by Honour:
Not for to hide it in a hedge,
Not for a train attendant;
But for the glorious privilege
Of being Independent."

—Robert Burns.

Contents

Preface	ix
A Fable	xi
1 Industry	1
2 Habits of Thrift	9
3 Improvidence	22
4 Means of Saving	31
5 Examples of Thrift	49
6 Methods of Economy	66
7 Economy in Life Assurance	82
8 Savings Banks	91
9 Little Things	117
10 Masters and Men	132
11 The Crossleys—Masters and Men (Continued)	151
12 Living Beyond the Means	171
13 Great Debtors	190
14 Riches and Charity	210
15 Healthy Homes	231
16 The Art of Living	259

Preface

This book is intended as a sequel to "Self-Help," and "Character." It might, indeed, have appeared as an introduction to these volumes; for Thrift is the basis of Self-Help, and the foundation of much that is excellent in Character.

The author has already referred to the Use and Abuse of Money; but the lesson is worthy of being repeated and enforced. As he has already observed,—Some of the finest qualities of human nature are intimately related to the right use of money; such as generosity, honesty, justice, and self-denial; as well as the practical virtues of economy and providence. On the other hand, there are their counterparts of avarice, fraud, injustice, and selfishness, as displayed by the inordinate lovers of gain; and the vices of thoughtlessness, extravagance, and improvidence, on the part of those who misuse and abuse the means entrusted to them.

Sir Henry Taylor has observed that "industry must take an interest in its own fruits, and God has appointed that the mass of mankind shall be moved by this interest, and have their daily labour sweetened by it." The earnings and savings of industry should be intelligent for a purpose beyond mere earnings and savings. We do not work and strive for ourselves alone, but for the benefit of those who dependent upon us. Industry must know how to earn, how to spend, and how to save. The man who knows, like St. Paul, how to spare and how to abound, has a great knowledge.

Every man is bound to do what he can to elevate his social state, and to secure his independence. For this purpose he must spare from his means in order to be independent in his condition. Industry enables men to earn their living; it should also enable them to learn to live. Independence can only be established by the exercise of forethought, prudence, frugality, and self-denial. To be just as well as generous, men must deny themselves. The essence of generosity is self-sacrifice.

Preface

The object of this book is to induce men to employ their means for worthy purposes, and not to waste them upon selfish indulgences. Many enemies have to be encountered in accomplishing this object. There are idleness, thoughtlessness, vanity, vice, intemperance. The last is the worst enemy of all. Numerous cases are cited in the course of the following book, which show that one of the best methods of abating the Curse of Drink, is to induce old and young to practise the virtue of Thrift.

Much of this book was written, and some of it published, years ago; but an attack of paralysis, which compelled the author to give up writing for some time, has delayed its appearance until now. For much of the information recently received, he is indebted to Edward Crossley, Esq., Mayor of Halifax; Edward Akroyd, Esq., Halifax; George Chetwynd, Esq., General Post Office; S.A. Nichols, Esq., Over Darwen; Jeremiah Head, Esq., Middlesborough; Charles W. Sikes, Esq., Huddersfield: and numerous other correspondents in Durham, Renfrewshire, Yorkshire, Lancashire, Staffordshire, and South Wales.

The author trusts that the book will prove useful and helpful towards the purpose for which it is intended.

London, *November,* 1875.

A Fable

A grasshopper, half starved with cold and hunger, came to a well-stored beehive at the approach of winter, and humbly begged the bees to relieve his wants with a few drops of honey.

One of the bees asked him how he had spent his time all the summer, and why he had not laid up a store of food like them.

"Truly." said he, "I spent my time very merrily, in drinking, dancing, and singing, and never once thought of winter."

"Our plan is very different," said the bee; "we work hard in the summer, to lay by a store of food against the season when we foresee we shall want it; but those who do nothing but drink, and dance, and sing in the summer, must expect to starve in the winter."

Chapter 1

Industry

"Not what I have, but what I do, is my kingdom." —Carlyle.

"Productive industry is the only capital which enriches a people, and spreads national prosperity and well-being. In all labour there is profit, says Solomon. What is the science of Political Economy, but a dull sermon on this text?" —Samuel Laing.

"God provides the good things of the world to serve the needs of nature, by the labours of the ploughman, the skill and pains of the artizan, and the dangers and traffic of the merchant. . . . The idle person is like one that is dead, unconcerned in the changes and necessities of the world; and he only lives to spend his time, and eat the fruits of the earth: like a vermin or a wolf, when their time comes they die and perish, and in the meantime do no good." —Jeremy Taylor.

"For the structure that we raise, Time is with materials filled; Our todays and yesterdays Are the blocks with which we build." —Longfellow.

Thrift began with civilization. It began when men found it necessary to provide for tomorrow, as well as for today. It began long before money was invented.

Thrift means private economy. It includes domestic economy, as well as the order and management of a family.

While it is the object of Private Economy to create and promote the well-being of individuals, it is the object of Political Economy to create and increase the wealth of nations.

Industry

Private and public wealth have the same origin. Wealth is obtained by labour; it is preserved by savings and accumulations; and it is increased by diligence and perseverance.

It is the savings of individuals which compose the wealth—in other words, the well-being—of every nation. On the other hand, it is the wastefulness of individuals which occasions the impoverishment of states. So that every thrifty person may be regarded as a public benefactor, and every thriftless person as a public enemy.

There is no dispute as to the necessity for Private Economy. Everybody admits it, and recommends it. But with respect to Political Economy, there are numerous discussions,—for instance, as to the distribution of capital, the accumulations of property, the incidence of taxation, the Poor Laws, and other subjects,—into which we do not propose to enter. The subject of Private Economy, of Thrift, is quite sufficient by itself to occupy the pages of this book.

Economy is not a natural instinct, but the growth of experience, example, and forethought. It is also the result of education and intelligence. It is only when men become wise and thoughtful that they become frugal. Hence the best means of making men and women provident is to make them wise.

Prodigality is much more natural to man than thrift. The savage is the greatest of spendthrifts, for he has no forethought, no tomorrow. The prehistoric man saved nothing. He lived in caves, or in hollows of the ground covered with branches. He subsisted on shellfish which he picked up on the seashore, or upon hips and haws which he gathered in the woods. He killed animals with stones. He lay in wait for them, or ran them down on foot. Then he learnt to use stones as tools; making stone arrow-heads and spear-points, thereby utilizing his labour, and killing birds and animals more quickly.

The original savage knew nothing of agriculture. It was only in comparatively recent times that men gathered seeds for food, and saved a portion of them for next year's crop. When minerals were discovered, and fire was applied to them, and the minerals were smelted into metal, man made an immense stride. He could then fabricate hard tools, chisel stone, build houses, and proceed by unwearying industry to devise the manifold means and agencies of civilization.

The dweller by the ocean burnt a hollow in a felled tree, launched it, went to sea in it, and fished for food. The hollowed tree became a boat, held together with iron nails. The boat became a galley, a ship, a paddle-boat, a screw steamer, and the world was opened up for colonization and civilization.

Man would have continued uncivilized, but for the results of the useful labours of those who preceded him. The soil was reclaimed by his predecessors, and made to grow food for human uses. They invented tools and fabrics, and we reap the useful results. They discovered art and science, and we succeed to the useful effects of their labours.

All nature teaches that no good thing which has once been done passes utterly away. The living are ever reminded of the buried millions who have worked and won before them. The handicraft and skill displayed in the buildings and sculptures of the long-lost cities of Nineveh, Babylon, and Troy, have descended to the present time. In nature's economy, no human labour is altogether lost. Some remnant of useful effect continues to reward the race, if not the individual.

The mere material wealth bequeathed to us by our forefathers forms but an insignificant item in the sum of our inheritance. Our birthright is made up of something far more imperishable. It consists of the sum of the useful effects of human skill and labour. These effects were not transmitted by learning, but by teaching and example. One generation taught another, and thus art and handicraft, the knowledge of mechanical appliances and materials, continued to be preserved. The labours and efforts of former generations were thus transmitted by father to son; and they continue to form the natural heritage of the human race—one of the most important instruments of civilization.

Our birthright, therefore, consists in the useful effects of the labours of our forefathers; but we cannot enjoy them unless we ourselves take part in the work. All must labour, either with hand or head. Without work, life is worthless; it becomes a mere state of moral coma. We do not mean merely physical work. There is a great deal of higher work—the work of action and endurance, of trial and patience, of enterprise and philanthropy, of spreading truth and civilization, of diminishing suffering and relieving the poor, of helping the weak, and enabling them to help themselves.

"A noble heart," says Barrow, "will disdain to subsist, like a drone, upon others' labours; like a vermin to filch its food out of the public granary; or, like a shark, to prey upon the lesser fry; but it will rather outdo his private obligations to other men's care and toil, by considerable service and beneficence to the public; for there is no calling of any sort, from the sceptre to the spade, the management whereof, with any good success, any credit, any satisfaction, doth not demand much work of the head, or of the hands, or of both."

Labour is not only a necessity, but it is also a pleasure. What would otherwise be a curse, by the constitution of our physical system becomes a blessing. Our life is a conflict with nature in some respects, but it is also a co-operation with nature in others. The sun, the air, and the earth are constantly abstracting from us our vital forces. Hence we eat and drink for nourishment, and clothe ourselves for warmth.

Nature works with us. She provides the earth which we furrow; she grows and ripens the seeds that we sow and gather. She furnishes, with the help of human labour, the wool that we spin and the food that we eat. And it ought never to be forgotten, that however rich or poor we may be, all that we eat, all that we are clothed with, all that shelters us, from the palace to the cottage, is the result of labour.

Men co-operate with each other for the mutual sustenance of all. The husbandman tills the ground and provides food; the manufacturer weaves tissues, which the tailor and seamstress make into clothes; the mason and the bricklayer build the houses in which we enjoy household life. Numbers of workmen thus contribute and help to create the general result.

Labour and skill applied to the vulgarest things invest them at once with precious value. Labour is indeed the life of humanity; take it away, banish it, and the race of Adam were at once stricken with death. "He that will not work," said St. Paul, "neither shall he eat;" and the apostle glorified himself in that he had laboured with his own hands, and had not been chargeable to any man.

There is a well-known story of an old farmer calling his three idle sons around him when on his deathbed, to impart to them an important secret. "My sons," said he, "a great treasure lies hid in the estate which I am about to leave to you." The old man gasped. "Where is it hid?" exclaimed the sons in a breath. "I am about to tell you," said the old man; "you will have to dig for it—" but his breath failed him before he could impart the weighty secret; and he died. Forthwith the sons set to work with spade and mattock upon the long neglected fields, and they turned up every sod and clod upon the estate. They discovered no treasure, but they learnt to work; and when fields were sown, and the harvests came, lo! the yield was prodigious, in consequence of the thorough tillage which they had undergone. Then it was that they discovered the treasure concealed in the estate, of which their wise old father had advised them.

Industry

Labour is at once a burden, a chastisement, an honour, and a pleasure. It may be identified with poverty, but there is also glory in it. It bears witness, at the same time, to our natural wants and to our manifold needs. What were man, what were life, what were civilization, without labour? All that is great in man comes of labour;—greatness in art, in literature, in science. Knowledge—"the wing wherewith we fly to heaven"—is only acquired through labour. Genius is but a capability of labouring intensely: it is the power of making great and sustained efforts. Labour may be a chastisement, but it is indeed a glorious one. It is worship, duty, praise, and immortality,—for those who labour with the highest aims, and for the purest purposes.

There are many who murmur and complain at the law of labour under which we live, without reflecting that obedience to it is not only in conformity with the Divine will, but also necessary for the development of intelligence, and for the thorough enjoyment of our common nature. Of all wretched men, surely the idle are the most so;—those whose life is barren of utility, who have nothing to do except to gratify their senses. Are not such men the most querulous, miserable, and dissatisfied of all, constantly in a state of *ennui*, alike useless to themselves and to others—mere cumberers of the earth, who when removed are missed by none, and whom none regret? Most wretched and ignoble lot, indeed, is the lot of the idlers.

Who have helped the world onward so much as the workers; men who have had to work for necessity or from choice? All that we call progress—civilization, well-being, and prosperity—depends upon industry, diligently applied,—from the culture of a barley-stalk, to the construction of a steamship,—from the stitching of a collar, to the sculpturing of "the statue that enchants the world."

All useful and beautiful thoughts, in like manner, are the issue of labour, of study, of observation, of research, of diligent elaboration. The noblest poem cannot be elaborated, and send down its undying strains into the future, without steady and painstaking labour. No great work has ever been done "at a heat." It is the result of repeated efforts, and often of many failures. One generation begins, and another continues—the present co-operating with the past. Thus, the Parthenon began with a mud-hut; the Last Judgment with a few scratches on the sand. It is the same with individuals of the race; they begin with abortive efforts, which, by means of perseverance, lead to successful issues.

The history of industry is uniform in the character of its illustrations. Industry enables the poorest man to achieve honour, if not distinction.

Industry

The greatest names in the history of art, literature, and science, are those of labouring men. A working instrument-maker gave us the steam-engine; a barber, the spinning-machine; a weaver, the mule; a pitman perfected the locomotive;—and working men of all grades have, one after another, added to the triumphs of mechanical skill.

By the working man, we do not mean merely the man who labours with his muscles and sinews. A horse can do this. But *he* is pre-eminently the working man who works with his brain also, and whose whole physical system is under the influence of his higher faculties. The man who paints a picture, who writes a book, who makes a law, who creates a poem, is a working man of the highest order,—not so necessary to the physical sustainment of the community as the ploughman or the shepherd; but not less important as providing for society its highest intellectual nourishment.

Having said so much of the importance and the necessity of industry, let us see what uses are made of the advantages derivable from it. It is clear that man would have continued uncivilized but for the accumulations of savings made by his forefathers,—the savings of skill, of art, of invention, and of intellectual culture.

It is the savings of the world that have made the civilization of the world. Savings are the result of labour; and it is only when labourers begin to save, that the results of civilization accumulate. We have said that thrift began with civilization: we might almost have said that thrift produced civilization. Thrift produces capital; and capital is the conserved result of labour. The capitalist is merely a man who does not spend all that is earned by work.

But thrift is not a natural instinct. It is an acquired principle of conduct. It involves self-denial—the denial of present enjoyment for future, good—the subordination of animal appetite to reason, forethought, and prudence. It works for today, but also provides for tomorrow. It invests the capital it has saved, and makes provision for the future.

"Man's right of seeing the future," says Mr. Edward Denison, "which is conferred on him by reason, has attached to it the duty of providing for that future; and our language bears witness to this truth by using, as expressive of active precaution against future want, a word which in its radical meaning implies only a passive foreknowledge of the same. Whenever we speak of the *virtue of providence*, we assume that forewarned is fore-armed, To know the future is no virtue, but it is the greatest of virtues to prepare for it."[1]

But a large proportion of men do not provide for the future. They do not remember the past. They think only of the present. They preserve nothing. They spend all that they earn. They do not provide for themselves: they do not provide for their families. They may make high wages, but eat and drink the whole of what they earn. Such people are constantly poor, and hanging on the verge of destitution.

It is the same with nations. The nations which consume all that they produce, without leaving a store for future production, have no capital. Like thriftless individuals, they live from hand to mouth, and are always poor and miserable. Nations that have no capital, have no commerce. They have no accumulations to dispose of; hence they have no ships, no sailors, no docks, no harbours, no canals, and no railways. Thrifty industry lies at the root of the civilization of the world.

Look at Spain. There, the richest soil is the least productive. Along the banks of the Guadalquiver, where once twelve thousand villages existed, there are now not eight hundred; and they are full of beggars. A Spanish proverb says, "El cielo y suelo es bueno, el entresuelo malo"—The sky is good, the earth is good; that only is bad which lies between the sky and the earth. Continuous effort, or patient labour, is for the Spaniard an insupportable thing. Half through indolence, half through pride, he cannot bend to work. A Spaniard will blush to work; he will not blush to beg![2]

It is in this way that society mainly consists of two classes—the savers and the wasters, the provident and the improvident, the thrifty and the thriftless, the Haves and the Have-nots. The men who economize by means of labour become the owners of capital which sets other labour in motion. Capital accumulates in their hands, and they employ other labourers to work for them. Thus trade and commerce begin.

The thrifty build houses, warehouses, and mills. They fit manufactories with tools and machines. They build ships, and send them to various parts of the world. They put their capital together, and build railroads, harbours, and docks. They open up mines of coal, iron, and copper; and erect pumping engines to keep them clear of water. They employ labourers to work the mines, and thus give rise to an immense amount of employment.

---

1. Letters of the late Edward Denison. p. 240.
2. Eugene Poitou—Spain and its People. pp. 184—188.

All this is the result of thrift. It is the result of economizing money, and employing it for beneficial purposes. The thriftless man has no share in the progress of the world. He spends all that he gets, and can give no help to anybody. No matter how much money he makes, his position is not in any respect raised. He husbands none of his resources. He is always calling for help. He is, in fact, the born thrall and slave of the thrifty.

Chapter 2

Habits of Thrift

"Die Hauptsache ist dass man lerne sich selbst zu beherrschen." [The great matter is to learn to rule oneself.] —Goethe.

"Most men work for the present, a few for the future. The wise work for both—for the future in the present, and for the present in the future." —Guesses at Truth.

"The secret of all success is to know how to deny yourself. . . . If you once learn to get the whip-hand of yourself, that is the best educator. Prove to me that you can control yourself, and I'll say you're an educated man; and without this, all other education is good for next to nothing." —Mrs. Oliphant.

"All the world cries, 'Where is the man who will save us? We want a man! Don't look so far for this man. You have him at hand. This man—it is you, it is I, it is each one of us! . . . How to constitute oneself a man? Nothing harder, if one knows not how to will it; nothing easier, if one wills it." —Alexandre Dumas.

Competence and comfort lie within the reach of most people, were they to take the adequate means to secure and enjoy them. Men who are paid good wages might also become capitalists, and take their fair share in the improvement and well-being of the world. But it is only by the exercise of labour, energy, honesty, and thrift, that they can advance their own position or that of their class.

Society at present suffers far more from waste of money than from want of money. It is easier to make money than to know how to spend it. It is not what a man gets that constitutes his wealth, but his manner of spending and economizing. And when a man obtains by his labour more than enough for his personal and family wants, and can lay by a little store of savings besides, he unquestionably possesses the elements of social well-being. The savings may amount to little, but they may be sufficient to make him independent.

There is no reason why the highly-paid workman of today may not save a store of capital. It is merely a matter of self-denial and private economy. Indeed, the principal industrial leaders of today consist, for the most part, of men who have sprung directly from the ranks. It is the accumulation of experience and skill that makes the difference between the workman and the *no*-workman; and it depends upon the workman himself whether he will save his capital or waste it. If he save it, he will always find that he has sufficient opportunities for employing it profitably and usefully.

"When I was down in Lancashire the other day," said Mr. Cobden to his fellow-townsmen at Midhurst, "I visited a mill, in company with some other gentlemen, and that mill belonged to a person whose real name I will not mention, but whom for the present purpose I will call Mr. Smith. There could not have been less than three or four thousand persons engaged in this mill when it was at work, and there were seven hundred power-looms under one roof. As we were coming away, one of the friends who accompanied me patted the owner of the mill on the shoulder, and with that frank and manly familiarity which rather distinguishes the Lancashire race, he said, 'Mr. Smith was a working man himself twenty-five years ago, and he owes all this entirely to his own industry and frugality.' To which Mr. Smith immediately replied, in the same frank and good-humoured manner, 'Nay, I do not owe it all to myself; I married a wife with a fortune; for she was earning 9*s* 6*d*. a week as a weaver at the power-loom, when she married me.'"

Thrift of Time is equal to thrift of money. Franklin said, "Time is gold." If one wishes to earn money, it may be done by the proper use of time. But time may also be spent in doing many good and noble actions. It may be spent in learning, in study, in art, in science, in literature. Time can be economized by system. System is an arrangement to secure certain ends, so that no time may be lost in accomplishing them. Every business man must be systematic and orderly. So must every housewife. There must be a place for everything, and everything in its place. There must also be a time for everything, and everything must be done in time.

It is not necessary to show that economy is useful. Nobody denies that thrift may be practised. We see numerous examples of it. What many men have already done, all other men *may* do. Nor is thrift a painful virtue. On the contrary, it enables us to avoid much contempt and many indignities. It requires us to deny ourselves, but not to abstain from any proper enjoyment. It provides many honest pleasures, of which thriftlessness and extravagance deprive us.

Let no man say that he cannot economize. There are few persons who could not contrive to save a few shillings weekly. In twenty years, three shillings saved weekly would amount to two hundred and forty pounds; and in ten years more, by addition of interest, to four hundred and twenty pounds. Some may say that they cannot save nearly so much. Well! begin with two shillings, one shilling, or even sixpence. Begin somewhere; but, at all events, make a beginning. Sixpence a week, deposited in the savings bank, will amount to forty pounds in twenty years, and seventy pounds in thirty years. It is the *habit* of economizing and denying oneself that needs to be formed.

Thrift does not require superior courage, nor superior intellect, nor any superhuman virtue. It merely requires common sense, and the power of resisting selfish enjoyments. In fact, thrift is merely common sense in every-day working action. It needs no fervent resolution, but only a little patient self-denial. *Begin* is its device! The more the habit of thrift is practised, the easier it becomes; and the sooner it compensates the self-denier for the sacrifices which it has imposed.

The question may be asked,—Is it possible for a man working for small wages to save anything, and lay it by in a savings bank, when he requires every penny for the maintenance of his family? But the fact remains, that it *is* done by many industrious and sober men; that they do deny themselves, and put their spare earnings into savings banks, and the other receptacles provided for poor men's savings. And if some can do this, all may do it under similar circumstances,—without depriving themselves of any genuine pleasure, or any real enjoyment.

How intensely selfish is it for a person in the receipt of good pay to spend everything upon himself,—or, if he has a family, to spend his whole earnings from week to week, and lay nothing by. When we hear that a man, who has been in the receipt of a good salary, has died and left nothing behind him—that he has left his wife and family destitute—left them to chance—to live or perish anywhere,—we cannot but regard it as the most selfish thriftlessness. And yet, comparatively little is thought of such cases. Perhaps the hat goes round. Subscriptions may produce something—perhaps nothing; and the ruined remnants of the unhappy family sink into poverty and destitution.

Habits of Thrift

Yet the merest prudence would, to a great extent, have obviated this result. The curtailment of any sensual and selfish enjoyment—of a glass of beer or a screw of tobacco—would enable a man, in the course of years, to save at least something for others, instead of wasting it on himself. It is, in fact, the absolute duty of the poorest man to provide, in however slight a degree, for the support of himself and his family in the season of sickness and helplessness which often comes upon men when they least expect such a visitation.

Comparatively few people can be rich; but most have it in their power to acquire, by industry and economy, sufficient to meet their personal wants. They may even become the possessors of savings sufficient to secure them against penury and poverty in their old age. It is not, however, the want of opportunity, but the want of will, that stands in the way of economy. Men may labour unceasingly with hand or head; but they cannot abstain from spending too freely, and living too highly.

The majority prefer the enjoyment of pleasure to the practice of self-denial. With the mass of men, the animal is paramount. They often spend all that they earn. But it is not merely the working people who are spendthrifts. We hear of men who for years have been earning and spending hundreds a year, who suddenly die,—leaving their children penniless. Everybody knows of such cases. At their death, the very furniture of the house they have lived in belongs to others. It is sold to pay their funeral expenses and debts which they have incurred during their thriftless lifetime.

Money represents a multitude of objects without value, or without real utility; but it also represents something much more precious,—and that is independence. In this light it is of great moral importance.

As a guarantee of independence, the modest and plebeian quality of economy is at once ennobled and raised to the rank of one of the most meritorious of virtues. "Never treat money affairs with levity," said Bulwer; "Money is Character." Some of man's best qualities depend upon the right use of money,—such as his generosity, benevolence, justice, honesty, and forethought. Many of his worst qualities also originate in the bad use of money,—such as greed, miserliness, injustice, extravagance, and improvidence.

No class ever accomplished anything that lived from hand to mouth. People who spend all that they earn, are ever hanging on the brink of destitution. They must necessarily be weak and impotent—the slaves of time and circumstance. They keep themselves poor. They lose self-respect, as well as the respect of others. It is impossible that they can be free and independent. To be thriftless, is enough to deprive one of all manly spirit and virtue.

But a man with something saved, no matter how little, is in a different position. The little capital he has stored up, is always a source of power. He is no longer the sport of time and fate. He can boldly look the world in the face. He is, in a manner, his own master. He can dictate his own terms. He can neither be bought nor sold. He can look forward with cheerfulness to an old age of comfort and happiness.

As men become wise and thoughtful, they generally become provident and frugal. A thoughtless man, like a savage, spends as he gets, thinking nothing of tomorrow, of the time of adversity, or of the claims of those whom he has made dependent on him. But a wise man thinks of the future; he prepares in good time for the evil day that may come upon him and his family; and he provides carefully for those who are near and dear to him.

What a serious responsibility does the man incur who marries! Not many seriously think, of this responsibility. Perhaps this is wisely ordered. For, much serious thinking might end in the avoidance of married life and its responsibilities. But, once married, a man ought forthwith to determine that, so far as his own efforts are concerned, want shall never enter his household; and that his children shall not, in the event of his being removed from the scene of life and labour, be left a burthen upon society.

Economy with this object is an important duty. Without economy, no man can be just—no man can be honest. Improvidence is cruelty to women and children; though the cruelty is born of ignorance. A father spends his surplus means in drink, providing little, and saving nothing; and then he dies, leaving his destitute family his lifelong victims. Can any form of cruelty surpass this? Yet this reckless course is pursued to a large extent among every class. The middle and upper classes are equally guilty with the lower class. They live beyond their means. They live extravagantly. They are ambitious of glare and glitter—frivolity and pleasure. They struggle to be rich, that they may have the means of spending,—of drinking rich wines, and giving good dinners.

When Mr. Hume said in the House of Commons, some years ago, that the tone of living in England was altogether too high, his observation was followed with "loud laughter." Yet his remark was perfectly true. It is far more true now than it was then. Thinking people believe that life is now too fast, and that we are living at high-pressure. In short, we live extravagantly. We live beyond our means. We throw away oar earnings, and often throw our lives after them.

Many persons are diligent enough in making money, but do not know how to economize it,—or how to spend it. They have sufficient skill and industry to do the one, but they want the necessary wisdom to do the other. The temporary passion for enjoyment seizes us, and we give way to it without regard to consequences. And yet it may be merely the result of forgetfulness, and might be easily controlled by firmness of will, and by energetic resolution to avoid the occasional causes of expenditure for the future. The habit of saving arises, for the most part, in the desire to ameliorate our social condition, as well as to ameliorate the condition of those who are dependent upon us. It dispenses with everything which is not essential, and avoids all methods of living that are wasteful and extravagant. A purchase made at the lowest price will be dear, if it be a superfluity. Little expenses lead to great. Buying things that are not wanted, soon accustoms us to prodigality in other respects.

Cicero said, "Not to have a mania for buying, is to possess a revenue." Many are carried away by the habit of bargain-buying. "Here is something wonderfully cheap: let us buy it." "Have you any use for it?" "No, not at present; but it is sure to come in useful, some time." Fashion runs in this habit of buying. Some buy old china—as much as will furnish a china-shop. Others buy old pictures—old furniture—old wines,—all great bargains! There would be little harm in buying these old things, if they were not so often bought at the expense of the connoisseur's creditors. Horace Walpole once said, "I hope that there will not be another sale, for I have not an inch of room nor a farthing left."

Men must prepare in youth and in middle age the means of enjoying old age pleasantly and happily. There can be nothing more distressing than to see an old man who has spent the greater part of his life in well-paid-for-labour, reduced to the necessity of begging for bread, and relying entirely on the commiseration of his neighbours, or upon the bounty of strangers. Such a consideration as this should inspire men in early life with a determination to work and to save, for the benefit of themselves and their families in later years.

It is, in fact, in youth that economy should be practised, and in old age that men should dispense liberally, provided they do not exceed their income. The young man has a long future before him, during which he may exercise the principles of economy; whilst the other is reaching the end of his career, and can carry nothing out of the world with him.

Habits of Thrift

This, however, is not the usual practice. The young man now spends, or desires to spend, quite as liberally, and often much more liberally, than his father, who is about to end his career. He begins life where his father left off. He spends more than his father did at his age, and soon finds himself up to his ears in debt. To satisfy his incessant wants, he resorts to unscrupulous means, and to illicit gains. He tries to make money rapidly; he speculates, over-trades, and is speedily wound up. Thus he obtains experience; but it is the result, not of well-doing, but of ill-doing.

Socrates recommends fathers of families to observe the practice of their thrifty neighbours—of those who spend their means to the best advantage,—and to profit by their example. Thrift is essentially practical, and can best be taught by facts. Two men earn, say, five shillings a day. They are in precisely the same condition as respects family living, and expenditure Yet the one says he cannot save, and does not; while the other says he can save, and regularly deposits part of his savings in a savings bank, and eventually becomes a capitalist.

Samuel Johnson fully knew the straits of poverty. He once signed his name *Impransus,* or *Dinnerless.* He had walked the streets with Savage, not knowing where to lay his head at night. Johnson never forgot the poverty through which he passed in his early life, and he was always counselling his friends and readers to avoid it. Like Cicero, he averred that the best source of wealth or well-being was economy. He called it the daughter of Prudence, the sister of Temperance, and the mother of Liberty. his mind, his character. Self-respect, originating in self-love, instigates the first step of improvement. It stimulates a man to rise, to look upward, to develop his intelligence, to improve his condition. Self-respect is the root of most of the virtues—of cleanliness, chastity, reverence, honesty, sobriety. To think meanly of one's self is to sink; sometimes to descend a precipice at the bottom of which is infamy.

Every man can help himself to some extent. We are not mere straws thrown upon the current to mark its course; but possessed of freedom of action, endowed with power to stem the waves and rise above them, each marking out a course for himself. We can each elevate ourselves in the scale of moral being. We can cherish pure thoughts. We can perform good actions. We can live soberly and frugally. We can provide against the evil day. We can read good books, listen to wise teachers, and place ourselves under the divinest influences on earth. We can live for the highest purposes, and with the highest aims in view.

"Self-love and social are the same," says one of our poets. The man who improves himself, improves the world. He adds one more true man to the mass. And the mass being made up of individuals, it is clear that were each to improve himself, the result would be the improvement of the whole. Social advancement is the consequence of individual advancement. The whole cannot be pure, unless the individuals composing it are pure. Society at large is but the reflex of individual conditions. All this is but the repetition of a truism, but truisms have often to be repeated to make their full impression.

Then again, a man, when he has improved himself, is better able to improve those who are brought into contact with him. He has more power. His sphere of vision is enlarged. He sees more clearly the defects in the condition of others that might be remedied. He can lend a more active helping hand to raise them. He has done his duty by himself, and can with more authority urge upon others the necessity of doing the like duty to themselves. How can a man be a social elevator, who is himself walking in the mire of self-indulgence? How can he teach sobriety or cleanliness, if he be himself drunken or foul? "Physician, heal thyself," is the answer of his neighbours.

The sum and substance of our remarks is this: In all the individual reforms or improvements that we desire, we must begin with ourselves. We must exhibit our gospel in our own life. We must teach by our own example. If we would have others elevated, we must elevate ourselves. Each man can exhibit the results in his own person. He can begin with self-respect.

The uncertainty of life is a strong inducement to provide against the evil day. To do this is a moral and social, as well as a religious duty. "He that provideth not for his own, and especially for those of his own household, hath denied the faith, and is worse than an infidel."

The uncertainty of life is proverbially true. The strongest and healthiest man may be stricken down in a moment, by accident or disease. If we take human life in the mass, we cannot fail to recognize the uncertainty of life as much as we do the certainty of death.

There is a striking passage in Addison's "Vision of Mirza," in which life is pictured as a passage over a bridge of about a hundred arches. A black cloud hangs over each end of the bridge. At the entrance to it there are hidden pitfalls very thickly set, through which throngs disappear, so soon as they have placed their feet upon the bridge. They grow thinner towards the centre; they gradually disappear; until at length only a few persons reach the further side, and these also having dropped through the pitfalls, the bridge at its further extremity becomes entirely clear. The description of Addison corresponds with the results of the observations made as to the duration of human life.

Thus, of a hundred thousand persons born in this country, it has been ascertained that a fourth of them die before they have reached their fifth year; and one-half before they have reached their fiftieth year. One thousand one hundred will reach their ninetieth year. Sixteen will live to a hundred. And only two persons out of the hundred thousand—like the last barks of an innumerable convoy, will reach the advanced and helpless age of a hundred and five years.

Two things are very obvious,—the uncertainty as to the hour of death in individuals, but the regularity and constancy of the circumstances which influence the duration of human life in the aggregate. It is a matter of certainty that the *average* life of all persons born in this country extends to about forty-five years. This has been proved by a very large number of observations of human life and its duration.

Equally extensive observations have been made as to the average number of persons of various ages who die yearly. It is always the number of the experiments which gives the law of the probability. It is on such observations that the actuary founds his estimates of the mortality that exists at any given period of life. The actuary tells you that he has been guided by the Laws of Mortality. Now the results must be very regular, to justify the actuary in speaking of Mortality as governed by Laws. And yet it is so.

Indeed, there would seem to be no such thing as chance in the world. Man lives and dies in conformity to a law. A sparrow falls to the ground in obedience to a law. Nay, there are matters in the ordinary transactions of life, such as one might suppose were the mere result of chance, which are ascertained to be of remarkable accuracy when taken in the mass. For instance, the number of letters put in the post-office without an address; the number of letters wrongly directed; the number containing money; the number unstamped; continue nearly the same, in relation to the number of letters posted, from one year to another.

Now it is the business of man to understand the laws of health, and to provide against their consequences,—as, for instance, in the matter of sickness, accident, and premature death. We cannot escape the consequences of transgression of the natural laws, though we may have meant well. We must have done well. The Creator does not alter His laws to accommodate them to our ignorance. He has furnished us with intelligence, so that we may understand them and act upon them: otherwise we must suffer the consequences in inevitable pain and sorrow.

We often hear the cry raised, "Will nobody help us?" It is a spiritless, hopeless cry. It is sometimes a cry of revolting meanness, especially when it issues from those who with a little self-denial, sobriety, and thrift, might easily help themselves.

Many people have yet to learn, that virtue, knowledge, freedom, and prosperity must spring from themselves. Legislation can do very little for them: it cannot make them sober, intelligent, and well-doing. The prime miseries of most men have their origin in causes far removed from Acts of Parliament.

The spendthrift laughs at legislation. The drunkard defies it, and arrogates the right of dispensing with forethought and self-denial,— throwing upon others the blame of his ultimate wretchedness. The mob orators, who gather "the millions" about them, are very wide of the mark, when, instead of seeking to train their crowd of hearers to habits of frugality, temperance, and self-culture, they encourage them to keep up the cry, "Will nobody help us?"

The cry sickens the soul. It shows gross ignorance of the first elements of personal welfare. Help is in men themselves. They were born to help and to elevate themselves. They must work out their own salvation. The poorest men have done it; why should not every man do it? The brave, upward spirit ever conquers.

The number of well-paid workmen in this country has become very large, who might easily save and economize, to the improvement of their moral well-being, of their respectability and independence, and of their status in society as men and citizens. They are improvident and thriftless to an extent which proves not less hurtful to their personal happiness and domestic comfort, than it is injurious to the society of which they form so important a part.

In "prosperous times" they spend their gains recklessly, and when adverse times come, they are at once plunged in misery. Money is not used, but abused; and when wage-earning people should be providing against old age, or for the wants of a growing family, they are, in too many cases, feeding folly, dissipation, and vice. Let no one say that this is an exaggerated picture. It is enough to look round in any neighbourhood, and see how much is spent and how little is saved; what a large proportion of earnings goes to the beershop, and how little to the savings bank or the benefit society.

"Prosperous times" are very often the least prosperous of all times. In prosperous times, mills are working full time; men, women, and children are paid high wages; warehouses are emptied and filled; goods are manufactured and exported; wherries full of produce pass along the streets; immense luggage trains run along the railways, and heavily-laden ships leave our shores daily for foreign ports, full of the products of our industry. Everybody seems to be becoming richer and more prosperous. But we do not think of whether men and women are becoming wiser, better trained, less self-indulgent, more religiously disposed, or living for any higher purpose than the satisfaction of the animal appetite.

If this apparent prosperity be closely examined, it will be found that expenditure is increasing in all directions. There are demands for higher wages; and the higher wages, when obtained, are spent as soon as earned. Intemperate habits are formed, and, once formed, the habit of intemperance continues. Increased wages, instead of being saved, are for the most part spent in drink.

Thus, when a population is thoughtless and improvident, no kind of material prosperity will benefit them. Unless they exercise forethought and economy, they will alternately be in a state of "hunger and burst." When trade falls off, as it usually does after exceptional prosperity, they will not be comforted by the thought of what they *might* have saved, had it ever occurred to them that the "prosperous times" might not have proved permanent.

During prosperous times, Saint Monday is regularly observed. The Bank Holiday is repeated weekly. "Where are all the workmen?" said a master to his foreman on going the rounds among his builders,—this work must be pushed on and covered in while the fine weather lasts." "Why, sir," said the foreman, "this is Monday; and they have not spent all their money yet." Dean Boyd, preaching at Exeter on behalf of the Devonshire hospitals, expressed his belief that the annual loss to the workpeople engaged in the woollen manufacture, the cotton trade, the bricklaying and building trade, by Idle Monday, amounted to over seven millions sterling. If man's chief end were to manufacture cloth, silk, cotton, hardware, toys, and china; to buy in the cheapest market, and to sell in the dearest; to cultivate land, grow corn, and graze cattle; to live for mere money profit, and hoard or spend, as the case might be, we might then congratulate ourselves upon our National Prosperity. But is this the chief end of man? Has he not faculties, affections, and sympathies, besides muscular organs? Has not his mind and heart certain claims, as well as his mouth and his back? Has he not a soul as well as a stomach? And ought not "prosperity" to include the improvement and well-being of his morals and intellect as well as of his bones and muscles?

Mere money is no indication of prosperity. A man's nature may remain the same. It may even grow more stunted and deformed, while he is doubling his expenditure, or adding cent, per cent, to his hoards yearly. It is the same with the mass. The increase of their gains may merely furnish them with increased means for gratifying animal indulgences, unless their moral character keeps pace with their physical advancement. Double the gains of an uneducated, overworked man, in a time of prosperity, and what is the result? Simply that you have furnished him with the means of eating and drinking more! Thus, not even the material well-being of the population is secured by that condition of things which is defined by political economists as "National Prosperity." And so long as the moral elements of the question are ignored, this kind of "prosperity" is, we believe, calculated to produce far more mischievous results than good. It is knowledge and virtue alone that can confer dignity on a man's life; and the growth of such qualities in a nation are the only true marks of its real prosperity; not the infinite manufacture and sale of cotton prints, toys, hardware, and crockery. The Bishop of Manchester, when preaching at a harvest thanksgiving near Preston, referred to a letter which he had received from a clergyman in the south of England, who, after expressing his pleasure at the fact that the agricultural labourers were receiving higher wages, lamented "that at present the only result he could discover from their higher wages was that a great deal *more beer* was consumed. If this was the use we were making of this prosperity, we could hardly call it a blessing for which we had a right or ground to thank God. The true prosperity of the nation consisted not so much in the fact that the nation was growing in wealth—though wealth was a necessary attribute of prosperity—but that it was growing in virtue; and that there was a more equable distribution of comfort, contentment, and the things of this lower world."

In making the preceding observations we do not in the least advocate the formation of miserly, penurious habits; for we hate the scrub, the screw, the miser. All that we contend for is, that man should provide for the future,—that they should provide during good times for the bad times which almost invariably follow them,—that they should lay by a store of savings as a breakwater against want, and make sure of a little fund which may maintain them in old age, secure their self-respect, and add to their personal comfort and social well-being. Thrift is not in any way connected with avarice, usury, greed, or selfishness. It is, in fact, the very reverse of these disgusting dispositions.

It means economy for the purpose of securing independence. Thrift requires that money should be used and not abused—that it should be honestly earned and economically employed—

> "Not for to put it in a hedge,
> Not for a train attendent,
> —But for the glorious privilege
> Of being Independent."

Chapter 3

Improvidence

"*The man who has a wife and children has given hostages to fortune.*"—Lord Bacon.

"*In all conditions and circumstances, well-being is in the power of those who have power over themselves.*"—J.J. Gurney.

"*Where is their common sense? Alas, what imprudence! Early marriages; many children; poor-rates, and the workhouse. . . . They are born; they are wretched; they die. . . . In no foreign country of far less civilization than England, is there the same improvidence.*"—Lord Lytton.

"*No man oppresses thee, O free and independent franchiser; but does not this stupid pewter pot oppress thee? No son of Adam can bid thee come or go, but this absurd pot of heavy-wet can and does, Thou art the thrall, not of Cedric the Saxon, but of thy own brutal appetites, and this accursed dish of liquor. And thou pratest of thy 'liberty,' thou entire blockhead!*"—Carlyle.

"*Never did any publike misery Rise of it selfe; God's plagues still grounded are On common staines of our Humanity: And to the flame, which ruineth Mankind, Man gives the matter, or at least gives winde.*"—Daniell.

England is one of the richest countries in the world. Our merchants are enterprising, our manufacturers are industrious, our labourers are hardworking. There is an accumulation of wealth in the country to which past times can offer no parallel. The Bank is gorged with gold. There never was more food in the empire; there never was more money. There is no end to our manufacturing productions, for the steam-engine never tires. And yet notwithstanding all this wealth, there is an enormous mass

Improvidence

of poverty. Close alongside the Wealth of Nations, there gloomily stalks the Misery of Nations,—luxurious ease resting upon a dark background of wretchedness.

Parliamentary reports have again and again revealed to us the miseries endured by certain portions of our working population. They have described the people employed in factories, workshops, mines, and brickfields, as well as in the pursuits of country life. We have tried to grapple with the evils of their condition by legislation, but it seems to mock us. Those who sink into poverty are fed, but they remain paupers. Those who feed them, feel no compassion; and those who are fed, return no gratitude. There is no bond of sympathy between the givers and the receivers. Thus the Haves and the Have-nots, the opulent and the indigent, stand at the two extremes of the social scale, and a wide gulf is fixed between them.

Among rude and savage people, the condition of poverty is uniform. Provided the bare appetites are satisfied, suffering is scarcely felt. Where slavery exists, indigence is little known; for it is the master's interest to keep the slave in a condition fit for labour, and the employer generally takes care to supply the animal wants of the employed. It is only when society becomes civilized and free, and man enters into competition with his fellows, that he becomes exposed to indigence, and experiences social misery. Where civilization, as in this country, has reached its highest point, and where large accumulations of wealth have been made, the misery of the indigent classes is only rendered more acute by the comfort and luxury with which it is placed in immediate contrast.

Much of the existing misery is caused by selfishness—by the greed to accumulate wealth on the one hand, and by improvidence on the other. Accumulation of money has become the great desire and passion of the age. The wealth of nations, and not the happiness of nations, is the principal aim. We study political economy, and let social economy shift for itself. Regard for "Number One" is the prevailing maxim.

High profits are regarded as the *summum bonum,*—no matter how obtained, or at what sacrifice. Money is our god: "Devil take the hindmost" our motto. The spirits of darkness rule supreme—

"Mammon has led them on, Mammon, the least erect of all the spirits That fell from Heaven."

With respect to the poorer classes,—what has become of them in the midst of our so-called civilization? An immense proportion of them remain entirely uncivilized. Though living in a Christian country, Christianity has never reached them. They are as uncivilized and unchristianized as the Trinobantes were at the landing of Julius Caesar, about nineteen hundred years ago. Yet these uncivilized people live in our midst. St. James's and St. Giles's lie close together. In the Parks of London, you may see how gold is worshipped; in the East End of London, you may see to what depths human misery may fall.

They work, eat, drink, and sleep: that constitutes their life. They think nothing of providing for tomorrow, or for next week, or for next year. They abandon themselves to their sensual appetites; and make no provision whatever for the future. The thought of adversity, or of coming sorrow, or of the helplessness that comes with years and sickness, never crosses their minds. In these respects, they resemble the savage tribes, who know no better, and do no worse. Like the North American Indians, they debase themselves by the vices which accompany civilization, but make no use whatever of its benefits and advantages.

Captain Parry found the Esquimaux near the North Pole as uncivilized as the miserable creatures who inhabit the dens of our great cities. They were, of course, improvident; for, like savages generally, they never save. They were always either feasting or famished.

When they found a quantity of whale's blubber, they would eat as much of it as they could, and hide the rest. Yet their improvidence gave them no concern. Even when they had been without food or fuel for days together, they would be as gay and good-humoured as usual. They never thought of how they should be provided for tomorrow. Saving for the future forms no part of the savage economy.

Amongst civilized peoples, cold is said to be the parent of frugality. Thus the northern nations of Europe owe a portion of their prosperity to the rigour of their climate. Cold makes them save during summer, to provide food, coal, and clothing during winter. It encourages house-building and housekeeping. Hence Germany is more industrious than Sicily; Holland and Belgium than Andalusia; North America and Canada than Mexico.

When the late Edward Denison, M.P. for Newark, with unexampled self-denial, gave up a large portion of his time and labour to reclaim the comparatively uncivilized population of the East End of London, the first thing he did was to erect an iron church of two stories, the lower part of which was used as a school and lecture room, and also as a club where men and boys might read, play games, and do anything else that might keep them out of the drinking-houses. "What is so bad in this quarter," said Mr. Denison, "is the habitual condition of this mass of humanity—its uniform mean level, the absence of anything more civilizing than a

Improvidence

grinding organ to raise the ideas beyond the daily bread and beer, the utter want of education, the complete indifference to religion, with the fruits of all this—improvidence, dirt, and their secondaries, crime and disease. . . . There is no one to give a push to struggling energy, to guide aspiring intelligence, or to break the fall of unavoidable misfortune. . . . The Mission Clergyman," he goes on to say, "is a sensible, energetic man, in whose hands the work of *civilizing the people* is making as much progress as can be expected. But most of his energy is taken up in serving tables, nor can any great advance be made while every nerve has to be strained to keep the people from absolute starvation. And this is what happens every winter. . . . What a monstrous thing it is that in the richest country in the world, large masses of the population should be condemned annually, by a natural operation of nature, to starvation and death. It is all very well to say, how can it be helped? Why, it was not so in our grandfathers' time. Behind us they were in many ways, but they were not met every winter with the spectacle of starving thousands. The fact is, we have accepted the marvellous prosperity which has in the last twenty years been granted us, without reflecting on the conditions attached to it, and without nerving ourselves to the exertion and the sacrifices which their fulfilment demands."

And yet Mr. Denison clearly saw that if the people were sufficiently educated, and taught to practise the virtue of Thrift, much of this misery might be prevented. "The people," he elsewhere says, "*create* their destitution and their disease. Probably there are hardly any of the most needy who, if they had been only moderately frugal and provident, could not have placed themselves in a position to tide over the occasional months of want of work, or of sickness, which there always must be. . . . I do not underrate the difficulty of laying by out of weekly earnings, but I say it *can* be done. A dock-labourer, while a young, strong, unmarried man, could lay by half his weekly wages, and such men are almost sure of constant employment."

After showing how married men might also save, Mr. Denison goes on to say, "Saving is within the reach of nearly every man, even if quite at the bottom of the tree; but if it were of anything like *common* occurrence, the destitution and disease of this city would be kept within quite manageable limits. And this will take place. I may not live to see it, but it will be within two generations. For, unfortunately, this amount of change may be effected without the least improvement in the spiritual condition of the people. Good laws, energetically enforced, with compulsory education, supplemented by gratuitous individual exertion (which will then have a much reduced field and much fairer prospects), will certainly succeed in giving the mass of the people so much light as will generally guide them into so much industry and morality as is clearly conducive to their bodily ease and advancement in life."

The difference in thriftiness between the English workpeople and the inhabitants of Guernsey is thus referred to by Mr. Denison: "The difference between poverty and pauperism is brought home to us very strongly by what I see here. In England, we have people faring sumptuously while they are getting good wages, and coming on the parish paupers the moment those wages are suspended. Here, people are never dependent upon any support but their own; but they live, of their own free will, in a style of frugality which a landlord would be hooted at for suggesting to his cottagers. We pity Hodge, reduced to bacon and greens, and to meat only once a week. The principal meal of a Guernsey farmer consists of *soupe à la graisse,* which is, being interpreted, cabbage and peas stewed with a little dripping. This is the daily dinner of men who *own* perhaps three or four cows, a pig or two, and poultry. But the produce and the flesh of these creatures they sell in the market, investing their gains in extension of land, or stock, or in "quarters," that is, rent-charges on land, certificates of which are readily bought and sold in the market."[1]

Mr. Dension died before he could accomplish much. He was only able to make a beginning. The misery, arising from improvidence, which he so deeply deplored, still exists, and is even more widely spread. It is not merely the artizan who spends all that he earns, but the classes above him, who cannot plead the same excuse of ignorance. Many of what are called the "upper" classes are no more excusable than the "lower." They waste their means on keeping up appearances, and in feeding folly, dissipation, and vice.

No one can reproach the English workman with want of industry. He works harder and more skilfully than the workman of any other country; and he might be more comfortable and independent in his circumstances, were he as prudent as he is laborious. But improvidence is unhappily the defect of the class. Even the best-paid English workmen, though earning more money than the average of professional men, still for the most part belong to the poorer classes because of their thoughtlessness. In prosperous times they are not accustomed to make provision for adverse

---

1. Letters and other writings of the late Edward Denison, M.P., pp. 141, 142.

times; and when a period of social pressure occurs, they are rarely found more than a few weeks ahead of positive want.

Hence, the skilled workman, unless trained in good habits, may exhibit no higher a life than that of the mere animal; and the earning of increased wages will only furnish him with increased means for indulging in the gratification of his grosser appetites. Mr. Chadwick says, that during the Cotton Famine, "families trooped into the relief rooms in the most abject condition, whose previous aggregate wages exceeded the income of many curates,—as had the wages of many of the individual workmen."[2] In a time of prosperity, working-people feast, and in a time of adversity they "clem." Their earnings, to use their own phrase, "come in at the spigot and go out at the bunghole." When prosperity comes to an end, and they are paid off, they rely upon chance and providence—the providence of the Improvident!

Though trade has invariably its cycles of good and bad years, like the lean and fat kine in Pharaoh's dream—its bursts of prosperity, followed by glut, panic, and distress—the thoughtless and spendthrift take no heed of experience, and make no better provision for the future. Improvidence seems to be one of the most incorrigible of faults. "There are whole neighbourhoods in the manufacturing districts," says Mr. Baker in a recent Report, "where not only are there no savings worth mentioning, but where, within a fortnight of being out of work, the workers themselves are starving for want of the merest necessaries." Not a strike takes place, but immediately the workmen are plunged in destitution; their furniture and watches are sent to the pawnshop, whilst deplorable appeals are made to the charitable, and numerous families are cast upon the poor-rates.

This habitual improvidence—though of course there are many admirable exceptions—is the real cause of the social degradation of the artizan. This too is the prolific source of social misery. But the misery is entirely the result of human ignorance and self-indulgence. For though the Creator has ordained poverty, the poor are not necessarily, nor as a matter of fact, the miserable. Misery is the result of moral causes,—most commonly of individual vice and improvidence.

The Rev. Mr. Norris, in speaking of the habits of the highly paid miners and iron-workers of South Staffordshire, says, "Improvidence is too tame a word for it—it is recklessness; here young and old, married and unmarried, are uniformly and almost avowedly self-indulgent spendthrifts. One

---

2. Address on Economy and Trade. By Edwin Chadwick, C.B., p. 22.

sees this reckless character marring and vitiating the nobler traits of their nature. Their gallantry in the face of danger is akin to foolhardiness; their power of intense labour is seldom exerted except to compensate for time lost in idleness and revelry; their readiness to make 'gatherings' for their sick and married comrades seems only to obviate the necessity of previous saving; their very creed—and, after their sort, they are a curiously devotional people, holding frequent prayer-meetings in the pits—often degenerates into fanatical fatalism. But it is seen far more painfully and unmistakably in the alternate plethora and destitution between which, from year's end to year's end, the whole population seems to oscillate. The prodigal revelry of the *reckoning night,* the drunkenness of Sunday, the refusal to work on Monday and perhaps Tuesday, and then the untidiness of their home towards the latter part of the two or three weeks which intervene before the next pay-day; their children kept from school, their wives and daughters on the pit-bank, their furniture in the pawnshop; the crowded and miry lanes in which they live, their houses often cracked from top to bottom by the 'crowning in' of the ground, without drainage, or ventilation, or due supply of water;—such a state of things as this, co-existing with earnings which might ensure comfort and even prosperity, seems to prove that no legislation can cure the evil."

We have certainly had numerous "Reforms." We have had household suffrage, and vote by ballot. We have relieved the working classes of the taxes on corn, cattle, coffee, sugar, and provisions generally; and imposed a considerable proportion of the taxes from which they have been relieved on the middle and upper ranks. Yet these measures have produced but little improvement in the condition of the working people. They have not applied the principle of Reform to themselves. They have not begun at home. Yet the end of all Reform is the improvement of the individual. Everything that is wrong in Society results from that which is wrong in the Individual. When men are bad, society is bad.

Franklin, with his shrewd common sense, observed, "The taxes are indeed very heavy; and if those laid on by the Government were the only ones we had to pay, we might more easily discharge them; but we have many others, and much more grievous to some of us. We are taxed quite as much by our idleness, three times as much by our pride, and four times as much by our folly; and from these taxes the Commissioners cannot ease or deliver us by allowing an abatement."

Lord John Russell once made a similar statement to a body of working men who waited upon him for the purpose of asking relief from taxation.

Improvidence

"You complain of the taxes," he said; "but think of how you tax yourselves. You consume about fifty millions yearly in drink. Is there any Government that would dare to tax you to that extent? You have it in your own power greatly to reduce the taxes, and that without in any way appealing to us."

Complaining that the laws are bad, and that the taxes are heavy, will not mend matters. Aristocratic government, and the tyranny of masters, are nothing like so injurious as the tyranny of vicious appetites. Men are easily led away by the parade of their miseries, which are for the most part voluntary and self-imposed,—the results of idleness, thriftlessness, intemperance, and misconduct. To blame others for what we suffer, is always more agreeable to our self-pride, than to blame ourselves. But it is perfectly clear that people who live from day to day without plan, without rule, without forethought—who spend all their earnings, without saving anything for the future—are preparing beforehand for inevitable distress. To provide only for the present, is the sure means to sacrificing the future. What hope can there be for a people whose only maxim seems to be, "Let us eat and drink, for tomorrow we die"?

All this may seem very hopeless; yet it is not entirely so. The large earnings of the working classes is an important point to start with. The gradual diffusion of education will help them to use, and not abuse, their means of comfortable living. The more extended knowledge of the uses of economy, frugality, and thrift, will help them to spend their lives more soberly, virtuously, and religiously. Mr. Denison was of opinion that much of this might be accomplished "within two generations." Social improvement is always very slow. How extremely tardy has been the progress of civilization! How gradually have its humanizing influences operated in elevating the mass of the people! It requires the lapse of generations before its effects can be so much as discerned: for a generation is but as a day in the history of civilization. It has cost most nations ages of wars, before they could conquer their right of existence as nations. It took four centuries of persecutions and martyrdoms to establish Christianity, and two centuries of civil wars to establish the Reformation. The emancipation of the bondsmen from feudal slavery was only reached through long ages of misery. From the days in which our British progenitors rushed to battle in their war-paint,—or those more recent times when the whole of the labouring people were villeins and serfs, bought and sold with the soil which they tilled,—to the times in which we now live,—how wide the difference, how gratifying the contrast. Surely it ought not to be so difficult to put an end to the Satanic influences of thriftlessness, drunkenness, and improvidence!

Chapter 4

Means of Saving

"Self-reliance and self-denial will teach a man to drink out of his own cistern, and eat his own sweet bread, and to learn and labour truly to get his own living, and carefully to save and expend the good things committed to his trust."—Lord Bacon.

"Love, therefore, labour: if thou should'st not want it for food, thou may'st for physic. It is wholesome for the body, and good for the mind; it prevents the fruit of idleness."—William Penn.

"The parent who does not teach his child a trade, teaches him to be a thief."—Brahminical Scriptures.

Those who say that "It can't be done," are probably not aware that many of the working classes are in the receipt of incomes considerably larger than those of professional men.

That this is the case, is not, by any means, a secret. It is published in blue-books, it is given in evidence before parliamentary committees, it is reported in newspapers. Any coal-owner, or iron-master, or cotton-spinner, will tell you of the high wages that he pays to his workpeople.

Families employed in the cotton manufacture are able to earn over three pounds a week, according to the number of the children employed.[1] Their annual incomes will thus amount to about a hundred and fifty pounds a year,—which is considerably larger than the incomes of many

---

1. A return of seven families employed by Henry Ashworth, New Cayley Mills, Lancashire, is given in the Blue Book, entitled, "Report of the Paris Universal Exhibition, 1867, containing the Returns relative to the New Order of Reward," p. 163. Of the seven families, the lowest earnings per family amounted to £2 14s. 6d.; and the highest to £3 19s. a week.

professional men—higher than the average of country surgeons, higher than the average of the clergy and ministers of all denominations, higher than the average of the teachers of common schools, and probably higher than the average income of the middle classes of the United Kingdom generally.

An employer at Blackburn informs us that many persons earn upwards of five pounds a week,—or equal to an average income of two hundred and sixty pounds a year. Such families, he says, "ought not to expend more than three pounds weekly. The rest should be saved. But most of them, after feeding and clothing themselves, spend the rest in drink and dissipation."

The wages are similar in the Burnley district, where food, drink, and dress absorb the greater part of the workpeople's earnings. In this, as in other factory districts, "the practice of young persons (mill-workers) boarding with their parents is prevalent, and is very detrimental to parental authority." Another reporter says, "Wages are increasing: as there is more money, and more time to spend it in, sobriety is not on the increase, especially amongst females."

The operatives employed in the woollen manufacture receive about forty shillings a week, and some as much as sixty,[2] besides the amount earned by their children.

A good mechanic in an engine shop makes from thirty-five to forty-five shillings a week, and some mechanics make much larger wages. Multiply these figures, and it will be found that they amount to an annual income of from a hundred to a hundred and twenty pounds a year.

But the colliers and iron-workers are paid much higher wages. One of the largest iron-masters recently published in the newspapers the names of certain colliers in his employment who were receiving from four to five pounds a week,—or equal to an annual income of from two hundred to two hundred and fifty pounds a year.[3]

---

2. See the above Blue Book, p. 57, certifying the wages paid by Bliss and Son, of Chipping Norton Woollen Factory.

3. Richard Fothergill, Esq., M.P. He published a subsequent letter, from which we extract the following:—

"No doubt such earnings seem large to clerks, and educated men, who after receiving a costly education have often to struggle hard for bread; but they are nevertheless the rightful earnings of steady manual labour; and I have the pleasure of adding that, while all steady, well-disposed colliers, in good health, could make equally good wages, many hundreds in South Wales are quietly doing as much or more: witness a steady collier in my

Iron-workers are paid a still higher rate of wages. A plate-roller easily makes three hundred a year.[4] The rollers in rail mills often make much more. In busy times they have made as much as from seven to ten guineas a week, or equal to from three to five hundred a year.[5] But, like the workers in cotton mills, the iron workers are often helped by their sons, who are also paid high wages. Thus, the under-hands are usually boys from fourteen years of age and upwards, who earn about nineteen shillings a week, and the helpers are boys of under fourteen, who earn about nine shillings a week.

These earnings are far above the average incomes of the professional classes. The rail rollers are able to earn a rate of pay equal to that of Lieutenant-Colonels in Her Majesty's Foot Guards; plate-rollers equal to that of Majors of Foot; and roughers equal to that of Lieutenants and Adjutants.

Goldsmith spoke of the country curate as "passing rich with forty pounds a year." The incomes of curates have certainly increased since the time when Goldsmith wrote, but nothing like the incomes of skilled and unskilled workmen. If curates merely worked for money, they would certainly change their vocation, and become colliers and iron-workers.

When the author visited Renfrewshire a few years ago, the colliers were earning from ten to fourteen shillings a day. According to the common saying, they were "making money like a minting machine." To take an instance, a father and three sons were earning sixty pounds a month,—or equal to a united income of more than seven hundred pounds a year. The father was a sober, steady, "eident" man. While the high wages lasted, he was the first to enter the pit in the morning, and the last to leave it at night. He only lost five days in one year (1873–4),—the loss being

---

employment, with his two sons living at home, whose monthly pay ticket has averaged £30 for the past twelvemonth.

"Another steady collier within my information, aided by his son, h as earned during the past five months upwards of £20 a month on the average, and from his manual labour as an ordinary collier—for it is of the working colliers and firemen I am speaking all along—he has built fifteen good houses, and, disregarding all menaces, he continues his habits of steady industry, whereby he hopes to accumulate an independence for his family in all events."

4. See Messrs. Fox, Head, and Co.'s return, in the Blue Book above referred to. This was the rate of wages at Middlesborough, in Yorkshire. In South Wales, the wages of the principal operatives engaged in the iron manufacture, recently, were—Puddlers. 9s. a day; first heaters on the rail mills. 8s. 9d. a day: second heaters, 11s. 7d.: roughers, 10s. 9d.: rollers, 13s. 2d., or equal to that amount.

5. Even at the present time, when business is so much depressed, the mill-rollers make an average wage of £5 10s. a week.

occasioned by fast-days and holidays. Believing that the period of high wages could not last long, he and his sons worked as hard as they could. They saved a good deal of money, and bought several houses; besides educating themselves to occupy higher positions.

In the same neighbourhood, another collier, with four sons, was earning money at about the same rate per man, that is about seventy-five-pounds a mouth, or nine hundred pounds a year. This family bought five houses within a year, and saved a considerable sum besides. The last information we had respecting them was that the father had become a contractor,—that he employed about sixty colliers and "reddsmen,"[6] and was allowed so much for every ton of coals brought to bank. The sons were looking after their father's interests. They were all sober, diligent, sensible men; and took a great deal of interest in the education and improvement of the people in their neighbourhood.

At the same time that these two families of colliers were doing so well, it was very different with the majority of their fellow-workmen. These only worked about three days in every week. Some spent their earnings at the public-house; others took a whisky "ploy" at the seaside. For that purpose they hired all the gigs, droskies, cabs, or "machines," about a fortnight beforehand. The results were seen, as the successive Monday mornings come round. The magistrate sat in the neighbouring town, where a number of men and women, with black eyes and broken heads, were brought before him for judgment. Before the time of high wages, the Court-house business was got through in an hour: sometimes there was no business at all. But when the wages were doubled, the magistrate could scarcely get through the business in a day. It seemed as if high wages meant more idleness, more whisky, and more broken heads and faces.

These were doubtless "roaring times" for the colliers, who, had they possessed the requisite self-denial, might have made little fortunes. Many of the men who worked out the coal remained idle three or four days in the week; while those who burnt the coal, were famished and frozen for want of it. The working people who were *not* colliers, will long remember that period as the time of the *coal famine*. While it lasted, Lord Elcho went over to Tranent—a village in East Lothian—to address the colliers upon their thriftlessness, their idleness, and their attempted combinations to keep up the price of coal.

---

6. "Reddsmen" are the men who clear the way for the colliers. They "redd up" the debris, and build up the roof (in the long wall system) as the colliery advances.

He had the moral courage—a quality much wanted in these days—to tell his constituents some hard but honest truths. He argued with them about the coal famine, and their desire to prolong it. They were working three days a week, and idling the other days. Some of them did not do a stroke of work during a week or a fortnight; others were taking about a hundred Bank holidays yearly. But what were they doing with the money they earned? Were they saving it for a rainy day; or, when the "roaring times" no longer existed, were they preparing to fall back upon the poor-rates? He found that in one case a man, with his two sons, was earning seven pounds in a fortnight. "I should like," he said, "to see those Scotchmen who are in the mining business taking advantage of these happy times, and endeavouring by their industry to rise from their present position—to exercise self-help, to acquire property, and possibly to become coal masters themselves."

It had been said in a newspaper, that a miner was earning wages equal to that of a Captain, and that a mining boy was earning wages equal to that of a Lieutenant in Her Majesty's service. "I only know," said Lord Elcho, "that I have a boy who, when he first joined Her Majesty's service, was an Ensign, and that his wage—to earn which, remember, he had, under the purchase system, to pay five hundred pounds,—was not the wage you are now receiving, but the wage which you were receiving in bad times,—and that was only five shillings a day." It might be said that the collier risks his life in earning his wages; but so does the soldier; and the gallant boy to whom Lord Elcho referred, afterwards lost his life in the Ashantee campaign.

The times of high wages did not leave a very good impression on the public mind. Prices became higher, morals became lower, and the work done was badly done. There was a considerable deterioration in the character of British workmanship. "We began to rely too much upon the foreigner. Trade was to a large extent destroyed, and an enormous loss of capital was sustained, both by the workmen and by the masters. Lord Aberdare was of opinion that three millions sterling were lost by *the workmen alone,* during the recent strike in South Wales. One hundred and twenty thousand workmen were in enforced idleness at once, and one hundred and fifty thousand pounds were lost every week in wages during the time that they remained idle.

What the employers think of the recent flash of "prosperity," can easily be imagined. But it may not be unnecessary to quote some of the statements of correspondents. A large employer of labour in South

Lancashire says: "Drunkenness increases, and personal violence is not sufficiently discouraged. High wages and household suffrage came upon the people before education had prepared them for the change."

In a large iron-work near Newcastle, where the men were paid the highest wages for rolling plates and rails—and where they were earning between three and four hundred pounds a year—the proprietors observe: "Except in a few instances, we are afraid that workmen and their families spend most of their earnings." Another employer in South Staffordshire says: In the majority of cases, the men employed in the iron-work spend the whole of their wages before the end of the following week. There are, of course, some exceptions; but they are, unhappily, very few." Another, in South Wales, says: "As to the thrifty habits of the men, a small minority are careful and saving; they generally invest their money in cottage property. But the great majority of the men spend their money often before they earn it, and that in the most reckless way. Large sums are spent in drink: this leads to idleness; and, owing to drinking and idling, the works are kept short of men until about Wednesday in each week, when the greater part of the most idly disposed have become sobered down. Of course, when wages are low, the men work more regularly. There is less drinking, and altogether the condition of the place is healthier in every respect both in a moral and physical sense."

Another observer remarks, that the miners of Bilston are about six thousand in number, and they spend more than fifty thousand pounds annually in the purchase of ale and liquors. Their improvidence may be studied with advantage in the Bilston Market. No other market is supplied with finer poultry, or comparatively to the population, in greater abundance; and this is chiefly, if not entirely, for, the consumption of the labouring classes,—for the resident inhabitants, not directly associated with those classes are few in number. Sordid and ill-favoured men may there be seen buying on Saturday, chickens, ducks, and geese, which they eat for supper; and in some instances, bottled porter and wine. Yet, so little have they beforehand in the world, that if the works were to stop, they would begin within a fortnight to pawn the little furniture of their cottages, and their clothes, for subsistence and for drink.

Mr. Chambers, of Edinburgh, in his description of the working classes of Sunderland makes these remarks: "With deep sorrow I mention that everywhere one tale was told. Intemperance prevails to a large extent; good wages are squandered on mean indulgences; there is little care for the morrow, and the workhouse is the ultimate refuge. One man, a skilled worker in an iron-foundry, was pointed out as having for years received a wage of one guinea a day, or six guineas a week; he had spent all, mostly in drink, and was now reduced to a lower department at a pound a week."

Another illustration occurs. A clerk at Blackburn took a house for twenty pounds a year, and sublet the cellars underneath to a factory operative at a rental of five pounds a year. The clerk had a wife, four children, and a servant; the operative had a wife and five children. The clerk and his family were well dressed, their children went to school, and all went to church on Sundays. The operative's family went, some to the factory, others to the gutter, but none to school; they were ill-dressed, excepting on Sundays, when they obtained their clothes from the pawnshop. As the Saturdays came round, the frying-pan in the cellar was almost constantly at work until Monday night; and as regularly as Thursday arrived, the bundle of clothes was sent to the pawnshop. Yet the income of the upper-class family in the higher part of the house was a hundred a year; and the income of the lower class family in the cellar was fifty pounds more—that is, a hundred and fifty pounds a year!

An employer in the same neighbourhood used to say, "I cannot afford lamb, salmon, young ducks and green peas, new potatoes, strawberries and such-like, until after my hands have been consuming these delicacies of the season for some three or four weeks."

The intense selfishness, thriftlessness, and folly of these highly paid operatives, is scarcely credible. Exceptions are frequently taken to calling the working classes "the lower orders;" but "the lower orders" they always will be, so long as they indicate such sensual indulgence and improvidence. In cases such as these, improvidence is not only a great sin, and a feeder of sin, but it is a great *cruelty*. In the case of the father of a family, who has been instrumental in bringing a number of helpless beings into the world, it is heartless and selfish in the highest degree to spend money on personal indulgences such as drink, which do the parent no good, and the mother and the children, through the hereditary bad example, an irreparable amount of mischief. The father takes sick, is thrown out of work, and his children are at once deprived of the means of subsistence. The reckless parent has not even taken the precaution to enter a Provident or a Benefit Society; and while he is sick, his wife and children are suffering the pangs of hunger. Or, he dies; and the poor creatures are thrown upon the charity of strangers, or on the miserable pittance wrung from the poor-rates.

It would seem to be of little use preaching up an extension of rights to a people who are so supinely indifferent to their own well-being,—who are really unconcerned about their own elevation. The friends of the industrious should faithfully tell them that they must exercise prudence, economy, and self-denial, if they would really be raised from selfish debasement, and become elevated to the dignity of thinking beings. It is only by practising the principles of self-dependence that they can achieve dignity, stability, and consideration in society; or that they can acquire such influence and power as to raise them in the scale of social well-being.

Brown, the Oxford shoemaker, was of opinion that "a good mechanic is the most independent man in the world." At least he ought to be such. He has always a market for his skill; and if he be ordinarily diligent, sober, and intelligent, he may be useful, healthy, and happy. With a thrifty use of his means, he may, if he earns from thirty to forty shillings a week, dress well, live well, and educate his children creditably.

Hugh Miller never had more than twenty-four shillings a week while working as a journeyman stonemason, and here is the result of his fifteen years' experience:—

"Let me state, for it seems to be very much the fashion to draw dolorous pictures of the condition of the labouring classes, that from the close of the first year in which I worked as a journeyman until I took final leave of the mallet and chisel, I never knew what it was to want a shilling; that my two uncles, my grandfather, and the mason with whom I served my apprenticeship—all working men—had had a similar experience; and that it was the experience of my father also. I cannot doubt that deserving mechanics may, in exceptional cases, be exposed to want; but I can as little doubt that the cases *are* exceptional, and that much of the suffering of the class is a consequence either of improvidence on the part of the competently skilled, or of a course of trifling during the term of apprenticeship, quite as common as trifling at school, that always lands those who indulge in it in the hapless position of the inferior workman."

It is most disheartening to find that so many of the highest paid workmen in the kingdom should spend so large a portion of their earnings in their own personal and sensual gratification. Many spend a third, and others half their entire earnings, in drink. It would be considered monstrous, on the part of any man whose lot has been cast among the educated classes to exhibit such a degree of selfish indulgence; and to spend even one-fourth of his income upon objects in which his wife and children have no share.

Means of Saving

Mr. Roolmck recently asked, at a public meeting,[7] "Why should the mail who makes £200 or £300 a year by his mechanical labour, be a rude, coarse, brutal fellow? There is no reason why he should be so.

Why should he not be like a gentleman? Why should not his house be like my house? When I go home from my labour, what do I find? I find a cheerful wife—I find an elegant, educated woman. I have a daughter; she is the same. Why should not you find the same happy influences at home? I want to know, when the working man comes from his daily labour to his home, why he should not find his table spread as mine is spread; why he should not find his wife well dressed, cleanly, loving, kind, and his daughter the same? . . . We all know that many working men, earning good wages, spend their money in the beerhouse and in drunkenness, instead of in clothing their wives and families. Why should not these men spend their wages as I spend my small stipend, in intellectual pleasures, in joining with my family in intellectual pursuits? Why should not working men, after enjoying their dinners and thanking God for what they have got, turn their attention to intellectual enjoyments, instead of going out to get drunk in the nearest pothouse! Depend on it these things ought to go to the heart of a working man; and he is not a friend to the working man who talks to him and makes him believe that he is a great man in the State, and who don't tell him what are the duties of his position."

It is difficult to account for the waste and extravagance of working people. It must be the hereditary remnant of the original savage. It must be a survival. The savage feasts and drinks until everything is gone; and then he hunts or goes to war. Or it may be the survival of slavery in the State. Slavery was one of the first of human institutions. The strong man made the weak man work for him. The warlike race subdued the less warlike race, and made them their slaves. Thus slavery existed from the earliest times. In Greece and Rome the righting was done by freemen, the labour by helots and bondsmen. But slavery also existed in the family. The wife was the slave of her husband as much as the slave whom he bought in the public market.

Slavery long existed among ourselves. It existed when Caesar lauded. It existed in Saxon times, when the household work was done by slaves. The Saxons were notorious slave-dealers, and the Irish were their best customers. The principal mart was at Bristol, from whence the Saxons

---

7. Meeting of the Mechanics' Institutes at Dewsbury, Yorkshire.

Means of Saving

exported large numbers of slaves into Ireland so that, according to Irish historians, there was scarcely a house in Ireland without a British slave in it.

When the Normans took possession of England, they continued slavery. They made slaves of the Saxons themselves whom they decreed villeins and bondsmen. Domesday Book shows that the toll of the market at Lewes in Sussex was a penny for a cow, and fourpence for a slave—not a serf (*adscriptus glebae*), but an unconditional bondsman. From that time slavery continued in various forms. It is recorded of "the good old times," that it was not till the reign of Henry IV. (1320—1413) that villeins, farmers, and mechanics were permitted by law to put their children to school; and long after that, they dared not educate a son for the Church without a licence from the lord.[8] The Kings of England, in their contests with the feudal aristocracy, gradually relaxed the slave laws. They granted charters founding Royal Burghs; and when the slaves fled into them, and were able to conceal themselves for a year and a day, they then became freemen of the burgh, and were declared by law to be free.

The last serfs in England were emancipated in the reign of Queen Elizabeth; but the last serfs in Scotland, were not emancipated until the reign of George III, at the end of last century. Before then, the colliers and salters belonged to the soil. They were bought and sold with it. They had no power to determine what their wages should be. Like the slaves in the Southern States of America, they merely accepted such sustenance as was sufficient to maintain their muscles and sinews in working order.

They were never required to save for any purpose, for they had no right to their own savings. They did not need to provide for tomorrow; their masters provided for them. The habit of improvidence was thus formed; and it still continues. The Scotch colliers, who were recently earning from ten to fourteen shillings a day, are the grandsons of men who were slaves down to the end of last century. The preamble of an Act passed in 1799 (39th Geo. III., c. 56), runs as follows: "Whereas, before the passing of an Act of the fifteenth of his present Majesty, many colliers, coal-bearers, and salters *were bound for life to, and transferable with, the collieries and salt-works where they worked,* but by the said Act their bondage was taken off and they were declared to be free, notwithstanding which many colliers and coalbearers and salters still continue in a state of bondage from not having complied with the provisions, or from having become

---

8. Henry's History of England, Book v., chap. 4

subject to the penalties of that Act," etc. The new Act then proceeds to declare them free from servitude. The slaves formerly earned only enough to keep them, and laid by nothing whatever for the future. Hence we say that the improvidence of the colliers, as of the iron-workers, is but a survival of the system of slavery in our political constitution.

Matters have now become entirely different. The workman, no matter what his trade, is comparatively free. The only slavery from which he suffers, is his passion for drink. In this respect he still resembles the Esquimaux and the North American Indians. Would he be really free? Then he must exercise the powers of a free, responsible man. He must exercise self-control and self-constraint,—and sacrifice present personal gratifications for prospective enjoyments of a much higher kind. It is only by self-respect and self-control that the position of the workman can be really elevated.

The working man is now more of a citizen than he ever was before. He is a recognized power, and has been admitted within the pale of the constitution. For him mechanics' institutes, newspapers, benefit societies, and all the modern agencies of civilization, exist in abundance. He is admitted to the domain of intellect; and, from time to time, great thinkers, artists, engineers, philosophers, and poets, rise up from his order, to proclaim that intellect is of no rank, and nobility of no exclusive order. The influences of civilization are rousing society to its depths; and daily evidences are furnished of the rise of the industrious classes to a position of social power. Discontent may, and does, exhibit itself; but discontent is only the necessary condition of improvement; for a man will not be stimulated to rise up into a higher condition unless he be first made dissatisfied with the lower condition out of which he has to rise. To be satisfied is to repose; while, to be rationally dissatisfied, is to contrive, to work, and to act, with an eye to future advancement.

The working classes very much under-estimate themselves. Though they receive salaries or wages beyond the average earnings of professional men, yet many of them have no other thought than that of living in mean houses, and spending their surplus time and money in drink. They seem wanting in respect for themselves as well as for their class. They encourage the notion that there is something degrading in labour,—than which nothing can be more false. Labour of all kinds is dignifying and honourable; it is the idler, above all others, who is undignified and dishonourable.

"Let the working man," says Mr. Sterling, "try to connect his daily task, however mean, with the highest thoughts he can apprehend, and he thereby secures the rightfulness of his lot, and is raising his existence to his utmost good. It is because the working man has failed to do this, and because others have failed to help him as they ought, that the lot of labour has hitherto been associated with what is mean and degrading."

With respect to remuneration, the average of skilled mechanics and artisans, as we have already said, are better paid than the average of working curates. The working engineer is better paid than the ensign in a marching regiment. The foreman in any of our large engineering establishments is better paid than an army surgeon. The rail-roller receives over a guinea a day, while an assistant navy surgeon receives fourteen shillings, and after three years' service, twenty-one shillings, with rations. The majority of dissenting ministers are much worse paid than the better classes of skilled mechanics and artizans; and the average of clerks employed in counting-houses and warehouses receive wages very much lower.

Skilled workmen might—and, if they had the will, they would—occupy a social position as high as the educated classes we refer to. What prevents them rising? Merely because they will not use their leisure to cultivate their minds. They have sufficient money; it is culture that they want. They ought to know that the position of men in society does not depend so much upon their earnings, as upon their character and intelligence. And it is because they neglect their abundant opportunities,—because they are thriftless and spend their earnings in animal enjoyments,—because they refuse to cultivate the highest parts of their nature,—that they are excluded, or rather self-excluded, from those social and other privileges in which they are entitled to take part.

Notwithstanding their high wages, they for the most part cling to the dress, the language, and the manners of their class. They appear, during their leisure hours, in filthy dresses, and unwashed hands. No matter how skilled the workman may be, he is ready to sink his mind and character to the lowest level of his co-workers. Even the extra money which he earns by his greater skill, often contributes to demoralize and degrade him. And yet he might dress as well, live as well, and be surrounded by the physical comforts and intellectual luxuries of professional men. But no! From week to week his earnings are wasted. He does not save a farthing; he is a public-house victim; and when work becomes slack, and his body becomes diseased, his only refuge is the workhouse.

How are these enormous evils to be cured? Some say by better education; others by moral and religious instruction; others by better homes, and better wives and mothers. All these influences will doubtless contribute much towards the improvement of the people. One thing is perfectly clear, that an immense amount of ignorance prevails, and that such ignorance must be dissipated before the lower classes can be elevated. Their whole character must be changed, and they must be taught in early life habits of forecast and self-control.

We often hear that "Knowledge is Power;" but we never hear that Ignorance is Power. And yet Ignorance has always had more power in the world than Knowledge. Ignorance dominates. It is because of the evil propensities of men that the costly repressive institutions of modern governments exist.

Ignorance arms men against each other; provides gaols and penitentiaries; police and constabulary. All the physical force of the State is provided by Ignorance; is required by Ignorance; is very often wielded by Ignorance. We may well avow, then, that Ignorance is Power.

Ignorance is powerful, because Knowledge, as yet, has obtained access only to the minds of the few. Let Knowledge become more generally diffused; let the multitude become educated, thoughtful, and wise; and then Knowledge may obtain the ascendancy over Ignorance. But that time has not yet arrived.

Look into the records of crime, and you will find that, for one man possessed of wisdom or knowledge who commits a crime, there are a hundred ignorant. Or, into the statistics of drunkenness and improvidence of all sorts; still Ignorance is predominant. Or, into the annals of pauperism; there, again, Ignorance is Power.

The principal causes of anxiety in this country, are the social suffering and disease which proceed from Ignorance. To mitigate these, we form associations, organize societies, spend money, and labour in committees. But the power of Ignorance is too great for us. We almost despair while we work. We feel that much of our effort is wasted. We are often ready to give up in dismay, and recoil from our encounter with the powers of evil.

"How forcible are right words!" exclaimed Job. Yes! But, with equal justice, he might have said, "How forcible are wrong words!" The wrong words have more power with ignorant minds than the right words. They fit themselves into wrong heads, and prejudiced heads, and empty heads; and have power over them. The right words have often no meaning for them, any more than if they were the words of some dead language. The wise man's thoughts do not reach the multitude, but fly over their heads. Only the few as yet apprehend them.

The physiologist may discuss the laws of health, and the Board of Health may write tracts for circulation among the people; but half the people cannot so much as read; and of the remaining half, but a very small proportion are in the habit of *thinking*. Thus the laws of health are disregarded; and when fever comes, it finds a wide field to work upon: in undrained and filthy streets and back-yards,—noisome, pestilential districts,—foul, uncleansed dwellings,—large populations ill-supplied with clean water and with pure air. There death makes fell havoc; many destitute widows and children have to be maintained out of the poor's-rates; and then we reluctantly confess to ourselves that Ignorance is Power.

The only method of abating this power of Ignorance, is by increasing that of Knowledge. As the sun goes up the sky, the darkness disappears; and the owl, the bat, and the beasts of prey, slink out of sight. Give the people knowledge,—give them better education,—and thus, crime will be abated,—drunkenness, improvidence, lawlessness, and all the powers of evil, will, to a certain extent, disappear.[9]

It must, however, be admitted that education is not enough. The clever man may be a clever rogue; and the cleverer he is, the cleverer rogue he will be. Education, therefore, must be based upon religion and morality; for education by itself will not eradicate vicious propensities. Culture of intellect has but little effect upon moral conduct. You may see clever, educated, literary men, with no conduct whatever,—wasteful, improvident, drunken, and vicious. It follows, therefore, that education must be based upon the principles of religion and morality.

Nor has the poverty of the people so much to do with their social degradation as is commonly supposed. The question is essentially a

---

9. The recent reports of Mr. Tremenheere to the Secretary of State for the Home Department, with respect to the condition of the population in the iron and coal districts, show that he places considerable reliance upon the effect of Education. The evidence which he brought together from all parts of the country, shows that the increase of immorality with the increase of wages was attributed to the low tastes and desires of the people.—that the obstinate refusal of the men to exert more than two-thirds of their fair powers of work, by which the cost of production is largely enhanced, capital crippled, and the public mulcted, was due to the same cause,—that their readiness to become the prey of unionists and agitators is traceable to their want of the most elementary principles of thought,—that most of the accidents, which are of weekly occurrence, are occasioned by their stupidity and ignorance,—that wherever they have advanced in intelligence, they have become more skilful, more subordinate, and more industrious. These facts have convinced the more thoughtful and far-sighted masters, that the only sure means of maintaining their ground under increasing foreign competition, and averting a social crisis, is to reform the character of the rising generation of operatives by education,

moral one. If the income of the labouring community could be suddenly doubled, their happiness will not necessarily be increased; for happiness does not consist in money. In fact, the increased wages might probably prove a curse instead of a blessing. In the case of many, there would be an increased consumption of drink, with the usual results,—an increase of drunken violence, and probably an increase of crime.

The late Mr. Clay, chaplain of the Preston House of Correction, after characterizing drunkenness as the *great sin*, proceeds: "It still rises in savage hostility, against everything allied to order and religion; it still barricades every avenue by which truth and peace seek to enter the poor man's home and heart. . . . Whatever may be the predominant cause of crime, it is very clear that ignorance, religious ignorance, is the chief ingredient in the character of the criminal. This combines with the passion for liquor, and offences numberless are engendered by the union."

The late Sir Arthur Helps, when speaking of high and low wages, and of the means of getting and spending money, thus expresses himself on the subject, in his "Friends in Council":"My own conviction is, that throughout England every year there is sufficient wages given, even at the present low rate, to make the condition of the labouring poor quite different from what it is. But then these wages must be well spent. I do not mean that the poor could of themselves alone effect this change; but were they seconded by the advice, the instruction, and the aid (not given in money, or only in money lent to produce the current interest of the day) of the classes above them, the rest the poor might accomplish for themselves. And, indeed, all that the rich could do to elevate the poor could hardly equal the advantage that would be gained by the poor themselves, if they could thoroughly subdue that one vice of drunkenness, the most wasteful of all the vices.

"In the living of the poor (as indeed of all of us) there are two things to be considered; how to get money, and how to spend it. Now, I believe, the experience of employers will bear me out in saying, that it is frequently found that the man with 20s. a week does not live more comfortably, or save more, than the man with 14s.,—the families of the two men being the same in number and general circumstances. It is probable that unless he have a good deal of prudence and thought, the man who gets at all more than the average of his class does not know what to do with it, or only finds in it a means superior to that which his fellows possess of satisfying his appetite for drinking."

Notwithstanding, however, the discouraging circumstances to which we have referred, we must believe that in course of time, as men's nature becomes improved by education—secular, moral, and religious—they may be induced to make a better use of their means, by considerations of prudence, forethought, and parental responsibility. A German writer speaks of the education given to a child as *a capital*—equivalent to a store of money—placed at its disposal by the parent. The child, when grown to manhood, may employ the education, as he might employ the money, badly; but that is no argument against the possession of either. Of course, the value of education, as of money, chiefly consists in its proper use. And one of the advantages of knowledge is, that the very acquisition of it tends to increase the capability of using it aright; which is certainly not the case with the accumulation of money.

Education, however obtained, is always an advantage to a man. Even as a means of material advancement, it is worthy of being sought after,—not to speak of its moral uses as an elevator of character and intelligence. And if, as Dr. Lyon Playfair insists, the composition between industrial nations must before long become a competition mainly of intelligence, it is obvious that England must make better provision for the education of its industrial classes, or be prepared to fall behind in the industrial progress of nations.

"It would be of little avail," said Dr. Brewster of Edinburgh, "to the peace and happiness of society, if the great truths of the material world were confined to the educated and the wise. The organization of science thus limited would cease to be a blessing. Knowledge secular, and knowledge divine, the double current of the intellectual life-blood of man, must not merely descend through the great arteries of the social frame; it must be taken up by the minutest capillaries before it can nourish and purify society. Knowledge is at once the manna and the medicine of our moral being. Where crime is the bane, knowledge is the antidote. Society may escape from the pestilence and may survive the famine; but the demon of ignorance, with his grim adjutants of vice and riot, will pursue her into her most peaceful haunts, destroying our institutions, and converting into a wilderness the paradise of social and domestic life. The State has, therefore, a great duty to perform. As it punishes crime, it is bound to prevent it. As it subjects us to laws, it must teach us to read them; and while it thus teaches, it must teach also the ennobling truths which display the power and the wisdom of the great Lawgiver, thus diffusing knowledge while it is extending education; and thus making men contented, and happy, and humble, while it makes them quiet and obedient subjects."

A beginning has already been made with public school education. Much still remains to be done to establish the system throughout the empire. At present we are unable to judge of the effects of what has been done. But if general education accomplish as much for England as it has already accomplished for Germany, the character of this country will be immensely improved during the next twenty years. Education has almost banished drunkenness from Germany; and had England no drunkenness, no thriftlessness, no reckless multiplication, our social miseries would be comparatively trivial.

We must therefore believe that as intelligence extends amongst the working class, and as a better moral tone pervades them, there will be a rapid improvement in their sober, thrifty and provident habits; for these form the firmest and surest foundations for social advancement. There is a growing desire, on the part of the more advanced minds in society, to see the working men take up their right position. They who do society's work,—who produce, under the direction of the most intelligent of their number, the wealth of the nation,—are entitled to a much higher place than they have yet assumed. We believe in this "good time coming," for working men and women,—when an atmosphere of intelligence shall pervade them—when they will prove themselves as enlightened, polite, and independent as the other classes of society; and, as the first and surest step towards this consummation, we counsel them to *provide*—to provide for the future as well as for the present—to provide, in times of youth and plenty, against the times of adversity, misfortune, and old age.

"If any one intends to improve his condition," said the late William Felkin, Mayor of Nottingham, himself originally a working man, "he must earn all he can, spend as little as he can, and make what he does spend, bring him and his family all the real enjoyment he can. The first saving which a working man makes out of his earnings is the first step,—and because it is the first, the most important step towards true independence. Now independence is as practicable in the case of an industrious and economic, though originally poor, workman, as in that of the tradesman or merchant,—and is as great and estimable a blessing. The same process must be attended to,—that is, the entire expenditure being kept below the clear income, all contingent claims being carefully considered and provided for, and the surplus held sacred, to be employed for those purposes, and those only, which duty or conscience may point out as important or desirable. This requires a course of laborious exertion and strict economy, a little foresight, and possibly some privation. But this is only what is common to all desirable objects. And inasmuch as I know what it is to labour with the hands long hours, and for small wages, as well as any workman to whom I address myself, and to practise self-denial withal, I am emboldened to declare from experience that the gain of independence, or rather self-dependence, for which I plead, is worth infinitely more than all the cost of its attainment; and, moreover, that to attain it in a greater or less degree, according to circumstances, is within the power of by far the greater number of skilled workmen engaged in our manufactories."

Chapter 5

Examples of Thrift

"Examples demonstrate the possibility of success."—Cotton.

"The force of his own merit, makes his way."—Shakespeare.

"Reader, attend, whether thy soul Soars Fancy's flight beyond the Pole, Or darkling grubs this earthly hole In low pursuit—Know, prudent, cautious self-control, Is wisdom's root."—Burns.

"In the family, as in the State, the best source of wealth is Economy."—Cicero.

"Right action is the result of right faith; but a true and right faith cannot be sustained, deepened, extended, save in a course of right action."—M'Combie.

Thrift is the spirit of order applied to domestic management and organization. Its object is to manage frugally the resources of the family; to prevent waste; and avoid useless expenditure. Thrift is under the influence of reason and forethought, and never works by chance or by fits. It endeavours to make the most and the best of everything. It does not save money for saving's sake. It makes cheerful sacrifices for the present benefit of others; or it submits to voluntary privation for some future good.

Mrs. Inchbald, author of the "Simple Story," was, by dint of thrift, able to set apart the half of her small income for the benefit of her infirm sister. There was thus about two pounds a week for the maintenance of each. "Many times," she says, "during the winter, when I was crying with cold, have I said to myself, 'Thank God, my dear sister need not leave her chamber; she will find her fire ready for her each morning; for she is now far less able than I am to endure privation.'" Mrs. Inchbald's family were, for the most part very poor; and she felt it right to support them during their numerous afflictions. There is one thing that may be say of Benevolence,—that it has never ruined anyone; though selfishness and dissipation have ruined thousands.

The words "Waste not, want not," carved in stone over Sir Walter Scott's kitchen fireplace at Abbotsford, expresses in a few words the secret of Order in the midst of abundance. Order is most useful in the management of everything,—of a household, of a business, of a manufactory, of an army. Its maxim is—A place for everything, and everything in its place. Order is wealth; for, whoever properly regulates the use of his income, almost doubles his resources. Disorderly persons are rarely rich; and orderly persons are rarely poor.

Order is the best manager of time; for unless work is properly arranged, Time is lost; and, once lost, it is gone for ever. Order illustrates many important subjects. Thus, obedience to the moral and natural law, is order. Respect for ourselves and our neighbours, is order. Regard for the rights and obligations of all, is order. Virtue is order. The world began with order. Chaos prevailed, before the establishment of order.

Thrift is the spirit of order in human life. It is the prime agent in private economy. It preserves the happiness of many a household. And as it is usually woman who regulates the order of the household, it is mainly upon her that the well-doing of society depends. It is therefore all the more necessary that she should early be educated in the habit and the virtue of orderliness.

The peer, the merchant, the clerk, the artizan, and the labourer, are all of the same nature, born with the same propensities and subject to similar influences. They are, it is true, born in different positions, but it rests with themselves whether they shall live their lives nobly or vilely. They may not have their choice of riches or poverty; but they have their choice of being good or evil,—of being worthy or worthless.

People of the highest position, in point of culture and education, have often as great privations to endure as the average of working people. They have often to make their incomes go much further. They have to keep up a social standing. They have to dress better; and live sufficiently well for the purpose of health. Though their income may be less than that of colliers and iron-workers, they are under the moral necessity of educating their sons and bringing them up as gentlemen, so that they may take their fair share of the world's work.

Thus, the tenth Earl of Buchan brought up a numerous family of children, one of whom afterwards rose to be Lord Chancellor of England,

Examples of Thrift

upon an income not exceeding two hundred a year. It is not the amount of income, so much as the good use of it, that marks the true man; and viewed in this light, good sense, good taste, and sound mental culture, are among the best of all economists.

The late Dr. Aiton said that his father brought up a still larger family on only half the income of the Earl of Buchan. The following dedication, prefixed to his work on "Clerical Economics," is worthy of being remembered: "This work is respectfully dedicated to a Father, now in the eighty-third year of his age, who, on an income which never exceeded a hundred pounds yearly, educated, out of a family of twelve children, four sons to liberal professions, and who has often sent his last shilling to each of them, in their turn, when they were at college."

The author might even cite his own case as an illustration of the advantages of thrift. His mother was left a widow, when her youngest child—the youngest of eleven—was only three weeks old. Notwithstanding a considerable debt on account of a suretyship, which was paid, she bravely met the difficulties of her position, and perseveringly overcame them. Though her income was less than that of many highly paid working men, she educated her children well, and brought them up religiously and virtuously. She put her sons in the way of doing well, and if they have not done so, it was through no fault of hers.

Hume, the historian, was a man of good family; but being a younger brother, his means were very small. His father died while he was an infant; he was brought up by his mother, who devoted herself entirely to the rearing and educating of her children. At twenty-three, young Hume went to France to prosecute his studies. "There," says he, in his Autobiography, "I laid down that plan of life which I have steadily and successfully pursued. I resolved to make a very rigid frugality supply my deficiency of fortune, to maintain unimpaired my independency, and to regard every object as contemptible, except the improvement of my talents in literature." The first book he published was a complete failure. But he went on again; composed and published another book, which was a success. But he made no money by it. He became secretary to the military embassy at Vienna and Turin; and at thirty-six he thought himself rich. These are his own words: "My appointments, with my frugality, had made me reach a fortune which I called independent, though most of my friends were inclined to smile when I said so: in short, I was now master of near a thousand pounds." Every one knows that a thousand pounds, at five per cent., means fifty pounds a year; and Hume considered himself independent with that income. His friend Adam Smith said of him: "Even in the lowest state of his fortune, his great and necessary frugality never hindered him from exercising, upon proper occasions, acts both of charity and generosity. It was a frugality founded not on avarice, but upon the love of independency."

But one of the most remarkable illustrations of Thrift is to be found in the history of the Rev. Robert Walker—the Wonderful Robert Walker, as he is still called in the district of Cumberland where he resided. He was curate of Leathwaite during the greater part of last century. The income of the curacy, at the time of his appointment (1735), was only five pounds a year. His wife brought him a fortune of forty pounds. Is it possible that he could contrive to live upon his five pounds a year, the interest of his wife's fortune, and the result of his labours as a clergyman? Yes, he contrived to do all this; and he not only lived well, though plainly, but he saved money, which he left for the benefit of his family. He accomplished all this by means of industry, frugality, and temperance.

First, about his industry. He thoroughly did the work connected with his curacy. The Sabbath was in all respects regarded by him as a holy day. After morning and evening service, he devoted the evening to reading the Scriptures and family prayer. On weekdays, he taught the children of the parish, charging nothing for the education, but only taking so much as the people chose to give him. The parish church was his school; and while the children were repeating their lessons by his side, he was, like Shenstone's schoolmistress, engaged in spinning wool. He had the right of pasturage upon the mountains for a few sheep and a couple of cows, which required his attendance. With this pastoral occupation he joined the labours of husbandry, for he rented two or three acres of land in addition to his own acre of glebe, and he also possessed a garden,—the whole of which was tilled by his own hand. The fuel of the house consisted of peat, procured by his labour from the neighbouring mosses. He also assisted his parishioners in haymaking and shearing their flocks,—in which latter art he was eminently dexterous. In return, the neighbours would present him with a haycock, or a fleece, as a general acknowledgment of his services.

After officiating as curate of Leathwaite for about twenty years, the annual value of the living was increased to seventeen pounds ten shillings. His character being already well known and highly appreciated, the Bishop of Carlisle offered Mr. Walker the appointment of the adjoining curacy of Ulpha; but he conscientiously refused it, on the ground that the annexation "would be apt to cause a general discontent among the inhabitants of both places, by either thinking themselves slighted, being only served alternately, or neglected in the duty, or attributing it to covetousness in me; all which occasions of murmuring I would willingly avoid." Yet at this time Mr. Walker had a family of eight children. He afterwards maintained one of his sons at Trinity College Dublin, until he was ready for taking Holy Orders.

The parish pastor was, of course, a most economical man. Yet no act of his life savoured in the least degree of meanness or avarice. On the other hand, his conduct throughout life displayed the greatest disinterestedness and generosity. He knew very little of luxuries, and he cared less. Tea was only used in his house for visitors. The family used milk, which was indeed far better. Excepting milk, the only other drink used in the house was water—clear water drawn from the mountain spring. The clothing of the family was comely and decent; but it was all home-made: it was simple, like their diet. Occasionally one of the mountain sheep was killed for purposes of food; and towards the end of the year, a cow was killed and salted down for provision during winter. The hide was tanned, and the leather furnished shoes for the family. By these and other means, this venerable clergyman reared his numerous family; not only preserving them, as he so affectingly says, "from wanting the necessaries of life," but affording them "an unstinted education, and the means of raising themselves in society."[1]

Many men, in order to advance themselves in the world, and to raise themselves in society, have "scorned delights and lived laborious days." They have lived humbly and frugally, in order to accomplish greater things. They have supported themselves by their hand labour, until they could support themselves by their head labour. Some may allege that this is not justifiable—that it is a sin against the proletariat to attempt to rise in the world,—that "once a cobbler always a cobbler." But, until a better system has been established, the self-application of individuals is the only method by which science and knowledge can be conquered, and the world permanently advanced.

Goethe says, "It is perfectly indifferent within what circle an honest man acts, provided he do but know how to understand and completely fill out that circle;" and again, "An honest and vigorous will could make

---

1. The best account of Mr. Walker is to be found in the Appendix to the Poems of Wordsworth. The poet greatly appreciated the clergyman's character, and noticed him in his "Excursion," as well as in the Notes to the Sonnets entitled "The River Duddon."

itself a path and employ its activity to advantage under every form of society." "What is the best government?" he asks: "That which teaches us to govern ourselves!" All that we need, in his opinion, is individual liberty, and self-culture. "Let every one," he says, "only do the right in his place, without troubling himself about the turmoil of the world."

At all events, it is not by socialism, but by individualism, that anything has been done towards the achievement of knowledge, and the advancement of society. It is the will and determination of individual men that impels the world forward in art, in science, and in all the means and methods of civilization.

Individual men are willing to deny themselves, but associated communities will not. The masses are too selfish, and fear that advantage will be taken of any sacrifices which they may be called upon to make. Hence it is amongst the noble band of resolute spirits that we look for those who raise and elevate the world, as well as themselves. The recollection of what they have done, acts as a stimulus to others. It braces the mind of man, reanimates his will, and encourages him to further exertions.

When Lord Elcho addressed the East Lothian colliers, he named several men who had raised themselves from the coalpit; and first of all he referred to Mr. Macdonald, member for Stafford. "The beginning of my acquaintance with Mr. Macdonald," he said, "was, when I was told that a miner wanted to see me in the lobby of the House of Commons. I went out and saw Mr. Macdonald, who gave me a petition from this district, which he asked me to present. I entered into conversation with him, and was much struck by his intelligence. He told me that he had begun life as a boy in the pit in Lanarkshire, and that the money he saved as a youth in the summer, he spent at Glasgow University in the winter; and that is where he got whatever book-learning or power of writing he possesses. I say that is an instance that does honour to the miners of Scotland. Another instance was that of Dr. Hogg, who began as a pitman in this county; worked in the morning, attended school in the afternoon; then went to the University for four years and to the Theological Hall for five years; and afterwards, in consequence of his health failing, he went abroad, and is now engaged as a missionary in Upper Egypt. Or take the case of Mr. (now Sir George) Elliot, member for North Durham, who has spoken up for the miners all the better, for having had practical knowledge of their work. He began as a miner in the pit, and he worked his way up till he has in his employment many thousand men. He has risen to his great wealth and station from the humblest position; as every man who now hears me is capable of doing, to a greater or less degree, if he will only be thrifty and industrious."

Lord Elcho might also have mentioned Dr. Hutton, the geologist, a man of a much higher order of genius; who was the son of a coal-viewer. Bewick, the wood engraver, is also said to have been the son of a coal-miner. Dr. Campbell was the son of a Loanhead collier: he was the forerunner of Moffat and Livingstone, in their missionary journeys among the Bechuanas in South Africa. Allan Ramsay, the poet, was also the son of a miner.

George Stephenson worked his way from the pithead to the highest position as an engineer. George began his life with industry, and when he had saved a little money, he spent it in getting a little learning. What a happy man he was, when his wages were increased to twelve shillings a week. He declared upon that occasion that he was "made a man for life!" He was not only enabled to maintain himself upon his earnings, but to help his poor parents, and to pay for his own education. When his skill had increased, and his wages were advanced to a pound a week, he immediately began, like a thoughtful, intelligent workman, to lay by his surplus money; and when he had saved his first guinea, he proudly declared to one of his colleagues that he "was now a rich man!"

And he was right. For the man who, after satisfying his wants, has something to spare, is no longer poor. It is certain that from that day Stephenson never looked back; his advance as a self-improving man was as steady as the light of sunrise. A person of large experience has indeed stated that he never knew, amongst working people, a single instance of a man having out of his small earnings laid by a pound, who had in the end become a pauper.

When Stephenson proposed to erect his first locomotive, he had not sufficient means to defray its cost. But in the course of his life as a workman, he had established a character. He was trusted. He was faithful. He was a man who could be depended on. Accordingly, when the Earl of Havensworth was informed of Stephenson's desire to erect a locomotive, he at once furnished him with the means for enabling him to carry his wishes into effect.

Watt, also, when inventing the condensing steam-engine, maintained himself by making and selling mathematical instruments. He made flutes, organs, compasses,—anything that would maintain him, until he had completed his invention. At the same time he was perfecting his own education—learning French, German, mathematics, and the principles of natural philosophy. This lasted for many years; and by the time that Watt developed his steam-engine and discovered Mathew Boulton, he had, by his own efforts, become an accomplished and scientific man.

These great workers did not feel ashamed of labouring with their hands for a living; but they also felt within themselves the power of doing head-work as well as hand-work. And while thus labouring with their hands, they went on with their inventions, the perfecting of which has proved of so much advantage to the world. Hugh Miller furnished, in his own life, an excellent instance of that practical common sense in the business of life which he so strongly recommended to others. When he began to write poetry, and felt within him the growing powers of a literary man, he diligently continued his labour as a stone-cutter.

Horace Walpole has said that Queen Caroline's patronage of Stephen Duck, the thresher poet, ruined twenty men, who all turned poets. It was not so with the early success of Hugh Miller. "There is no more fatal error," he says, "into which a working man of a literary turn can fall, than the mistake of deeming himself too good for his humble employments; and yet it is a mistake as common as it is fatal. I had already seen several poor wrecked mechanics, who, believing themselves to be poets, and regarding the manual occupation by which they could alone live in independence as beneath them, and become in consequence little better than mendicants,—too good to work for their bread, but not too good virtually to beg it; and looking upon them as beacons of warning, I determined that, with God's help, I should give their error a wide offing, and never associate the idea of meanness with an honest calling, or deem myself too good to be independent."

At the same time, a man who feels that he has some good work in him, which study and labour might yet bring out, is fully justified in denying himself, and in applying his energies to the culture of his intellect. And it is astonishing how much carefulness, thrift, the reading of books, and diligent application, will help such men onward.

The author in his boyhood knew three men who worked in an agricultural implement maker's shop. They worked in wood and iron, and made carts, ploughs, harrows, drilling-machines, and such-like articles. Somehow or other, the idea got into their heads that they might be able to do something better than making carts and harrows. They did not despise the lot of hand-labour, but they desired to use it as a step towards something better. Their wages at that time could not have exceeded from eighteen to twenty shillings a week.

Examples of Thrift

Two of the young men, who worked at the same bench, contrived to save enough money to enable them to attend college during the winter. At the end of each session they went back to their hand-labour, and earned enough wages during the summer to enable them to return to their classes during the winter. The third did not adopt this course. He joined a mechanics' institute which had just been started in the town in which he lived. By attending the lectures and reading the books in the library, he acquired some knowledge of chemistry, of the principles of mechanics, and of natural philosophy. He applied himself closely, studied hard in his evening hours, and became an accomplished man.

It is not necessary to trace their history; but what they eventually arrived at, may be mentioned. Of the first two, one became the teacher and proprietor of a large public school; the other became a well-known dissenting minister; while the third, working his way strenuously and bravely, became the principal engineer and manager of the largest steamship company in the world.

Although mechanics' institutes are old institutions, they have scarcely been supported by working men. The public-house is more attractive and more frequented. And yet mechanics' institutes—even though they are scarcely known south of Yorkshire and Lancashire—have been the means of doing a great deal of good. By placing sound mechanical knowledge within the reach of even the few persons who have been disposed to take advantage of them, they have elevated many persons into positions of great social influence. "We have heard a distinguished man say publicly, that a mechanics' institution had made him; that but for the access which it had afforded him to knowledge of all kinds, he would have occupied a very different position. In short, the mechanics' institution had elevated him from the position of a licensed victualler to that of an engineer.

We have referred to the wise practice of men in humble position maintaining themselves by their trade until they saw a way towards maintaining themselves by a higher calling. Thus Herschell maintained himself by music, while pursuing his discoveries in astronomy. When playing the oboe in the pump-room at Bath, he would retire while the dancers were lounging round the room, go out and take a peep at the heavens through his telescope, and quietly return to his instrument. It was while he was thus maintaining himself by music, that he discovered the Georgium Sidus. When the Royal Society recognized his discovery, the oboe-player suddenly found himself famous.

Franklin long maintained himself by his trade of printing. He was a hard-working man,—thrifty, frugal and a great saver of time. He worked for character as much as for wages; and when it was found that he could be relied on, he prospered. At length he was publicly recognized as a great statesman, and as one of the most scientific men of his time.

Ferguson, the astronomer, lived by portrait painting, until his merits as a scientific man were recognized. John Dollond maintained himself as a silk weaver in Spitalfields. In the course of his studies he made great improvements in the refracting telescope; and the achromatic telescope, which he invented, gave him a high rank among the philosophers of his age. But during the greater part of his life, while he was carrying on his investigations, he continued, until the age of forty-six, to carry on his original trade. At length he confined himself entirely to making telescopes; and then he gave up his trade of a silk weaver. Winckelmann, the distinguished writer on classical antiquities and the fine arts, was the son of a shoemaker. His father endeavoured, as long as he could, to give his hoy a learned education; but becoming ill and worn-out, he had eventually to retire to the hospital. Winckelmann and his father were once accustomed to sing at night in the streets to raise fees to enable the boy to attend the grammar school. The younger Winckelmann then undertook, by hard labour, to support his father; and afterwards, by means of teaching, to keep himself at college. Every one knows how distinguished he eventually became.

Samuel Richardson, while writing his novels, stuck to his trade of a bookseller. He sold his books in the front shop, while he wrote them in the back. He would not give himself up to authorship, because he loved his independence. "You know," he said to his friend Defreval, "how my business engages me. You know by what snatches of time I write, that I may not neglect that, and that I may preserve that independency which is the comfort of my life. I never sought out of myself for patrons. My own industry and God's providence have been my whole reliance. The great are not great to me unless they are good, and it is a glorious privilege that a middling man enjoys, who has preserved his independency, and can occasionally (though not stoically) tell the world what he thinks of that world, in hopes to contribute, though by his mite, to mend it."

The late Dr. Olynthus Gregory, in addressing the Deptford Mechanics' Institution at their first anniversary, took the opportunity of mentioning various men in humble circumstances (some of whom he had been able to assist), who, by means of energy, application, and self-denial, had been able to accomplish great things in the acquisition of knowledge. Thus he described the case of a Labourer on the turnpike road, who had become an able Greek scholar; of a Fifer, and a Private Soldier, in a regiment of militia, both self-taught mathematicians, one of whom became a successful schoolmaster, the other a lecturer on natural philosophy; of a journeyman Tin-plate worker, who invented rules for the solution of cubic equations; of a country Sexton, who became a teacher of music, and who, by his love of the study of musical science, was transformed from a drunken sot to an exemplary husband and father; of a Coal Miner (a correspondent of Dr. Gregory's), who was an able writer on topics of the higher mathematics; of another correspondent, a labouring Whitesmith, who was also well acquainted with the course of pure mathematics, as taught at Cambridge, Dublin, and the military colleges; of a Tailor, who was an excellent geometrician, and had discovered curves which escaped the notice of Newton, and who laboured industriously and contentedly at his trade until sixty years of age, when, by the recommendation of his scientific friends, he was appointed Nautical Examiner at the Trinity House; of a ploughman in Lincolnshire, who, without aid of men or books, discovered the rotation of the earth, the principles of spherical astronomy, and invented a planetary system akin to the Tychonic; of a country Shoemaker, who became distinguished as one of the ablest metaphysical writers in Britain, and who, at more than fifty years of age, was removed by the influence of his talents and their worth, from his native country to London, where he was employed to edit some useful publications devoted to the diffusion of knowledge and the best interests of mankind.

Students of Art have had to practise self-denial in many ways. Quentin Matsys, having fallen in love with a painter's daughter, and determined to win her. Though but a blacksmith and a farrier, he studied art so diligently, and acquired so much distinction, that his mistress afterwards accepted the painter whom she had before rejected as the blacksmith. Flaxman, however, married his wife before he had acquired any distinction whatever as an artist. He was merely a skilful and promising pupil. When Sir Joshua Reynolds heard of his marriage, he exclaimed, "Flaxman is ruined for an artist!" But it was not so. When Flaxman's wife heard of the remark, she said, "Let us work and economize; I will never have it said that Ann Denbam ruined John Flaxman as an artist." They economized accordingly. To earn money, Flaxman undertook to collect the local rates; and what with art and industry, the patient, hard-working, thrifty couple, after five years of careful saving, set out for Rome together. There Flaxman studied and worked; there he improved his knowledge of art; and there he acquired the reputation of being the first of English sculptors.

The greater number of artists have sprung from humble life. If they had been born rich, they would probably never have been artists. They have had to work their way from one position to another; and to strengthen their nature by conquering difficulty. Hogarth began his career by engraving shop-bills. William Sharp began by engraving door-plates. Tassie the sculptor and medallist, began life as a stone-cutter. Having accidentally seen a collection of pictures, he aspired to become an artist and entered an academy to learn the elements of drawing. He continued to work at his old trade until he was able to maintain himself by his new one. He used his labour as the means of cultivating his skill in his more refined and elevated profession.

Chantry of Sheffield, was an economist both of time and money. He saved fifty pounds out of his earnings as a carver and gilder; paid the money to his master, and cancelled his indentures. Then he came up to London, and found employment as a journeyman carver; he proceeded to paint portraits and model busts, and at length worked his way to the first position as a sculptor.

Canova was a stone-cutter, like his father and his grandfather; and through stone-cutting he worked his way to sculpture. After leaving the quarry, he went to Venice, and gave his services to an artist, from whom he received but little recompense for his work. "I laboured," said he, "for a mere pittance, but it was sufficient. It was the fruit of my own resolution; and, as I then flattered myself, the foretaste of more honourable rewards,—for I never thought of wealth." He pursued his studies,—in drawing and modelling; in languages, poetry, history, antiquity, and the Greek and Roman classics. A long time elapsed before his talents were recognised, and then he suddenly became famous.

Lough, the English sculptor, is another instance of self-denial and hard work. When a boy, he was fond of drawing. At school, he made drawings of horses, dogs, cows, and men, for pins: that was his first pay; and he used to go home with his jacket sleeve stuck full of them. He and his brothers next made figures in clay. Pope's Homer lay on his father's window. The boys were so delighted with it, that they made thousands of models—one taking the Greeks, and the other the Trojans. An odd volume of Gibbon gave an account of the Coliseum. After the family were in bed, the brothers made a model of the Coliseum, and filled it with fighting gladiators. As the boys grew up, they were sent to their usual outdoor work, following the plough and doing the usual agricultural labour; but still adhering to their modelling at leisure hours. At Christmas-time, Lough was very much in demand. Everybody wanted him to make models in pastry for Christmas pies,—the neighbouring farmers especially, "It was capital practice," he afterwards said.

At length Lough went from Newcastle to London, to push his way in the world of art. He obtained a passage in a collier, the skipper of which he knew. When he reached London, he slept on board the collier as long as it remained in the Thames. He was so great a favourite with the men, that they all urged him to go back. He had no friends, no patronage, no money; What could he do with everything against him? But, having already gone so far, he determined to proceed. He would not go back—at least, not yet. The men all wept when he took farewell of them. He was alone in London; under the shadow of St. Paul's.

His next step was to take a lodging in an obscure first floor in Burleigh Street, over a greengrocer's shop; and there he began to model his grand statue of Milo. He had to take the roof off to let Milo's head out. There Haydon found him, and was delighted with his genius. "I went," he says, "to young Lough, the sculptor, who has just burst out, and has produced a great effect. His Milo is really the most extraordinary thing, considering all the circumstances, in modern sculpture. It is another proof of the efficacy of inherent genius." [2] That Lough must have been poor enough at this time, is evident from the fact that, during the execution of his Milo, he did not eat meat for three months; and when Peter Coxe found him out, he was tearing up his shirt to make wet rags for his figure, to keep the clay moist. He had a bushel and a half of coals during the whole winter; and he used to lie down by the side of his clay model of the immortal figure, damp as it was, and shiver for hours till he fell asleep.

Chantrey once said to Haydon, "When I have made money enough, I will devote myself to high art." But busts engrossed Chantrey's time. He was munificently paid for them, and never raised himself above the money-making part of his profession. When Haydon next saw Chantrey at Brighton, he said to him, "Here is a young man from the country, who has come to London; and he is doing precisely what you have so long been dreaming of doing."

The exhibition of Milo was a great success. The Duke of Wellington went to see it, and ordered a statue. Sir Matthew White Eidley was much

---

2. Haydon's Autobiography, vol. ii., p, 155.

struck by the genius of young Lough, and became one of his greatest patrons. The sculptor determined to strike out a new path for himself. He thought the Greeks had exhausted the Pantheistic, and that heathen gods had been overdone. Lough began and pursued the study of lyric sculpture: he would illustrate the great English poets. But there was the obvious difficulty of telling the story of a figure by a single attitude. It was like a flash of thought. "The true artist," he said, "must plant his feet firmly on the earth, and sweep the heavens with his pencil. I mean," he added, "that the soul must be combined with the body, the ideal with the real, the heavens with the earth."

It is not necessary to describe the success of Mr. Lough as a sculptor. His statue of "The Mourners" is known all over the world. He has illustrated Shakespeare and Milton. His Puck, Titania, and other great works, are extensively known, and their genius universally admired. But it may be mentioned that his noble statue of Milo was not cast in bronze until 1862, when it was exhibited at the International Exhibition of that year.

The Earl of Derby, in recently distributing the prizes to the successful pupils of the Liverpool College,[3] made the following observations:—

"The vast majority of men, in all ages and countries, must work before they can eat. Even those who are not under the necessity, are, in England, generally impelled by example, by custom, perhaps by a sense of what is fitted for them, to adopt what is called an active pursuit of some sort. . . . If there is one thing more certain than another, it is this—that every member of a community is bound to do something for that community, in return for what he gets from it; and neither intellectual cultivation, nor the possession of material wealth, nor any other plea whatever, except that of physical or mental incapacity, can excuse any of us from that plain and personal duty. . . . And though it may be, in a community like this, considered by some to be a heterodox view, I will say that it often appears to me, in the present day, that we are a little too apt in all classes to look upon ourselves as mere machines for what is called 'getting on,' and to forget that there are in every human being many faculties which cannot be employed, and many wants which cannot be satisfied, by that occupation. I have not a word to utter against strenuous devotion to business while you are at it. But one of the wisest and most thoroughly cultivated men whom I ever knew, retired before the age of fifty, from

---

3. A collection ought to be made and published of Lord Derby's admirable Addresses to Young Men.

a profession in which he was making an enormous income, because, he said, he had got as much as he or any one belonging to him could want, and he did not see why he should sacrifice the rest of his life to money-getting. Some people thought him very foolish. I did not. And I believe that the gentleman of whom I speak never once repented his decision."

The gentleman to whom Lord Derby referred was Mr. Nasmyth, the inventor of the steam hammer. And as he has himself permitted the story of his life to be published, there is no necessity for concealing his name. His life is besides calculated to furnish one of the best illustrations of our subject. When a boy, he was of a bright, active, cheerful disposition. To a certain extent he inherited his mechanical powers from his father, who, besides being an excellent painter, was a thorough mechanic. It was in his workshop that the boy made his first acquaintance with tools. He also had for his companion the son of an iron-founder, and he often went to the founder's shop to watch the moulding, iron-melting, casting, forging, pattern-making, and smith's work that was going on.

"I look back," Mr. Nasmyth says, "to the hours of Saturday afternoons spent in having the run of the workshops of this small foundry as the true and only apprenticeship of my life. I did not trust to reading about such things. I saw, handled, and helped when I could; and all the ideas in connection with them became in all details, ever after, permanent in my mind,—to say nothing of the no small acquaintance obtained at the same time of the nature of workmen."

In course of time, young Nasmyth, with the aid of his father's tools, could do little jobs for himself. He made steels for tinder-boxes, which he sold to his schoolfellows. He made model steam-engines, and sectional models, for use at popular lectures and in schools; and by selling such models, he raised sufficient money to enable him to attend the lectures on Natural Philosophy and Chemistry at the Edinburgh University. Among his works at that time, was a working model of a steam carriage for use on common roads. It worked so well that he was induced to make another on a larger scale. After having been successfully used, he sold the engine for the purpose of driving a small factory.

Nasmyth was now twenty years old, and wished to turn his practical faculties to account. His object was to find employment in one of the great engineering establishments of the day. The first, in his opinion, was that of Henry Maudslay, of London. To attain his object, he made a small steam-engine, every part of which was his own handiwork, including the casting and forging. He proceeded to London; introduced himself to the great engineer; submitted his drawings; showed his models; and was finally engaged as Mr. Maudslay's private workman.

Then came the question of wages. When Nasmyth finally left home to begin the world on his own account, he determined not to cost his father another farthing. Being the youngest of eleven children, he thought that he could maintain himself, without trenching farther upon the family means. And he nobly fulfilled his determination. He felt that the wages sufficient to maintain other workmen, would surely be sufficient to maintain him. He might have to exercise self-control and self-denial; but of course he could do that. Though but a youth, he had wisdom enough and self-respect enough to deny himself everything that was unnecessary, in order to preserve the valuable situation which he had obtained.

Well, about the wages. When Mr. Maudslay referred his young workman to the chief cashier as to his weekly wages, it was arranged that Nasmyth was to receive ten shillings a week. He knew that, by strict economy, he could live within this amount. He contrived a small cooking apparatus, of which we possess the drawings. It is not necessary to describe his method of cooking, nor his method of living; it is sufficient to say that his little cooking apparatus (in which he still takes great pride) enabled him fully to accomplish his purpose. He lived within his means, and did not cost his father another farthing.

Next year his wages were increased to fifteen shillings. He then began to save money. He did not put it in a bank, but used his savings for the purpose of making the tools with which he afterwards commenced business. In the third year of his service, his wages were again increased, on account, doubtless, of the value of his services. "I don't know," he has since said, "that any future period of my life abounded in such high enjoyment of existence as the three years I spent at Maudslay's. It was a glorious situation for one like myself,—so earnest as I was in all that related to mechanism—in the study of men as well as of machinery. I wish many a young man would do as I then did. I am sure they would find their reward in that feeling of constant improvement, of daily advancement, and true independence, which will ever have a charm for those who are earnest in their endeavours to make right progress in life and in the regard of all good men."

After three years spent at Maudslay's, Mr. Nasmyth returned to Edinburgh to construct a small stock of engineering tools suitable for starting him in business on his own account. He hired a workshop and did various engineering jobs, in order to increase his little store of money and to execute his little stock of tools. This occupied him for two years; and in 1834 he removed the whole of his tools and machinery to Manchester. He began business there in a very humble way, but it increased so rapidly that he was induced to remove to a choice piece of land on the banks of the Bridgewater Canal at Patricroft, and there make a beginning—at first in wooden sheds—of the now famous Bridgewater Foundry.

"There," says he, "I toiled right heartily until December 31st, 1856, when I retired to enjoy, in active leisure, the result of many an anxious and interesting day. I had there, with the blessing of God, devoted the best years of my life to the pursuit of a business of which I was proud. And I trust that, without undue vanity, I may be allowed to say that I have left my mark upon several useful inventions, which probably have had no small share in the mechanical works of the age. There is scarcely a steamship or locomotive that is not indebted to my steam hammer; and without it, Armstrong and Whitworth guns and iron-plated men-of-war could scarcely have existed."

But though Nasmyth retired from business at the age of forty-eight, he did not seek repose in idleness. He continues to be as busy as the busiest; but in an altogether different direction. Instead of being tied to the earth, he enjoys himself amongst the stars. By means of telescopes of his own making, he has investigated the sun, and discovered its "willow leaves;" he has examined and photographed the moon, and in the monograph of it which he has published, he has made us fully acquainted with its geography. He is also a thorough artist, and spends a considerable portion of his time in painting,—though he is too modest to exhibit. The last time we visited his beautiful home at Hammerfield, he was busy polishing glasses for one of his new telescopes,—the motive power being a windmill erected on one of his outhouses.

Another word before we have done. "If," said Nasmyth, "I were to try to compress into one sentence the whole of the experience I have had during an active and successful life, and offer it to young men as a rule and certain receipt for success in any station, it would be composed in these words—'Duty first! Pleasure second!' From what I have seen of young men and their after-progress, I am satisfied that what is generally termed 'bad fortune,' 'ill luck,' and 'misfortune,' is in nine cases out of ten, simply the result of inverting the above simple maxim. Such experience as I have had, convinces me that absence of success arises in the great majority of cases from want of self-denial and want of common sense. The worst of all maxims is 'Pleasure first! Work and Duty second!'"

Chapter 6

Methods of Economy

"It was with profound wisdom that the Romans called by the same name courage and virtue. There is in fact no virtue, properly so called, without victory over ourselves; and what cost us nothing, is worth nothing."—De Maistre.

"Almost all the advantages which man possesses above the inferior animals, arise from his power of acting in combination with his fellows; and of accomplishing by the united efforts of numbers what could not be accomplished by the detached efforts of indivduals."—J.S. Mill.

"For the future, our main security will be in the wider diffusion of Property, and in all such measures as will facilitate this result. With the possession of property will come Conservative instincts, and disinclination for rash and reckless schemes. . . . We trust much, therefore, to the rural population becoming Proprietors, and to the urban population becoming Capitalists."—W.R. Greg.

The methods of practising economy are very simple. Spend less than you earn. That is the first rule. A portion should always be set apart for the future. The person who spends more than he earns, is a fool. The civil law regards the spendthrift as akin to the lunatic, and frequently takes from him the management of his own affairs.

The next rule is to pay ready money, and never, on any account, to run into debt. The person who runs into debt is apt to get cheated; and if he runs into debt to any extent, he will himself be apt to get dishonest. "Who pays what he owes, enriches himself."

The next is, never to anticipate uncertain profits by expending them before they are secured. The profits may never come, and in that case you will have taken upon yourself a load of debt which you may never get rid of. It will sit upon your shoulders like the old man in Sinbad.

Another method of economy is, to keep a regular account of all that you earn, and of all that you expend. An orderly man will know beforehand what he requires, and will be provided with the necessary means for obtaining it. Thus his domestic budget will be balanced; and his expenditure kept within his income.

John Wesley regularly adopted this course. Although he possessed a small income, he always kept his eyes upon the state of his affairs. A year before his death, he wrote with a trembling hand, in his Journal of Expenses; "For more than eighty-six years I have kept my accounts exactly. I do not care to continue to do so any longer, having the conviction that I economize all that I obtain, and give all that I can,—that is to say, all that I have."[1]

Besides these methods of economy, the eye of the master or the mistress is always necessary to see that nothing is lost, that everything is put to its proper use and kept in its proper place, and that all things are done decently and in order. It does no dishonour to even the highest individuals to take a personal interest in their own affairs. And with persons of moderate means, the necessity for the eye of the master overlooking everything, is absolutely necessary for the proper conduct of business.

It is difficult to fix the precise limits of economy. Bacon says that if a man would live well within his income, he ought not to expend more than one-half, and save the rest. This is perhaps too exacting; and Bacon himself did not follow his own advice. What proportion of one's income should be expended on rent? That depends upon circumstances. In the country about one-tenth; in London about one-sixth. It is at all events better to save too much, than spend too much. One may remedy the first defect, but not so easily the latter. Wherever there is a large family, the more money that is put to one side and saved, the better.

Economy is necessary to the moderately rich, as well as to the comparatively poor man. Without economy, a man cannot be generous. He cannot take part in the charitable work of the world. If he spends all that he earns, he can help nobody. He cannot properly educate his children, nor put them in the way of starting fairly in the business of life. Even the example of Bacon shows that the loftiest intelligence cannot neglect thrift

---

1. Southey's Life of Wesley, vol. ii., p. 560.

without peril. But thousands of witnesses daily testify, that men even of the most moderate intelligence, can practise the virtue with success.

Although Englishmen are a diligent, hard-working, and generally self-reliant race, trusting to themselves and their own efforts for their sustenance and advancement in the world, they are yet liable to overlook and neglect some of the best practical methods of improving their position, and securing their social well-being. They are not yet sufficiently educated to be temperate, provident, and foreseeing. They live for the present, and are too regardless of the coming time. Men who are husbands and parents, generally think they do their duty if they provide for the hour that is, neglectful of the hour that is to come. Though industrious, they are improvident; though money-making, they are spendthrift. They do not exercise forethought enough, and are defective in the virtue of prudent economy.

Men of all classes are, as yet, too little influenced by these considerations. They are apt to live beyond their incomes,—at all events, to live up to them, The upper classes live too much for display; they must keep up their "position in society;" they must have fine houses, horses, and carriages; give good dinners, and drink rich wines, their ladies must wear costly and gay dresses. Thus the march of improvidence goes on over broken hearts, ruined hopes, and wasted ambitions.

The vice descends in society,—the middle classes strive to ape the patrician orders; they flourish crests, liveries, and hammercloths; their daughters must learn "accomplishments"—see "society"—ride and drive—frequent operas and theatres. Display is the rage, ambition rivalling ambition; and thus the vicious folly rolls on like a tide. The vice again descends. The working classes, too, live up to their means—much smaller means, it is true; but even when they are able, they are not sufficiently careful to provide against the evil day; and then only the poorhouse offers its scanty aid to protect them against want.

To save money for avaricious purposes is altogether different from saving it for economical purposes. The saving may be accomplished in the same manner—by wasting nothing, and saving everything. But here the comparison ends. The miser's only pleasure is in saving. The prudent economist spends what he can afford for comfort and enjoyment, and saves a surplus for some future time. The avaricious person makes gold his idol: it is his molten calf, before which he constantly bows down; whereas the thrifty person regards it as a useful instrument, and as a means of promoting his own happiness and the happiness of those who are dependent upon him. The miser is never satisfied. He amasses wealth that he can never consume, but leaves it to be squandered by others, probably by spendthrifts; whereas the economist aims at securing a fair share of the world's wealth and comfort, without any thought of amassing a fortune.

It is the duty of all persons to economize their means,—of the young as well as of the old. The Duke of Sully mentions, in his Memoirs, that nothing contributed more to his fortune than the prudent economy which he practised, even in his youth, of always preserving some ready money in hand for the purpose of meeting circumstances of emergency. Is a man married? Then the duty of economy is still more binding. His wife and children plead to him most eloquently. Are they, in the event of his early death, to be left to buffet with the world unaided? The hand of charity is cold, the gifts of charity are valueless, compared with the gains of industry, and the honest savings of frugal labour, which carry with them blessings and comforts, without inflicting any wound upon the feelings of the helpless and bereaved. Let every man, therefore, who can, endeavour to economize and to save; not to hoard, but to nurse his little savings, for the sake of promoting the welfare and happiness of himself while here, and of others when he has departed.

There is a dignity in the very effort to save with a worthy purpose, even though the attempt should not be crowned with eventual success. It produces a well-regulated mind; it gives prudence a triumph over extravagance; it gives virtue the mastery over vice; it puts the passions under control; it drives away care; it secures comfort. Saved money, however little, will serve to dry up many a tear—will ward off many sorrows and heartburnings, which otherwise might prey upon us. Possessed of a little store of capital, a man walks with a lighter step—his heart beats more cheerily. When interruption of work or adversity happens, he can meet them; he can recline on his capital, which will either break his fall, or prevent it altogether. By prudential economy, we can realize the dignity of man; life will be a blessing, and old age an honour. We can ultimately, under a kind Providence, surrender life, conscious that we have been no burden upon society, but rather, perhaps, an acquisition and ornament to it; conscious, also, that as we have been independent, our children after us, by following our example, and availing themselves of the means we have left behind us, will walk in like manner through the world in happiness and independence.

Every man's first duty is, to improve, to educate, and elevate himself—helping forward his brethren at the same time by all reasonable methods.

Methods of Economy

Each has within himself the capability of free will and free action to a large extent; and the fact is proved by the multitude of men who have successfully battled with and overcome the adverse circumstances of life in which they have been placed; and who have risen from the lowest depths of poverty and social debasement, as if to prove what energetic man, resolute of purpose, can do for his own elevation, progress, and advancement in the world. Is it not a fact that the greatness of humanity, the glory of communities, the power of nations, are the result of trials and difficulties encountered and overcome?

Let a man resolve and determine that he will advance, and the first step of advancement is already made. The first step is half the battle. In the very fact of advancing himself, he is in the most effectual possible way advancing others. He is giving them the most eloquent of all lessons—that of example; which teaches far more emphatically than words can teach. He is doing, what others are by imitation incited to do. Beginning with himself, he is in the most emphatic manner teaching the duty of self-reform and of self-improvement; and if the majority of men acted as he did, how much wiser, how much happier, how much more prosperous as a whole, would society become. For, society being made up of units, will be happy and prosperous, or the reverse, exactly in the same degree as the respective individuals who compose it.

Complaints about the inequality of conditions are as old as the world. In the "Economy" of Xenophon, Socrates asks, "How is it that some men live in abundance, and have something to spare, whilst others can scarcely obtain the necessaries of life, and at the same time run into debt?" "The reason is," replied Isomachus, "because the former occupy themselves with their business, whilst the latter neglect it."

The difference between men consists for the most part in intelligence, conduct, and energy. The best character never works by chance, but is under the influence of virtue, prudence, and forethought.

There are, of course, many failures in the world. The man who looks to others for help, instead of relying on himself, will fail. The man who is undergoing the process of perpetual waste, will fail. The miser, the scrub, the extravagant, the thriftless, will necessarily fail. Indeed, most people fail because they do not deserve to succeed. They set about their work in the wrong way, and no amount of experience seems to improve them. There is not so much in luck as some people profess to believe. Luck is only another word for good management in practical affairs. Richelieu used to say that he would not continue to employ an unlucky man,—in other words, a man wanting in practical qualities, and unable to profit by experience; for failures in the past are very often the auguries of failures in the future.

Some of the best and ablest of men are wanting in tact. They will neither make allowance for circumstances, nor adapt themselves to circumstances: they will insist on trying to drive their wedge the broad end foremost. They raise walls only to run their own heads against. They make such great preparations, and use such great precautions, that they defeat their own object,—like the Dutchman mentioned by Washington Irving, who, having to leap a ditch, went so far back to have a good run at it, that when he came up he was completely winded, and had to sit down on the wrong side to recover his breath.

In actual life, we want things done, not preparations for doing them; and we naturally prefer the man who has definite aims and purposes, and proceeds in the straightest and shortest way to accomplish his object, to the one who describes the thing to be done, and spins fine phrases about doing it. Without action, words are mere maundering.

The desire for success in the world, and even for the accumulation of money, is not without its uses. It has doubtless been implanted in the human heart for good rather than for evil purposes. Indeed the desire to accumulate, forms one of the most powerful instruments for the regeneration of society. It provides the basis for individual energy and activity. It is the beginning of maritime and commercial enterprise. It is the foundation of industry, as well as of independence. It impels men to labour, to invent, and to excel.

No idle nor thriftless man ever became great. It is amongst those who never lost a moment, that we find the men who have moved and advanced the world,—by their learning, their science, or their inventions. Labour of some sort is one of the conditions of existence. The thought has come down to us from pagan times, that "Labour is the price which the gods have set upon all that is excellent." The thought is also worthy of Christian times.

Everything depends, as we shall afterwards find, upon the uses to which accumulations of wealth are applied. On the tombstone of John Donough, of New Orleans, the following maxims are engraved as the merchant's guide to young men on their way through life:—

"Remember always that labour is one of the conditions of our existence.

Methods of Economy

"Time is gold; throw not one minute away, but place each one to account.

"Do unto all men as you would be done by.

"Never put off till tomorrow what can be done today.

"Never bid another do what you can do yourself.

"Never covet what is not your own.

"Never think any matter so trifling as not to deserve notice.

"Never give out what does not come in.

"Do not spend, but produce.

"Let the greatest order regulate the actions of your life.

"Study in your course of life to do the greatest amount of good.

"Deprive yourself of nothing that is necessary to your comfort, but live in honourable simplicity and frugality.

"Labour then to the last moment of your existence."

Most men have it in their power, by prudent arrangements, to defend themselves against adversity, and to throw up a barrier against destitution. They can do this by their own individual efforts, or by acting on the principle of co-operation, which is capable of an almost indefinite extension. People of the most humble condition, by combining their means and associating together, are enabled in many ways to defend themselves against the pressure of poverty, to promote their physical well-being, and even to advance the progress of the nation.

A solitary individual may be able to do very little to advance and improve society; but when he combines with his fellows for the purpose, he can do a very great deal. Civilization itself is but the effect of combining. Mr. Mill has said that "almost all the advantages which man possesses over the inferior animals, arise from his power of acting in combination with his fellows, and of accomplishing, by the united efforts of numbers, what could not be accomplished by the detached efforts of individuals."

The secret of social development is to be found in co-operation; and the great question of improved economical and social life can only receive a satisfactory solution through its means. To effect good on a large scale, men must combine their efforts; and the best social system is that in which the organization for the common good is rendered the most complete in all respects.

The middle classes have largely employed the principle of association. No class has risen so rapidly, or done more by their energy and industry to advance the power and progress of England. And why? Because the most

Methods of Economy

active have always been the most ready to associate, to co-operate, and to combine. They have combined when they were attacked, combined when they had an abuse to destroy, or a great object to accomplish. They have associated together to manufacture articles of commerce, to make canals, to construct railways, to form gas companies, to institute insurance and banking companies, and to do an immense amount of industrial work. By combining their small capitals together, they have been able to accumulate an enormous aggregate capital, and to execute the most gigantic undertakings.

The middle classes have accomplished more by the principle of co-operation than the classes who have so much greater need of it. All the joint stock companies are the result of association. The railways, the telegraphs, the banks, the mines, the manufactories, have for the most part been established and are carried on by means of the savings of the middle classes.

The working classes have only begun to employ the same principle. Yet how much might they accomplish by its means! They might co-operate in saving as well as in producing. They might, by putting their saved earnings together, become, by combination, their own masters. Within a few years past, many millions sterling have been expended in strikes for wages. A hundred millions a year are thrown away upon drink and other unnecessary articles. Here is an enormous capital. Men who expend or waste such an amount can easily become capitalists. It requires only will, energy, and self-denial. So much money spent on buildings, plant, and steam-engines, would enable them to manufacture for themselves, instead of for the benefit of individual capitalists. The steam-engine is impartial in its services. It is no respecter of persons; it will work for the benefit of the labourer as well as for the benefit of the millionaire. It will work for those who make the best use of it, and who have the greatest knowledge of its powers.

The greater number of workmen possess little capital save their labour; and, as we have already seen, many of them uselessly and wastefully spend most of their earnings, instead of saving them and becoming capitalists. By combining in large numbers for the purposes of economical working, they might easily become capitalists, and operate upon a large scale. As society is now constituted, every man is not only justified but bound in duty as a citizen, to accumulate his earnings by all fair and honourable methods, with the view of securing a position of ultimate competence and independence.

We do not say that men should save and hoard their gains for the mere sake of saving and hoarding; this would be parsimony and avarice. But we do say that all men ought to aim at accumulating a sufficiency—enough to maintain them in comfort during the helpless years that are to come—to maintain them in times of sickness and of sorrow, and in old age, which, if it does come, ought to find them with a little store of capital in hand, sufficient to secure them from dependence upon the charity of others.

Workmen are for the most part disposed to associate; but the association is not always of a healthy kind. It sometimes takes the form of Unions against masters; and displays itself in the Strikes that are so common, and usually so unfortunate. Workmen also strike against men of their own class, for the purpose of excluding them from their special calling. One of the principal objects of trades-unions is to keep up wages at the expense of the lower paid and unassociated working people. They endeavour to prevent poorer men learning their trade, and thus keep the supply of labour below the demand.[2] This system may last for a time, but it becomes ruinous in the end.

It is not the want of money that prevents skilled workmen from becoming capitalists, and opening the door for the employment of labouring men who are poorer and less skilled than themselves. The work-people threw away half a million sterling during the Preston strike, after which they went back to work at the old terms. The London building trades threw away over three hundred thousand pounds during their strike; and even had they obtained the terms for which they struck, it would have taken six years to recoup them for their loss. The colliers in the Forest of Dean went back to work at the old terms after eleven weeks' play, at the loss of fifty thousand pounds. The iron-workers of Northumberland and Durham, after spending a third of the year in idleness, and losing two hundred thousand pounds in wages, went back to work at a reduction of ten per cent. The colliers and iron-workers of South Wales, during the recent strike or lock-out, were idle for four months, and, according to Lord Aberdare, lost, in wages alone, not less than three millions sterling!

---

2. On the 31st January, 1875, a labourer in the employment of Messrs. Vickers, Sheffield, who had not served an apprenticeship, was put on to turn one of the lathes. This being contrary to the rules of the union, the men in the shop struck work. It is a usual course for men of the union to "strike" in this manner against persons of their own condition, and to exercise a force not resting in law or natural right, but merely on the will of a majority, and directly subversive of the freedom of the individual.

Here, then, is abundance of money within the power of workingmen,—money which they might utilize, but do not. Think only of a solitary million, out of the three millions sterling which they threw away during the coal strike, being devoted to the starting of collieries, or iron-mills, or manufactories, to be worked by co-operative production for the benefit of the operatives themselves. With frugal habits, says Mr. Greg, the well-conditioned workman might in ten years easily have five hundred pounds in the bank; and, combining his savings with twenty other men similarly disposed, they might have ten thousand pounds for the purpose of starting any manufacture in which they are adepts.[3]

That this is not an impracticable scheme, is capable of being easily proved. The practice of co-operation has long been adopted by workpeople throughout England. A large proportion of the fishery industry has been conducted on that principle for hundreds of years. Fishermen join in building, rigging, and manning a boat; the proceeds of the fish they catch at sea is divided amongst them—so much to the boat, so much to the fishermen. The company of oyster-dredgers of Whitstable "has existed time out of mind,"[4] though it was only in 1793 that they were incorporated by Act of Parliament. The tin-miners of Cornwall have also acted on the same principle. They have mined, washed, and sold the tin, dividing the proceeds among themselves in certain proportions,—most probably from the time that the Phoenicians carried away the produce to their ports in the Mediterranean.

In our own time, co-operation has been practised to a considerable extent. In 1795, the Hull Anti-Mill Industrial Society was founded. The reasons for its association are explained in the petition addressed to the Mayor and Aldermen of Hull by the first members of the society. The petition begins thus: "We, the poor inhabitants of the said town, have lately experienced much trouble and sorrow in ourselves and families, on the occasion of the exorbitant price of flour; and though the price is much reduced at present, yet we judge it needful to take every precaution to preserve ourselves from the invasions of covetous and merciless

---

3. "The annual expenditure of the working classes alone, on drink and tobacco, is not less than £60,000,000. Every year, therefore, the working classes have it in their power to become capitalists (simply by saving wasteful and pernicious expenditure) to an extent which would enable them to start at least 500 cotton mills, or coal mines, or iron works, on their own account, or to purchase at least 500,000 acres, and so set up 50,000 families each with a nice little estate of their own of ten acres, on fee simple. No one can dispute the facts. No one can deny the inference."—Quarterly Review, No. 263.

4. Reports on the Paris Universal Exhibition, 1867, vol. vi., p. 252.

men in future." They accordingly entered into a subscription to build a mill, in order to supply themselves with flour. The corporation granted their petition, and supported them by liberal donations. The mill was built, and exists to this day. It now consists of more than four thousand members, each holding a share of twenty-five shillings. The members belong principally to the labouring classes. The millers endeavoured by action at law to put down the society, but the attempt was successfully resisted. The society manufactures flour, and sells it to the members at market price, dividing the profits annually amongst the shareholders, according to the quantity consumed in each member's family. The society has proved eminently remunerative.

Many years passed before the example of the "poor inhabitants" of Hull was followed. It was only in 1847 that the co-operators of Leeds purchased a flour-mill, and in 1850 that those of Rochdale did the same; since which time they have manufactured flour for the benefit of their members. The corn-millers of Leeds attempted to undersell the Leeds Industrial Society. They soon failed, and the price of flour was permanently reduced. The Leeds mill does business amounting to more than a hundred thousand pounds yearly; its capital amounts to twenty-two thousand pounds; and it paid more than eight thousand pounds of profits and bonuses to its three thousand six hundred members in 1866, besides supplying them with flour of the best quality. The Rochdale District Co-operative Corn-mill Society has also been eminently successful. It supplies flour to consumers residing within a radius of about fifteen miles round Rochdale.[5] It also supplies flour to sixty-two co-operative societies, numbering over twelve thousand members. Its business in 1866 amounted to two hundred and twenty-four thousand pounds, and its profits to over eighteen thousand pounds.

The Rochdale Corn-mill grew out of the Rochdale Equitable Pioneers Society, which formed an epoch in the history of industrial co-operative institutions. The Equitable Pioneers Society was established in the year 1844, at a time when trade was in a very bad condition, and working people generally were heartless and hopeless as to their future state. Some twenty-eight or thirty men, mostly flannel weavers, met and formed themselves into a society for the purpose of economizing their hard-won earnings. It is pretty well known that working-men generally pay at least ten per cent. more for the articles they consume, than they

---

5. Its history is given in the Reports above referred to, p. 269.

need to do under a sounder system. Professor Fawcett estimates their loss at nearer twenty per cent. than ten per cent. At all events, these working-men wished to save this amount of profit, which before went into the pockets of the distributers of the necessaries,—in other words, into the pockets of the shopkeepers.

The weekly subscription was twopence each; and when about fifty-two calls of twopence each had been made, they found that they were able to buy a sack of oatmeal, which they distributed at cost-price amongst the members of the society. The number of members grew, and the subscriptions so increased, that the society was enabled to buy tea, sugar, and other articles, and distribute them amongst the members at cost-price. They superseded the shopkeepers, and became their own tradesmen. They insisted from the first on payments in cash. No credit was given.

The society grew. It established a store for the sale of food, firing, clothes, and other necessaries. In a few years the members set on foot the Co-operative Corn-mill. They increased the capital by the issue of one-pound shares, and began to make and sell clothes and shoes. They also sold drapery. But the principal trade consisted in the purchase and sale of provisions—butchers' meat, groceries, flour, and such-like. Notwithstanding the great distress during the period of the cotton famine, the society continued to prosper. From the first, it set apart a portion of its funds for educational purposes, and established a news-room, and a library, which now contains over six thousand volumes.

The society continued to increase until it possessed eleven branches for the sale of goods and stores in or near Rochdale, besides the original office in Toad Lane. At the end of 1866, it had 6,246 members, and a capital of £99,908. Its income for goods sold and cash received during the year was £249,122; and the gross profit £31,931.

But this was not all. Two and a half per cent. was appropriated from the net profits to support the news-rooms and library; and there are now eleven news and reading rooms at different places in or near the town where the society carries on its business; the sum devoted to this object amounting to over seven hundred pounds per annum. The members play at chess and draughts, and use the stereoscopic views, microscopes, and telescopes placed in the libraries. No special arrangements have been made to promote temperance; but the news-rooms and library exercise a powerful and beneficial influence in promoting sobriety. It has been said that the society has done more to remove drunkenness from Rochdale than all that the advocates of temperance have been able to effect.

The example of the Rochdale Pioneers has exercised a powerful influence on working-men throughout the northern counties of England. There is scarcely a town or village but has a co-operative institution of one kind or another. These societies have promoted habits of saving, of thrift, and of temperance. They have given the people an interest in money matters, and enabled them to lay out their earnings to the best advantage. They have also given the working people some knowledge of business; for the whole of their concerns are managed by committees selected at the general meetings of the members.

One of the most flourishing co-operative societies is that established at Over Darwen. The society has erected a row of handsome buildings in the centre of the town. The shops for the sale of provisions, groceries, clothing, and other necessaries, occupy the lower story. Over the shops are the library, reading rooms, and class rooms, which are open to the members and their families. The third story consists of a large public hall, which is used for lectures, concerts, and dances. There are six branches of the society established in different parts of the town. A large amount of business is done, and the profits are very considerable. These are divided amongst the members, in proportion to the purchases made by them. The profits are for the most part re-invested in joint-stock paper-mills, cotton-mills, and collieries, in the neighbourhood of Darwen. One of the most praiseworthy features of the society is the provision made for the free education of the members and their families. Two and a half per cent. of the profits are appropriated for the purpose. While inspecting the institution a few months ago, we were informed that the Science classes were so efficiently conducted, that one of the pupils had just obtained a Government Scholarship of fifty pounds a year, for three years, including free instruction at the School of Mines, Jermyn Street, London, with a free use of the laboratories during that period. There are also two other co-operative institutions in the same place; and we were informed that the working people of Darwen are, for the most part, hard-working, sober, and thrifty.

The example has also spread into Scotland and the south of England. At Northampton, a co-operative society exists for the purpose of buying and selling leather, and also for the manufacture of boots and shoes. At Padiham and other places in Lancashire, co-operative cotton-mills have been established. The Manchester and Salford Equitable Co-operative Society "combine the securities and facilities of a bank with the profits of a trade." But the business by which they mostly thrive, is by the purchase

Methods of Economy

and sale of food, provisions, groceries, draperies, and other articles, with the exception of intoxicating liquors.

The sole secret of their success consists in "ready money." They give no credit. Everything is done for cash; the profit of the trade being divided amongst the members. Every business man knows that cash payment is the soundest method of conducting business. The Rochdale Pioneers having discovered the secret, have spread it amongst their class. In their "advice to members of this and other societies," they say: "Look well after money matters. Buy your goods as much as possible in the first markets; or if you have the produce of your industry to sell, contrive, if possible, to sell it in the last. Never depart from the principle of buying and selling for ready money. Beware of long reckonings." In short, the co-operative societies became tradesmen on a large scale; and, besides the pureness of the food sold, their profit consisted in the discount for cash payments, which was divided amongst the members.

Land and Building Societies constitute another form of co-operation. These are chiefly supported by the minor middle-class men, but also to a considerable extent by the skilled and thrifty working-class men. By their means portions of land are bought, and dwelling-houses are built. By means of a building society, a person who desires to possess a house enters the society as a member, and instead of paying his rent to the landlord, pays his subscriptions and interest to a committee of his friends; and in course of time, when his subscriptions are paid up, the house is purchased, and conveyed to him by the society. The building-society is thus a savings bank, where money accumulates for a certain purpose. But even those who do not purchase a house, receive a dividend and bonus on their shares, which sometimes amounts to a considerable sum.

The accumulation of property has the effect which it always has upon thrifty men; it makes them steady, sober, and diligent. It weans them from revolutionary notions, and makes them conservative. When workmen, by their industry and frugality, have secured their own independence, they will cease to regard the sight of others' well-being as a wrong inflicted on themselves; and it will no longer be possible to make political capital out of their imaginary woes.

It has been said that Freehold Land Societies, which were established for political objects, had the effect of weaning men from political reform. They were first started in Birmingham, for the purpose of enabling men to buy land, and divide it into forty-shilling freeholds, so that the owners might become electors and vote against the corn-laws. The corn-laws have been done away with; but the holders of freehold land still exist, though many of them have ceased to be politicians. "Mr. Arthur Ryland informs me," said Mr. Holyoake, in a recent paper on Building Societies, "that in Birmingham, numbers of persons under the influence of these societies have forsaken patriotism for profits. And I know both co-operators and Chartists who were loud-mouthed for social and political reform, who now care no more for it than a Whig government; and decline to attend a public meeting on a fine night, while they would crawl like the serpent in Eden, through a gutter in a storm, after a good security. They have tasted land, and the gravel has got into their souls."

"Yet to many others," he adds, "these societies have taught a healthy frugality they never else would have known; and enabled many an industrious son to take to his home his poor old father—who expected and dreaded to die in the workhouse—and set him down to smoke his pipe in the sunshine in the garden, of which the land and the house belonged to his child."[6]

The Leeds Permanent Building Society, which has furnished healthy tenements for about two hundred families, sets forth the following recommendations of the influence which it has exercised amongst the working classes of that town: "It is truly cheering to hear the members themselves, at occasional meetings tell how, from small savings hitherto deemed too little for active application, they began to invest in the society: then to build or buy; then to advance in life, and come to competence, from extending their savings in this manner. . . . The provident habits and knowledge thus induced are most beneficial to the members. And the result is, that the careless become thoughtful, and, on saving, become orderly, respectable, propertied, and in every way better citizens, neighbours, and more worthy and comfortable. The employment of money in this useful direction encourages trade, advances prices and wages, comforts the working classes, and at the same time provides the means of home enjoyments, without which such advances would be comparatively useless, and certainly uncertain."[7]

There are also exceptional towns and villages in Lancashire where large sums of money have been saved by the operatives for buying or building comfortable cottage dwellings. Last year Padiham saved about fifteen thousand pounds for this purpose, although its population is only

---

6. Paper read at York Meeting of the National Society for Promoting Social Science, 26th Sept. 1864.

7. Letter of Mr. John Holmes, in Reports of Paris Universal Exhibition, 1867 vol. vi., p. 240.

about 8,000. Burnley has also been very successful. The Building Society there has 6,600 investors, who saved last year £160,000 or an average of twenty-four pounds for each investor. The members consist principally of mill operatives, miners, mechanics, engineers, carpenters, stonemasons, and labourers. They also include women, both married and unmarried. Our informant states that "great numbers of the working classes have purchased houses in which to live. They have likewise bought houses as a means of investment. The building society has assisted in hundreds of these cases, by advancing money on mortgage,—such mortgages being repaid by easy instalments."

Building Societies are, on the whole, among the most excellent methods of illustrating the advantages of Thrift. They induce men to save money for the purpose of buying their own homes; in which, so long as they live, they possess the best of all securities.

Chapter 7

Economy in Life Assurance

"Do not, for one repulse, forego the purpose that you resolved to effect."—Shakespeare.

"We are helpers, fellow-creatures, of the right against the wrong."—E. Barrett.

"Life was not given us to be all used up in the pursuit of what we must leave behind us when we die."—Joseph May.

"Le bonheur ou le malheur de la vielillesse n'est souvent que l'extrait de notre vie passée." (The blessedness or misery of old age is often but the extract of our past life.) De Maistre.

Two other methods of co-operative saving remain to be mentioned. The first is by Life Assurance [insurance], which enables widows and children to be provided for at the death of the assured; and the second is by Friendly Societies, which enable working men to provide themselves with relief in sickness, and their widows and orphans with a small sum at their death. The first method is practised by the middle and upper classes; and the second by the working classes.

It might possibly take a long time to save enough money to provide for those who are dependent upon us; and there is always the temptation to encroach upon the funds set apart for death, which—as most people suppose—may be a far-distant event. So that saving bit by bit, from week to week, cannot always be relied upon.

The person who joins an assurance society is in a different position. His annual or quarterly saving becomes at once a portion of a general fund, sufficient to realize the intention of the assured. At the moment that he makes his first payment, his object is attained. Though he die on the day after his premium has been paid, his widow and children will receive the entire amount of his assurance.

This system, while it secures a provision to his survivors, at the same time incites a man to the moral obligation of exorcising foresight and prudence, since through its means these virtues may be practised, and their ultimate reward secured. Not the least of the advantages attending life assurance is the serenity of mind which attends the provident man when lying on a bed of sickness, or when he is in prospect of death,—so unlike that painful anxiety for the future welfare of a family, which adds poignancy to bodily suffering, and retards or defeats the power of medicine. The poet Burns, in writing to a friend a few days before his death, said that he was "still the victim of affliction. Alas! Clark, I begin to fear the worst. Burns' poor widow, and half a dozen of his dear little ones helpless orphans;—there, I am weak as a woman's tear. Enough of this,—'tis half my disease!"

Life assurance may be described as a joint-stock plan for securing widows, and children from want. It is an arrangement by means of which a large number of persons agree to lay by certain small sums called "premiums," yearly, to accumulate at interest, as in a savings bank, against the contingency of the assurer's death,—when the amount of the sum subscribed for is forthwith handed over to his survivors. By this means, persons possessed of but little capital, though enjoying regular wages or salaries, however small, may at once form a fund for the benefit of their family at death.

We often hear of men who have been diligent and useful members of society, dying and leaving their wives and families in absolute poverty. They have lived in respectable style, paid high rents for their houses, dressed well, kept up good visiting acquaintance, were seen at most places of amusement, and brought up their children with certain ideas of social position and respectability; but death has stricken them down, and what is the situation of their families? Has the father provided for their future? From twenty to twenty-five pounds a year, paid into an Assurance Society, would have secured their widows and orphans against absolute want. Have they performed this duty? No—they have done nothing of the kind; it turns out that the family have been living up to their means, if not beyond them, and the issue is, that they are thrown suddenly bankrupt upon the world.

Conduct such as this is not only thoughtless and improvident, but heartless and cruel in the last degree. To bring a family into the world, give them refined tastes, and accustom them to comforts, the loss of which is misery, and then to leave the family to the workhouse, the prison, or the street—to the alms of relatives, or to the charity of the public,—is nothing short of a crime done against society, as well as against the unfortunate individuals who are the immediate sufferers.

It will be admitted, that the number of men who can lay by a sufficient store of capital for the benefit of their families, is, in these times of intense competition, comparatively small. Perhaps the claims of an increasing family absorb nearly all their gains, and they find that the sum which they can put away in the bank is so small, that it is not put away at all. They become reckless of ever attaining so apparently hopeless an object as that of an accumulation of savings, for the benefit of their families at death.

Take the case of a married man with a family. He has begun business, and thinks that if his life were spared, he might in course of years be able to lay by sufficient savings to provide for his wife and family at his death. But life is most uncertain, and he knows that at any moment he may be taken away,—leaving those he holds most dear comparatively destitute. At thirty he determines to join a sound life office. He insures for five hundred pounds, payable to his survivors at his death, and pays from twelve to thirteen pounds yearly. From the moment on which he pays that amount, the five hundred pounds are secured for his family, although he died the very next day.

Now, if he had deposited this twelve or thirteen pounds yearly in a bank, or employed it at interest, it would have taken about twenty years before his savings would have amounted to five hundred pounds. But by the simple and beautiful expedient of life assurance, these twenty-six years of the best part of his life are, on this account at least, secured against anxiety and care. The anticipation of future evil no longer robs him of present enjoyment. By means of his annual fixed payment—which decreases according to the profits of the society—he is secure of leaving a fixed sum at his death for the benefit of his family.

In this way, life assurance may be regarded in the light of a contract, by which the inequalities of life are to a certain extent averaged and compensated, so that those who die soon—or rather their families—become sharers in the good fortune of those who live beyond the average term of life. And even should the assurer himself live beyond the period at which his savings would have accumulated to more than the sum insured, he will not be disposed to repine, if he takes into account his exemption from corroding solicitude during so many years of his life.

The reasons which induce a man to insure his house and stock of goods against the accident of fire, ought to be still more imperative in inducing him to insure his life against the accident of disease and the contingency of sudden death. What is worldly prudence in the one case, is something more in the other; it has superadded to it the duty of providing for the future maintenance of a possibly widowed wife, and orphaned children; and no man can justly stand excused who neglects so great and binding an obligation. Is it an obligation on the part of a husband and father to provide daily bread for his wife and children during his life? Then it is equally an obligation on his part to provide means for their adequate support in event of his death. The duty is so obvious, the means of performing it are so simple, and are now so easily placed within the reach of all men,—the arrangement is so eminently practical, rational, benevolent, and just,—it is, moreover, so calculated to increase every wise and prudent man's sense of self-respect, and to encourage him in the performance of all proper social duties,—that we cannot conceive of any possible objection that can be urged against it; and it is only to be regretted that the practice is not far more general and customary than it is, amongst all classes of the community.[1]

The Friendly or Benefit Societies of the working classes are also Co-operative Societies under another form. They cultivate the habit of prudent self-reliance amongst the people, and are consequently worthy of every encouragement. It is certainly a striking fact that some four millions of working men should have organized themselves into voluntary associations for the purpose of mutual support in time of sickness and distress. These societies are the outgrowth in a great measure of the English love of self-government and social independence,—in illustration of which it maybe stated, that whereas in France only one person in seventy-six is found belonging to a benefit society, and in Belgium one in sixty-four, the proportion in England is found to be one in nine. The English societies are said to have in hand funds amounting to more than eleven millions sterling; and they distribute relief amongst their members, provided by voluntary contributions out of their weekly earnings, amounting to above two millions yearly.

---

1. It may be mentioned that the total amount assured in existing British offices, mostly by the middle classes, is about three hundred and fifty millions sterling; and that the annual premiums payable amount to not less than eleven millions sterling. And yet no more than one person in twenty of the persons belonging to the classes to whom Life Assurance is especially applicable, have yet availed themselves of its benefits.

Although the working classes of France and Belgium do not belong to benefit societies to anything like the same extent, it must be stated, in their justification, that they are amongst the most thrifty and prudent people in the world. They invest their savings principally in land and in the public funds. The French and Belgians have a positive hunger for land. They save everything that they can for the purpose of acquiring more. And with respect to their investments in the public funds, it may be mentioned, as a well-known fact, that it was the French peasantry who, by investing their savings in the National Defence Loan, liberated French soil from the tread of their German conquerors.[2]

English benefit societies, notwithstanding their great uses and benefits, have numerous defects. There are faults in the details of their organization and management, whilst many of them are financially unsound. Like other institutions in their early stages, they have been tentative and in a great measure empirical,—more especially as regards their rates of contribution and allowances for sick relief. The rates have in many cases been fixed too low, in proportion to the benefits allowed; and hence the "box" is often declared to be closed, after the money subscribed has been expended. The society then comes to an end, and the older members have to go without relief for the rest of their lives. But life assurance societies themselves have had to undergo the same discipline of failure, and the operation of "winding up" has not unfrequently thrown discredit upon these middle-class associations.

To quote the words of the Registrar of Friendly Societies, in a recent report: "Though the information thus far obtained is not very encouraging as to the general system of management; on the whole, perhaps, the results of the investments of the poor are not worse than those which noblemen, members of Parliament, merchants, professed financiers, and speculators have contrived to attain in their management of railways, joint-stock banks, and enterprises of all kinds."

The workmen's societies originated for the most part in a common want, felt by persons of small means, unable to accumulate any considerable store of savings to provide against destitution in the event of

---

2. At the present time one individual out of every eight in the population of France has a share in the National Debt, the average amount held being 170 francs. The participants in the debt approach closely to the number of freeholders, or rather distinct freeholdings, which amount to 5,550,000, according to the last return. France certainly furnishes a singular exception to those countries of Central and Western Europe, where "the rich are getting more rich and the poor ever more poor." In France wealth becomes more and more distributed among the bulk of the population.

disablement by disease or accident. At the beginning of life, persons earning their bread by daily labour are able to save money with difficulty. Unavoidable expenses absorb their limited means and press heavily on their income. When unable to work, any little store they may have accumulated is soon spent, and if they have a family to maintain, there is then no choice before them but destitution, begging, or recourse to the poor-rates. In their desire to avoid either of these alternatives, they have contrived the expedient of the benefit society. By combining and putting a large number of small contributions together, they have found it practicable thus to provide a fund sufficiently large to meet their ordinary requirements during sickness.

The means by which this is accomplished are very simple. Each member contributes to a common fund at the rate of from fourpence to sixpence a week, and out of this fund the stipulated allowance is paid. Most benefit societies have also a Widows' and Orphans' Fund, raised in like manner, out of which a sum is paid to the survivors of members at their death. It will be obvious that such organizations, however faulty they may be in detail, cannot fail to exercise a beneficial influence upon society at large. The fact that one of such associations, the Manchester Unity of Odd Fellows, numbers about half a million of members; possesses a funded capital amounting to £3,706,366; and distributes in sick relief and payments of sums at death above £300,000 a year, illustrates in a striking light their beneficial action upon the classes for whom and by whom they have been established. By their means, working men are enabled to secure the results of economy at a comparatively small cost. For, mutual assurance is economy in its most economical form; and merely presents another illustration of that power of co-operation which is working out such extraordinary results in all departments of society, and is in fact but another name for Civilization.

Many persons object to Friendly Societies because they are conducted at public-houses; because many of them are got up by the keepers of public-houses in order to obtain custom from the members; and because, in their fortnightly meetings to pay their subscriptions, they acquire the pernicious habit of drinking, and thus waste quite as much as they save. The Friendly Societies doubtless rely very much on the social element. The public-house is everybody's house. The members can there meet together, talk together, and drink together. It is extremely probable that had they trusted solely to the sense of duty—the duty of insuring against sickness—and merely required the members to pay their weekly contributions to a collector, very few societies of the kind would have remained in existence. In a large number of cases, there is practically no choice between the society that meets at a public-house, and none at all.

It so happens that the world cannot be conducted on superfine principles. To most men, and especially to the men we are speaking of, it is a rough, working world, conducted on common principles, such as will wear. To some it may seem vulgar to associate beer, tobacco, or feasting with the pure and simple duty of effecting an insurance against disablement by sickness; but the world we live in is vulgar, and we must take it as we find it, and try to make the best of it. It must be admitted that the tendencies to pure good in man are very weak, and need much helping. But the expedient, vulgar though it be, of attracting him through his appetite for meat and drink to perform a duty to himself and neighbours, is by no means confined to societies of working men. There is scarcely a London charity or institution but has its annual dinner for the purpose of attracting subscribers. Are we to condemn the eighteenpenny annual dinner of the poor man, but excuse the guinea one of the rich?

A vigorous effort was made by Mr. Akroyd of Halifax, in 1856, to establish a Provident Sick Society and Penny Savings Bank for the working men in the West Riding of Yorkshire. An organization was set on foot with these objects; and though the Penny Bank proved a complete success, the Provident Society proved a complete failure. Mr. Akroyd thus explains the causes of the failure: "We found the ground preoccupied," he says, "by Friendly Societies, especially by the Odd Fellows, Druids, Foresters, etc.; and against their principles of self-government, mutual check against fraud, and brotherhood, no new and independent society can compete. Our rates were also of necessity much higher than theirs, and this was perhaps one of the chief causes of our failure."

Low rates of contribution have been the principal cause of the failure of Friendly Societies.[3] It was of course natural that the members, being persons of limited means, should endeavour to secure the objects of their organization at the lowest cost. They therefore fixed their rates

---

3. The Registrar of Friendly Societies, in his report for 1859, states that from 1793 to 1858, the number of societies enrolled and certified had been 28,550, of which 6,850 had ceased to exist. The causes of failure in most cases were reported to be, inadequacy of the rates of contribution, the granting of pensions as well as sick pay, and no increase of young members. The dissolution of a society, however, is frequently effected with a view of remodelling it, and starting afresh under better regulations, and with rates of premium such as increased knowledge has shown to be necessary for the risks which they have to incur.

as low as possible; and, as the results proved, they in most cases fixed them too low. So long as the societies consisted, for the most part, of young, healthy men, and the average amount of sickness remained low, the payments made seemed ample. The funds accumulated, and many flattered themselves that their societies were in a prosperous state, when they contained the sure elements of decay. For, as the members grew older, their average liability to sickness was regularly increasing. The effects of increased age upon the solvency of benefit clubs soon becoming known, young men avoided the older societies, and preferred setting up organizations of their own. The consequence was, that the old men began to draw upon their reserves at the same time that the regular contributions fell off; and when, as was frequently the case, a few constantly ailing members kept pressing upon the society, the funds were at length exhausted, "the box" was declared to be closed, and the society was broken up. The real injustice was done to the younger men who remained in the society. After paying their contributions for many years, they found, when sickness at length fell upon them, that the funds had been exhausted, by expenditure for superannuation and other allowances, which were not provided for by the rules of the society.

Even the best of the Benefit Societies have been slow to learn the essential importance of adequate rates of contribution, to enable them to fulfil their obligations and ensure their continued usefulness as well as solvency. The defect of most of them consists in their trying to do too much with too little means. The benefits paid out are too high for the rates of contribution paid in. Those who come first are served, but those who come late too often find an empty box. Not only have the rates of payment been generally fixed too low, but there has been little or no discrimination in the selection of members. Men advanced in years and of fragile health are often admitted on the same terms as the young and the healthy, the only difference being in the rate of entry money. Even young lodges, which start with inadequate rates, instead of growing stronger, gradually grow weaker; and in the event of a few constantly ailing members falling upon the funds, they soon become exhausted, and the lodge becomes bankrupt and is broken up. Such has been the history of thousands of Friendly Societies, doing good and serving a useful purpose in their time, but short-lived, ephemeral, and to many of their members disappointing, and even deceptive.

Attempts have been recently made—more especially by the officers of the Manchester Unity of Odd Fellows—to improve the financial condition of their society. Perhaps the best proof of the desire that exists on the part of the leading minds in the Unity to bring the organization into a state of financial soundness, is to be found in the fact that the Board of Management have authorized the publication of the best of all data for future guidance,—namely, the actual sickness experience of the Order. An elaborate series of tables has accordingly been prepared and published for their information by Mr. Ratcliffe, the corresponding secretary, at an expense of about £3,500. In the preface to the last edition it is stated that "this sum has not been abstracted from the funds set apart for relief during sickness, for assurances at death, or for providing for necessitous widows and orphans, but from the management funds of the lodges—funds which, being generally raised by direct levy on the members, are not therefore readily expended without careful consideration on the part of those most interested in the character and welfare of their cherished institution."

We believe that time and experience will enable the leaders of Friendly Societies generally to improve them, and introduce new ameliorations. The best institutions are things of slow growth, and are shaped by experience, which includes failures as well as successes; and finally, they require age to strengthen them and root them in habit. The rudest society established by working men for mutual help in sickness, independent of help from private charity or the poor-rates, is grounded on a right spirit, and is deserving of every encouragement. It furnishes a foundation on which to build up something better. It teaches self-reliance, and thus cultivates amongst the humblest classes habits of provident economy.

Friendly Societies began their operations before there was any science of vital statistics to guide them; and if they have made mistakes in mutual assurance, they have not stood alone. Looking at the difficulties they have had to encounter, they are entitled to be judged charitably. Good advice given them in a kindly spirit will not fail to produce good results. The defects which are mixed up with them are to be regarded as but the transient integument which will most probably fall away as the flower ripens and the fruit matures.

Chapter 8

Savings Banks

"I wish I could write all across the sky, in letters of gold, the one word savings bank."—Rev. Wm. Marsh.

"The only true secret of assisting the poor is to make them agents in bettering their own condition."—Archbishop Sumner.

"Qui à vingt ne sait, à trente ne peut, à quarante n'a,—jamais ne saura, ne pourra, n'aura." ["Who at twenty knows not, at thirty cannot, at forty has not—will never know, never be able, never have."]—French Proverb.

"Go to the ant, thou sluggard; consider her ways, and be wise: which having no guide, overseer, or ruler, provideth her meat in the summer, and gathereth her food in the harvest."—Proverbs vi. 6.

It is said that there is a skeleton in every household. The skeleton is locked up—put away in a cupboard—and rarely seen. Only the people inside the house know of its existence. But the skeleton, nevertheless, cannot long be concealed. It comes to light in some way or another. The most common skeleton is Poverty. Poverty, says Douglas Jerrold, is the great secret, kept at any pains by one-half the world from the other half. When there is nothing laid by—nothing saved to relieve sickness when it comes—nothing to alleviate the wants of old age,—this is the skeleton hid away in many a cupboard.

In a country such as this, where business is often brought to a standstill by over-trading and over-speculation, many masters, clerks, and workpeople are thrown out of employment. They must wait until better times come round. But in the meantime, how are they to live? If they have accumulated no savings, and have nothing laid by, they are comparatively destitute.

Even the Co-operative Cotton-mills, or Co-operative Banks, which are nothing more than Joint-stock Companies, Limited,[1] may become bankrupt. They may not be able, as was the case during the cotton famine, to compete with large capitalists in the purchase of cotton, or in the production of cotton twist. Co-operative companies established for the purpose of manufacturing, are probably of too speculative a character to afford much lasting benefit to the working classes; and it seems that by far the safer course for them to pursue, in times such as the present, is by means of simple, direct saving. There may be less chance of gain, but there is less risk of loss. What is laid by is not locked up and contingent for its productiveness upon times and trade, but is steadily accumulating, and is always ready at hand for use when the pinch of adversity occurs.

Mr. Bright stated in the House of Commons, in 1860,[2] that the income of the working classes was "understated at three hundred and twelve millions a year." Looking at the increase of wages which has taken place during the last fifteen years, their income must now amount to at least four hundred millions.

Surely, out of this large fund of earnings, the working classes might easily save from thirty to forty millions yearly. At all events, they might save such an amount as, if properly used and duly economized, could not fail to establish large numbers of them in circumstances of comfort and even of comparative wealth.

The instances which we have already cited of persons in the humbler ranks of life having by prudential forethought accumulated a considerable store of savings for the benefit of their families, and as a stay for their old age, need not by any means be the comparatively exceptional cases

---

1. "The new cotton factories which have been called co-operative, and which, under that name, have brought together large numbers of shareholders of the wage classes, are all now in reality common joint-stock companies, with limited liability. The so-called co-operative shareholders in the leading establishments decided, as I am informed, by large majorities, that the workers should only be paid wages in the ordinary manner, and should not divide profits. The wages being for piecework, it was held that the payment was in accordance with communistic principle, 'each according to his capacity, each according to his work.' The common spinner had had no share in the work of the general direction, nor had he evinced any of the capacity of thrift or foresight of the capitalist, and why should he share profits as if he had? The wage class, in their capacity of shareholders, decided that it was an unjust claim upon their profits, and kept them undivided to themselves."—Edwin Chadwick, C.B.

2. Speech on the Representation of the People Bill.

that they are now. What one well-regulated person is able to do, others, influenced by similar self-reliant motives, and practising like sobriety and frugality, might with equal ease and in one way or another accomplish. A man who has more money about him than he requires for current purposes, is tempted to spend it. To use the common phrase, it is apt to "burn a hole in his pocket." He may be easily entrapped into company; and where his home provides but small comfort, the public-house, with its bright fire, is always ready to welcome him.

It often happens that workmen lose their employment in "bad times." Mercantile concerns become bankrupt, clerks are paid off, and servants are dismissed when their masters can no longer employ them. If the disemployed people have been in the habit of regularly consuming all their salaries and wages, without laying anything by, their case is about the most pitiable that can be imagined. But if they have saved something, at home or in the savings bank, they will be enabled to break their fall. They will obtain some breathing-time, before they again fall into employment. Suppose they have as much as ten pounds saved. It may seem a very little sum, yet in distress it amounts to much. It may even prove a man's passport to future independence.

With ten pounds a workman might remove from one district to another where employment is more abundant. With ten pounds, he might emigrate to Canada or the United States, where his labour might be in request. Without this little store of savings, he might be rooted to his native spot, like a limpet to the rock. If a married man with a family, his ten pounds would save his home from wreckage, and his household from destitution. His ten pounds would keep the wolf from the door until better times came round. Ten pounds would keep many a servant-girl from ruin, give her time to recruit her health, perhaps wasted by hard work, and enable her to look about for a suitable place, instead of rushing into the first that offered.

We do not value money for its own sake, and we should be the last to encourage a miserly desire to hoard amongst any class; but we cannot help recognizing in money the means of life, the means of comfort, the means of maintaining an honest independence. We would therefore recommend every young man and every young woman to begin life by learning to save; to lay up for the future a certain portion of every week's earnings, be it little or much; to avoid consuming every week or every year the earnings of that week or year; and we counsel them to do this, as they would avoid the horrors of dependence, destitution, or beggary. We would have men and women of every class able to help themselves—relying upon their own resources—upon their own savings; for it is a true saying that "a penny in the purse is better than a friend at court." The first penny saved is a step in the world. The fact of its being saved and laid by, indicates self-denial, forethought, prudence, wisdom. It may be the germ of future happiness. It may be the beginning of independence.

Cobbett was accustomed to scoff at the "bubble" of Savings Banks, alleging that it was an insult to people to tell them that they had anything to save. Yet the extent to which savings banks have been used, even by the humblest classes, proves that he was as much mistaken in this as he was in many of the views which he maintained. There are thousands of persons who would probably never have thought of laying by a penny, but for the facility of the savings bank: it would have seemed so useless to try. The small hoard in the cupboard was too ready at hand, and would have become dissipated before it accumulated to any amount; but no sooner was a place of deposit provided, where sums as small as a shilling could be put away, than people hastened to take advantage of it.

The first savings bank was started by Miss Priscilla Wakefield, in the parish of Tottenham, Middlesex, towards the close of last century,—her object being mainly to stimulate the frugality of poor children. The experiment proved so successful that in 1799 the Rev. Joseph Smith, of Wendon, commenced a plan of receiving small sums from his parishioners during summer, and returning them at Christmas, with the addition of one-third as a stimulus to prudence and forethought. Miss Wakefield, in her turn, followed Mr. Smith's example, and in 1804 extended the plan of her charitable bank, so as to include adult labourers, female servants, and others. A similar institution was formed at Bath, in 1808, by several ladies of that city; and about the same time Mr. Whitbread proposed to Parliament the formation of a national institution, "in the nature of a bank, for the use and advantage of the labouring classes alone;" but nothing came of his proposal.

It was not until the Rev. Henry Duncan, the minister of Ruthwell, a poor parish in Dumfriesshire, took up the subject, that the savings-bank system may be said to have become fairly inaugurated. The inhabitants of that parish were mostly poor cottagers, whose average wages did not amount to more than eight shillings a week. There were no manufactures in the district, nor any means of subsistence for the population, except what was derived from the land under cultivation; and the landowners were for the most part non-resident. It seemed a very unlikely place in which to establish a bank for savings, where the poor people were already obliged to strain every nerve to earn a bare living, to provide the means of educating their children (for, however small his income, the Scottish peasant almost invariably contrives to save something wherewith to send his children to school), and to pay their little contributions to the friendly society of the parish. Nevertheless, the minister resolved, as a help to his spiritual instructions, to try the experiment.

Not many labouring men may apprehend the deep arguments of the religious teacher, but the least intelligent can appreciate a bit of practical advice that tells on the well-being of his household as well as on the labourer's own daily comfort and self-respect. Dr. Duncan knew that, even in the poorest family, there were odds and ends of income apt to be frittered away in unnecessary expenditure. He saw some thrifty cottagers using the expedient of a cow, or a pig, or a bit of garden-ground, as a savings bank,—finding their return of interest in the shape of butter and milk, winter's bacon, or garden produce; and it occurred to him that there were other villagers, single men and young women, for whom some analogous mode of storing away their summer's savings might be provided, and a fair rate of interest returned upon their little investments.

Hence originated the parish savings bank of Ruthwell, the first self-supporting institution of the kind established in this country. That the minister was not wrong in his anticipations, was proved by the fact that, in the course of four years, the funds of his savings bank amounted to nearly a thousand pounds. And if poor villagers out of eight shillings a week, and female labourers and servants out of much less, could lay aside this sum,—what might not mechanics, artizans, miners, and iron-workers accomplish, who earn from thirty to fifty shillings a week all the year round?

The example set by Dr. Duncan was followed in many towns and districts in England and Scotland. In every instance the model of the Ruthwell parish bank was followed; and the self-sustaining principle was adopted. The savings banks thus instituted, were not eleemosynary institutions, nor dependent upon anybody's charity or patronage; but their success rested entirely with the depositors themselves. They encouraged the industrious classes to rely upon their own resources, to exercise forethought and economy in the conduct of life, to cherish self-respect and self-dependence, and to provide for their comfort and maintenance in old age, by the careful use of the products of their industry, instead of having to rely for aid upon the thankless dole of a begrudged poor-rate.

The establishment of savings banks with these objects, at length began to be recognized as a matter of national concern; and in 1817 an Act was passed which served to increase their number and extend their usefulness. Various measures have since been adopted with the object of increasing their efficiency and security. But notwithstanding the great good which these institutions have accomplished, it is still obvious that the better-paid classes of workpeople avail themselves of them to only a very limited extent. A very small portion of the four hundred millions estimated to be annually earned by the working classes finds its way to the savings bank, while at least twenty times the amount is spent annually at the beershop and the public-house.

It is not the highly-paid class of working men and women who invest money in the savings banks; but those who earn comparatively moderate incomes. Thus the most numerous class of depositors in the Manchester and Salford Savings Bank is that of domestic servants. After them rank clerks, shopmen, porters, and miners. Only about a third part of the deposits belong to the operatives, artizans, and mechanics. It is the same in manufacturing districts generally. A few years since, it was found that of the numerous female depositors at Dundee, only one was a factory worker: the rest were for the most part servants.

There is another fact that is remarkable. The habit of saving does not so much prevail in those counties where wages are the highest, as in those counties where wages are the lowest. Previous to the era of Post Office Savings Banks, the inhabitants of Wilts and Dorset—where wages are about the lowest in England—deposited more money in the savings banks, per head of the population, than they did in Lancashire and Yorkshire, where wages are about the highest in England. Taking Yorkshire itself, and dividing it into manufacturing and agricultural,—the manufacturing inhabitants of the West Riding of York invested about twenty-five shillings per head of the population in the savings banks; whilst the agricultural population of the East Riding invested about three times that amount.

Private soldiers are paid much less wages per week than the lowest-paid workmen, and yet they put more money in the savings banks than workmen who are paid from thirty to forty shillings a week. Soldiers are generally supposed to be a particularly thoughtless class. Indeed, they are sometimes held up to odium as reckless and dissolute; but the Military Savings Bank Returns refute the vilification, and prove that the British soldier is as sober, well-disciplined, and frugal, as we already know him to be brave. Most people forget that the soldier must be obedient, sober, and honest. If he is a drunkard, he is punished; if he is dishonest, he is drummed out of the regiment.

Wonderful is the magic of Drill! Drill means discipline, training, education. The first drill of every people is military. It has been the first education of nations. The duty of obedience is thus taught on a large scale,—submission to authority; united action under a common head. These soldiers,—who are ready to march steadily against vollied fire, against belching cannon, up fortress heights, or to beat their heads against bristling bayonets, as they did at Badajos,—were once tailors, shoemakers, mechanics, delvers, weavers, and ploughmen; with mouths gaping, shoulders stooping, feet straggling, arms and hands like great fins hanging by their sides; but now their gait is firm and martial, their figures are erect, and they march along, to the sound of music, with a tread that makes the earth shake. Such is the wonderful power of drill.

Nations, as they become civilized, adopt other methods of discipline. The drill becomes industrial. Conquest and destruction give place to production in many forms. And what trophies Industry has won, what skill has it exercised, what labours has it performed! Every industrial process is performed by drilled bands of artizans. Go into Yorkshire and Lancashire, and you will find armies of drilled labourers at work, where the discipline is perfect, and the results, as regards the amount of manufactured productions turned out of hand, are prodigious.

On efficient drilling and discipline, men's success as individuals, and as societies entirely depends. The most self-dependent man is under discipline,—and the more perfect the discipline, the more complete his condition. A man must drill his desires, and keep them under subjection,—he must obey the word of command, otherwise he is the sport of passion and impulse. The religions man's life is full of discipline and self-restraint. The man of business is entirely subject to system and rule. The happiest home is that where the discipline is the most perfect, and yet where it is the least felt. We at length become subject to it as to a law of Nature, and while it binds us firmly, yet we feel it not. The force of Habit is but the force of Drill.

One dare scarcely hint, in these days, at the necessity for compulsory conscription; and yet, were the people at large compelled to pass through the discipline of the army, the country would be stronger, the people would be soberer, and thrift would become much more habitual than it is at present.

Savings Banks

Military savings banks were first suggested by Paymaster Fairfowl in 1816; and about ten years later the question was again raised by Colonel Oglander, of the 26th Foot (Cameronians). The subject was brought under the notice of the late Duke of Wellington, and negatived; the Duke making the following memorandum on the subject: "There is nothing that I know of to prevent a soldier, equally with others of His Majesty's subjects, from investing his money in savings banks. If there be any impediment, it should be taken away; but I doubt the expediency of going further."

The idea, however, seems to have occurred to the Duke, that the proposal to facilitate the saving of money by private soldiers might be turned to account in the way of a reduction in the army expenditure, and he characteristically added: "Has a soldier more pay than he requires? If he has, it should be lowered, not to those now in the service, but to those enlisted hereafter." No one, however, could allege that the pay of the private soldier was excessive, and it was not likely that any proposal to lower it would be entertained.

The subject of savings banks for the army was allowed to rest for a time, but by the assistance of Sir James McGregor and Lord Howick a scheme was at length approved and finally established in 1842. The result has proved satisfactory in an eminent degree, and speaks well for the character of the British soldier. It appears from a paper presented to the House of Commons some years ago,—giving the details of the savings effected by the respective corps,—that the men of the Royal Artillery had saved over twenty-three thousand pounds, or an average of sixteen pounds to each depositor. These savings were made out of a daily pay of one and threepence and a penny for beer-money, or equal to about nine and sixpence a week, subject to sundry deductions for extra clothing. Again, the men of the Royal Engineers—mostly drawn from the skilled mechanical class—had saved nearly twelve thousand pounds, or an average of about twenty pounds for each depositor. The Twenty-sixth regiment of the line (Cameronians), whose pay was a shilling a day and a penny for beer, saved over four thousand pounds. Two hundred and fifty men of the first battalion, or one-third of the corps, were depositors in the savings bank, and their savings amounted to about seventeen pounds per man.

But this is not all. Private soldiers, out of their small earnings, are accustomed to remit considerable sums through the post office, to their poor relations at home. In one year, twenty-two thousand pounds were thus sent from Aldershot,—the average amount of each money order being twenty-one shillings and fourpence. And if men with seven shillings and seven-pence a week can do so much, what might not skilled workmen do, whose earnings amount to from two to three pounds a week?

Soldiers serving abroad during arduous campaigns have proved themselves to be equally thoughtful and provident. During the war in the Crimea, the soldiers and seamen sent home through the money order office seventy-one thousand pounds, and the army works corps thirty-five thousand pounds. More than a year before the money order system was introduced at Scutari, Miss Nightingale took charge of the soldiers' savings. She found them most willing to abridge their own comforts or indulgences, for the sake of others dear to them, as well as for their own future well-being; and she devoted an afternoon in every week to receiving and forwarding their savings to England. She remitted many thousand pounds in this manner, and it was distributed by a friend in London,—much of it to the remotest corners of Scotland and Ireland. And it afforded some evidence that the seed fell in good places (as well as of the punctuality of the post office), that of the whole number of remittances, all but one were duly acknowledged.

Again, there is not a regiment returning from India but brings home with it a store of savings. In the year 1860, after the Indian mutiny, more than twenty thousand pounds were remitted on account of invalided men sent back to England; besides which there were eight regiments which brought home balances to their credits in the regimental banks amounting to £40.499.[3] The highest was the Eighty-fourth, whose savings amounted to £9,718. The Seventy-Eighth (Ross-shire Buffs), the heroes who followed Havelock in his march on Lucknow, saved £6,480; and the gallant Thirty-second, who held Lucknow under Inglis, saved £5,263. The Eighty-sixth, the first battalion of the Tenth, and the Ninth Dragoons, all brought home an amount of savings indicative of providence and forethought, which reflected the highest honour upon them as men as well as soldiers.[4]

And yet the private soldiers do not deposit all their savings in the military savings banks,—especially when they can obtain access to an

---

3. The sum sent home by soldiers serving in India for the benefit of friends and relatives are not included in these amounts, the remittances being made direct by the paymasters of regiments, and not through the savings banks.
4. The amount of the Fund for Military Savings Banks on the 5th of January, 1876, was £338,350.

ordinary savings bank. We are informed that many of the household troops stationed in London deposit their spare money in the savings banks rather than in the regimental banks; and when the question was on a recent occasion asked as to the cause, the answer given was, "I would not have my sergeant know that I was saving money." But in addition to this, the private soldier would rather that his comrades did not know that he was saving money; for the thriftless soldier, like the thriftless workman, when he has spent everything of his own, is very apt to set up a kind of right to borrow from the fund of his more thrifty comrade.

The same feeling of suspicion frequently prevents workmen depositing money in the ordinary savings bank. They do not like it to be known to their employers that they are saving money, being under the impression that it might lead to attempts to lower their wages. A working man in a town in Yorkshire, who had determined to make a deposit in the savings bank, of which his master was a director, went repeatedly to watch at the door of the bank before he could ascertain that his master was absent; and he only paid in his money, after several weeks' waiting, when ne had assured himself of this fact.

The miners at Bilston, at least such of them as put money in the savings bank, were accustomed to deposit it in other names than their own. Nor were they without reason. For some of their employers were actually opposed to the institution of savings banks,—fearing lest the workmen might apply their savings to their maintenance during a turn-out; not reflecting that they have the best guarantee of the steadiness of this class of men, in their deposits at the savings bank. Mr. Baker, Inspector of Factories, has said that "the supreme folly of a strike is shown by the fact that there is seldom or never a rich workman at the head of it."

A magistrate at Bilston, not connected with the employment of workmen, has mentioned the following case. "I prevailed," he says, "upon a workman to begin a deposit in the savings bank. He came most unwillingly. His deposits were small, although I knew his gains to be great. I encouraged him by expressing satisfaction at the course he was taking. His deposits became greater; and at the end of five years he drew out the fund he had accumulated, bought a piece of land, and has built a house upon it. I think if I had not spoken to him, the whole amount would have been spent in feasting or clubs, or contributions to the trades unions. That man's eyes are now open—his social position is raised—he sees and feels as we do, and will influence others to follow his example."

Savings Banks

From what we have said, it will be obvious that there can be no doubt as to the ability of a large proportion of the better-paid classes of working men to lay by a store of savings. When they set their minds upon any object, they have no difficulty in finding the requisite money. A single town in Lancashire contributed thirty thousand pounds to support their fellow-workmen when on strike in an adjoining town. At a time when there are no strikes, why should they not save as much money on their own account, for their own permanent comfort? Many workmen already save with this object; and what they do, all might do. We know of one large mechanical establishment,—situated in an agricultural district, where the temptations to useless expenditure are few,—in which nearly all the men are habitual economists, and have saved sums varying from two hundred to five hundred pounds each.

Many factory operatives, with their families, might easily lay by from five to ten shillings a week, which in a few years would amount to considerable sums. At Darwen, only a short time ago, an operative drew his savings out of the bank to purchase a row of cottages, now become his property. Many others, in the same place, and in the neighbouring towns, are engaged in building cottages for themselves, some by means of their contributions to building societies, and others by means of their savings accumulated in the bank.

A respectably dressed working man, when making a payment one day at the Bradford savings bank, which brought his account up to nearly eighty pounds, informed the manager how it was that he had been induced to become a depositor. He had been a drinker; but one day accidentally finding his wife's savings bank deposit book, from which he learnt that she had laid by about twenty pounds, he said to himself, "Well now, if this can be done while I am spending, what might we do if both were saving?" The man gave up his drinking, and became one of the most respectable persons of his class. "I owe it all," he said, "to my wife and the savings bank."

When well-paid workmen such as these are able to accumulate a sufficient store of savings, they ought gradually to give up hard work, and remove from the field of competition as old age comes upon them. They ought also to give place to younger men; and prevent themselves being beaten down into the lower-paid ranks of labour. After sixty a man's physical powers fail him; and by that time he ought to have made provision for his independent maintenance. Nor are the instances by any means uncommon, of workmen laying by money with this object, and thereby proving what the whole class might, to a greater or less extent, accomplish in the same direction.

The extent to which Penny Banks have been used by the very poorest classes, wherever started, affords a striking illustration how much may be done by merely providing increased opportunities for the practice of thrift. The first Penny Bank was started in Greenock, about thirty years since, as an auxiliary to the savings bank. The object of the projector (Mr. J.M. Scott) was to enable poor persons, whose savings amounted to less than a shilling (the savings bank minimum) to deposit them in a safe place. In one year about five thousand depositors placed £1,580 with the Greenock institution. The estimable Mr. Queckett, a curate in the east end of London, next opened a Penny Bank, and the results were very remarkable. In one year as many as 14,513 deposits were made in the bank. The number of depositors was limited to 2,000; and the demand for admission was so great that there were usually many waiting until vacancies occurred.

"Some save for their rent," said Mr. Queckett, "others for clothes and apprenticing their children; and various are the little objects to which the savings are to be applied. Every repayment passes through my own hands, which gives an opportunity of hearing of sickness, or sorrow, or any other cause which compels the withdrawal of the little fund. It is, besides, a feeder to the larger savings banks, to which many are turned over when the weekly payments tendered exceed the usual sum. Many of those who could at first scarcely advance beyond a penny a week, can now deposit a silver coin of some kind."

Never was the moral influence of the parish clergyman more wisely employed than in this case. Not many of those whom Mr. Queckett thus laboured to serve were amongst the church-going class; but by helping them to be frugal, and improving their physical condition, he was enabled gradually to elevate their social tastes, and to awaken in them a religious life to which the greater number of them had before been strangers.

A powerful influence was next given to the movement by Mr. Charles W. Sikes, cashier of the Huddersfield Banking Company, who advocated their establishment in connection with the extensive organization of mechanics' institutes. It appeared to him that to train working people when young in habits of economy, was of more practical value to themselves, and of greater importance to society, than to fill their minds with the contents of many books. He pointed to the perverted use of money by

Savings Banks

the working class as one of the greatest practical evils of the time. "In many cases," he said, "the higher the workmen's wages, the poorer are their families; and these are they who really form the discontented and the dangerous classes. How can such persons take any interest in pure and elevating knowledge?"

To show the thriftlessness of the people, Mr. Sikes mentioned the following instance. "An eminent employer in the West Riding," he said, "whose mills for a quarter of a century have scarcely run short time for a single week, has within a few days examined the rate of wages now paid to his men, and compared it with that of a few years ago. He had the pleasure of finding that improvements in machinery had led to improvement in wages. His spinners and weavers are making about twenty-seven shillings a week. In many instances some of their children work at the same mill, and in a few instances their wives, and often the family income reaches from a hundred to a hundred and fifty pounds per annum. Visiting the homes of some of these men, he has seen with feelings of disappointment the air of utter discomfort and squalor with which many are pervaded. Increase of income has led only to increase of improvidence. The savings bank and the building society are equally neglected, although at the same mill there are some with no higher wages, whose homes have every comfort, and who have quite a little competency laid by. In Bradford, I believe, a munificent employer on one occasion opened seven hundred accounts with the savings bank for his operatives, paying in a small deposit for each. The result was not encouraging. Rapidly was a small portion of the sums drawn out, and very few remained as the nucleus of further deposits."[5]

Mr. Sikes suggested that each mechanics' institute should appoint a preliminary savings bank committee, to attend once a week for the purpose of receiving deposits from the members and others.

"If a committee at each institution," he said, "were to adopt this course, taking an interest in their humble circumstances, and in a sympathizing and kindly spirit, to suggest, invite, nay win them over, not only by reading the lesson, but forming the habit of true economy and self-reliance (the noblest lessons for which classes could be formed), how cheering would be the results! Once established in better habits, their feet firmly set in the path of self-reliance, how generally would young

---

5. From Mr. Sikes's excellent little handbook entitled "Good Times, or the Savings Bank and the Fireside."

men grow up with the practical conviction that to their own advancing intelligence and virtues must they mainly look to work out their own social welfare!"

This admirable advice was not lost. One institution after another embraced the plan, and preliminary savings banks were, shortly established in connection with the principal mechanics' institutes throughout Yorkshire. Those established at Huddersfield, Halifax, Bradford, Leeds, and York, were exceedingly successful. The Penny Banks established at Halifax consisted of a central bank and seven subordinate branches. The number of members, and the average amount of the sums deposited with them, continued to increase from year to year. Fourteen Penny Banks were established at Bradford; and after the depositors had formed the habit of saving in the smaller banks, they transferred them in bulk to the ordinary Savings Bank.

Thirty-six Penny Banks were established in and around Glasgow. The committee, in their Report, stated they were calculated "to check that reckless expenditure of little sums which so often leads to a confirmed habit of wastefulness and improvidence;" and they urged the support of the Penny Banks as the best means of extending the usefulness of the savings banks. The Penny Bank established at the small country town of Farnham is estimated to have contributed within a few years a hundred and fifty regular depositors to the savings bank of the same place. The fact that as large a proportion as two-thirds of the whole amount deposited is drawn out within the year, shows that Penny Banks are principally used as places of safe deposit for very small sums of money, until they are wanted for some special object, such as rent, clothes, furniture, the doctor's bill, and such-like purposes.

Thus the Penny Bank is emphatically the poor man's purse. The great mass of the deposits are paid in sums not exceeding sixpence, and the average of the whole does not exceed a shilling. The depositors consist of the very humblest members of the working class, and by far the greatest number of them have never before been accustomed to lay by any portion of their earnings. The Rev. Mr. Clarke, of Derby, who took an active interest in the extension of these useful institutions, has stated that one-tenth of the whole amount received by the Derby Penny Bank was deposited in copper money, and a large portion of the remainder in threepenny and fourpenny pieces.

It is clear, therefore, that the Penny Bank reaches a class of persons of very small means, whose ability to save is much less than that of the highly-paid workman, and who, if the money were left in their pockets, would in most cases spend it in the nearest public-house. Hence, when a Penny Bank was established at Putney, and the deposits were added up at the end of the first year, a brewer, who was on the committee, made the remark, "Well, that represents thirty thousand pints of beer not drunk."

At one of the Penny Banks in Yorkshire, an old man in receipt of parish outdoor relief was found using the Penny Bank as a place of deposit for his pennies until he had accumulated enough to buy a coat. Others save, to buy an eight-day clock, or a musical instrument, or for a railway trip.

But the principal supporters of the Penny Banks are boys, and this is their most hopeful feature; for it is out of boys that men are made. At Huddersfield many of the lads go in bands from the mills to the Penny Banks; emulation as well as example urging them on. They save for various purposes—one to buy a chest of tools, another a watch, a third a grammar or a dictionary.

One evening a boy presented himself to draw £1 10. According to the rules of the Penny Bank a week's notice must be given before any sum exceeding 20s. can be withdrawn, and the cashier demurred to making the payment. "Well," said the boy, "the reason's this—mother can't pay her rent; I'm goin' to pay it, for, as long as I have owt, she shall hev' it." In another case, a youth drew £20 to buy off his brother who had enlisted. "Mother frets so," said the lad, "that, she'll break her heart if he isn't bought off, and I cannot bear that."

Thus these institutions give help and strength in many ways, and, besides enabling young people to keep out of debt and honestly to pay their way, furnish them with the means of performing kindly and generous acts in times of family trial and emergency. It is an admirable feature of the Ragged Schools that almost every one of them has a Penny Bank connected with it for the purpose of training the scholars in good habits, which they most need; and it is a remarkable fact that in one year not less than £8,880 were deposited, in 25,637 sums, by the scholars connected with the Ragged School Union. And when, this can be done by the poor boys of the ragged schools, what might not be accomplished by the highly-paid operatives and mechanics of England?

But another capital feature in the working of Penny Banks, as regards the cultivation of prudent habits among the people, is the circumstance that the example of boys and girls depositing their spare weekly pennies, has often the effect of drawing their parents after them. A boy goes on for weeks paying his pence, and taking home his pass-book. The book shows that he has a "leger folio" at the bank expressly devoted to him—that his pennies are all duly entered, together with the respective dates of their deposits—that these savings are not lying idle, but bear interest at 2-1/2 per cent. per annum—and that he can have them restored to him at any time,—if under 20s., without notice; and it above 20s., then after a week's notice has been given.

The book is a little history in itself, and cannot fail to be interesting to the boy's brothers and sisters, as well as to his parents. They call him "good lad," and they see he is a well-conducted lad. The father, if he be a sensible man, naturally bethinks him that, if his boy can do so creditable a thing, worthy of praise, so might he himself. Accordingly, on the next Saturday night, when the boy goes to deposit his threepence at the Penny Bank, the father often sends his shilling.

Thus a good beginning is often made, and a habit initiated, which, if persevered in, very shortly exercises a most salutary influence on the entire domestic condition of the family. The observant mother is quick to observe the effects of this new practice upon the happiness of the home, and in course of time, as the younger children grow up and earn money, she encourages them to follow the elder boy's example. She herself takes them by the hand, leads them to the Penny Bank, and accustoms them to invest their savings there. Women have even more influence in such matters than men, and where they do exercise it, the beneficial effects are much more lasting.

One evening a strong, muscular mechanic appeared at the Bradford savings bank in his working dress, bringing with him three children, one of them in his arms. He placed on the counter their deposit books, which his wife had previously been accustomed to present, together with ten shillings, to be equally apportioned amongst the three. Pressing to his bosom the child in his arms, the man said, "Poor things! they have lost their mother since they were here last; but I must do the best I can for them." And he continued the good lesson to his children which his wife had begun, bringing them with him each time to see their little deposits made.

There is an old English proverb which says, "He that would thrive must first ask his wife;" but the wife must not only let her husband thrive, but help him, otherwise she is not the "help meet" which is as needful for the domestic comfort and satisfaction of the working man, as of every other man who undertakes the responsibility of a family. Women form the moral atmosphere in which we grow when children, and they have a great deal to do with the life we lead when we become men. It is true that the men may hold the reins; but it is generally the women who tell them which way to drive. What Rousseau said is very near the truth—"Men will always be what women make them."

Not long ago, Mr. Sikes encountered, in a second-class carriage, a well-dressed workman travelling from Sheffield to Glasgow, during holiday times, to see his mother. "I am glad," said Mr. Sikes, "to find a workman travelling so great a distance, for a purpose like that." "Yes," said the man, "and I am glad to say that I can afford to do it." "And do many of the workmen employed in your workshop save money?" asked Mr. Sikes. "No," said the other, "not more than about two in the hundred. The spare earnings of the others go, not to the savings banks, but to the drink-shops." "And when did you begin to save?" "When I was no bigger than that," indicating the height of a little boy: "the first money I saved was in a Penny Bank, and I have gone on saving ever since."

Such being the influence of early practice and example, we are glad to find that Economy is now being taught at public schools. The Rev. Mr. Crallan, of the Sussex County Asylum, has long taught lessons of thrift to poor boys and girls. He urges the establishment of Penny Banks in connection with Savings Banks, in all elementary schools. He wisely contends that simple lessons on money, its nature, its value, and its uses, together with the various duties of giving, spending, and saving, would have a vast influence on the rising generation.

The practice of teaching children provident habits has been adopted for about eight years in the National Schools of Belgium. The School Board of Ghent is convinced of the favourable influence that saving has upon the moral and material well-being of the working classes, and believes that the best means of causing the spirit of economy to penetrate their habits is to teach it to the children under tuition, and to make them practise it.

It is always very difficult to teach anything new to adults,—and especially lessons of thrift to men who are thriftless. Their method of living is fixed. Traditional and inveterate habits of expenditure exist among them. With men, it is the drinking-shop; with women, it is dress. They spend what they earn, and think nothing of tomorrow. When reduced to a state of distress, they feel no shame in begging; for the feeling of human dignity has not yet been sufficiently developed in them.

With children it is very different. They have no inveterate habits to get rid of. They will, for the most part, do as they are taught. And they can be taught economy, just as they can be taught arithmetic. They can, at all events, be inspired by a clever teacher with habits of economy and thrift. Every child has a few pence at times. The master may induce them to save these for some worthy purpose. At Ghent, a savings bank has been introduced in every school, and the children deposit their pennies there. It is introduced into the paying schools as well as the free schools; for habits of thrift are as useful to men and women of the richer as of the poorer classes. The results of the lessons on Economy have been highly satisfactory.[6] The children belonging to the schools of Ghent have accumulated eighteen thousand pounds, which is deposited in the State Savings Bank at three per cent. interest. This system is spreading into Holland, France, and Italy. It has also, to a certain extent, been adopted in this country. Thus Glasgow, Liverpool, Birmingham, Great Ilford, and the London Orphan Asylum, all show specimens of School Banks; and we trust that, before long, they will be established in every school throughout the kingdom.

It will be obvious, from what has been said, that the practice of economy depends very much upon the facilities provided for the laying by of small sums of money. Let a convenient savings bank be provided, and deposits gradually flow into it. Let a military savings bank be established, and private soldiers contrive to save something out of their small pay. Let penny banks be opened, and crowds of depositors immediately present themselves; even the boys of the ragged schools being able to put into them considerable sums of money. It is the same with school banks, as we have seen from the example of the school-children of Ghent.

Now, fifteen years ago, this country was very insufficiently provided with savings banks for the people. There were then many large towns and villages altogether unprovided with them. Lancashire had only thirty savings banks for upwards of two millions of people. The East Riding

---

6. A pamphlet published at Ghent says of the paying schools: "The spirit of economy is introduced there under the form of charity. The young girls buy with their pocket money, firstly materials, say cotton or linen, of which they afterwards make articles of dress during the hours set aside for manual work: afterwards the shirts, stockings, dresses, handkerchiefs, or aprons, are distributed to the poorer children of the free schools. The distribution Becomes the object of a little holiday: we know of nothing that can be more touching. The poor children are assembled in the Collier school; our young ladies go were also; one of them says a few words feelingly to her sisters in the poorer classes; one of the girls of the free schools replies. Then the pretty and useful things which have been made during the last year are distributed. It is the donors themselves who present the fruits of their labour to the poorest among the poor. The distribution is intermingled with singing. Need we reiterate the blessings of this blessed economy?"

of Yorkshire had only four savings banks. There were fifteen counties in the United Kingdom which had not a single savings bank. There were only about six hundred savings banks for about thirty millions of people. These were open only for two or three hours in the week; some were open for only four hours in the month. The workman who had money to save, had to carry his spare shillings in his pocket for some time before he could lay them by; and in the meantime he might be exposed to constant temptations to spend them. To keep his shillings safe, he must have acquired the habit of saving, which it was the object of savings banks to train and establish.

Dr. Guthrie, in his book on Ragged Schools, published in 1860, said: "How are our manufacturing and handicraft youth situated? By public-houses and spirit-shops they are surrounded with innumerable temptations; while to many of them savings banks are hardly known by name. Dissipation has her nets drawn across every street. In many of our towns, sobriety has to run the gauntlet of half-a-dozen spirit-shops in the space of a bow-shot. These are near at hand—open by day, and blazing by night, both on Sabbath and Saturday. Drunkenness finds immediate gratification; while economy has to travel a mile, it may be, for her savings bank; and that opens its door to thrift but once or twice a week."[7]

Many suggestions had been made by friends of the poorer classes, whether it might not be possible to establish a more extended system of savings banks throughout the country. As long ago as 1807, Mr. Whitbread introduced a Bill into Parliament for the purpose of enabling small deposits to be made at an office to be established in London; the money to be remitted by the postmasters of the districts in which the deposits were made. The Bill further contemplated the establishment of a National Assurance Society, by means of which working people were to be enabled to effect assurances to an extent not exceeding two hundred pounds, and to secure annuities to an amount not exceeding twenty pounds. Mr. Whitbread's bill was rejected, and nothing came of his suggestions.

The exertions of Sir Rowland Hill having given great vitality to the Post Office system, and extended its usefulness as a public institution in all directions, it was next suggested that the money-order offices (which were established in 1838) might be applied for the purpose of

---

7. Seed-Time and Harvest of Ragged Schools, or a Third Plea, with new editions of the First and Second Plea, p. 99.

depositing as well as for transmitting money. Professor Hancock published a pamphlet on the subject in 1852. In November, 1856, Mr. John Bullar, the eminent counsel—whose attention had been directed to the subject by the working of the Putney Penny Bank—suggested to the Post Office authorities the employment of money-order offices as a means of extending the savings-bank system; but his suggestion did not meet with approval at the time, and nothing came of it. Similar suggestions were made by other gentlemen—by Mr. Hume, by Mr. M'Corquodale, by Captain Strong, by Mr. Ray Smee, and others.

But it was not until Mr. Sikes, of Huddersfield, took up the question, that these various suggestions became embodied in facts. Suggestions are always useful. They arouse thinking. The most valuable are never lost, but at length work themselves into facts. Most inventions are the result of original suggestions. Some one attempts to apply the idea. Failures occur at first; but with greater knowledge, greater experience, and greater determination, the suggestion at last succeeds.

Post Office Savings Banks owe their success, in the first place, to the numerous suggestions made by Mr. Whitbread and others; next to Sir Rowland Hill who by establishing the Branch Post Offices for the transmission of money, made the suggestions practicable; next to Mr. Sikes, who took up the question in 1850, pushed it, persevered with it, and brought it under the notice of successive Chancellors of the Exchequer; and lastly to Mr. Gladstone, who, having clearly foreseen the immense benefits of Post Office Savings Banks, brought in a Bill and carried it through Parliament in 1861.

The money-order department of the Post Office had suggested to Mr. Sikes, as it had already done to other observers, that the organization already existed for making Post Office Savings Banks practicable throughout the kingdom. Wherever the local inspector found that as many as five money-orders were required in a week, the practice was to make that branch of the Post Office a money-order office. It was estimated that such an office was established on an average within three miles of every working man's door in the kingdom. The offices were open daily. They received money from all comers, and gave vouchers for the amounts transmitted through them. They held the money until it was drawn, and paid it out on a proper voucher being presented. The Post Office was, in fact, a bank for the transmission of money, holding it for periods of from twenty-four hours to weeks and months. By enabling it to receive more money from more depositors, and by increasing the time of holding it, allowing the usual interest, it became to all intents and purposes a National bank of deposit.

The results of the Post Office Savings Banks Act have proved entirely satisfactory. The money-order offices have been largely extended. They are now about four thousand in number; consequently the facilities for saving have been nearly doubled since the banks were established. The number in the London district is now about four hundred and sixty, so that from any point in the thickly populated parts of the metropolis, a Savings Bank may be found within a distance of a few hundred yards. The number of the depositors at the end of 1873 amounted to more than a million and a half; while the amount of deposits reached over twenty-one millions sterling.[8] At the same time the amount deposited with the original Savings Banks remained about the same.

Post Office Savings Banks possess several great advantages which ought to be generally known. The banks are very widely diffused, and are open from nine in the morning until six in the evening, and on Saturdays until nine at night. Persons may make a deposit of a shilling, or of any number of shillings, provided more than thirty pounds is not deposited in any one year. The Post Office officers furnish the book in which the several deposits are entered. The book also contains the regulations of the Post Office Savings Banks. Interest is allowed at the rate of two pounds ten shillings per cent, per annum.

Another most important point is, the Security. Government is responsible for the full amount paid in; so that the money deposited with the Post Office Savings Bank is as safe as if it were in the Bank of England. The money saved may also be transferred from place to place, without expense, and may be easily paid to the depositor when required, no matter where it was originally deposited. All that is done, is done in perfect secrecy between the depositor and the postmaster, who is forbidden to disclose the names of the depositors.

We have frequently alluded to Mr. Charles William Sikes in connection with Penny Banks and Post Office Savings Banks. His name must always hold a distinguished place in connection with those valuable institutions. He is the son of a private banker in Huddersfield. When at school he was presented, as a prize, with a copy of Dr. Franklin's Essays and Letters. He perused the book with avidity. It implanted in his mind the germs of many useful thoughts, and exercised a powerful influence in giving a

---

8. The amount reached £23,157,469 at the end of 1874.

practical character to his life. Huddersfield is a busy manufacturing town. Although workmen were well paid for their labour, there were many ups and downs in their business. When trade became slack, and they had spent all that they had earned, numbers of them were accustomed to apply for charity in the streets or by the wayside. Young Sikes often wondered whether these people had ever heard of Dr. Franklin, and of his method of avoiding beggary or bad times by saving their money when trade was brisk and they were well off.

Early in 1833, Mr. Sikes entered the service of the Huddersfield Banking Company. It was the second joint stock bank that had been established in England. The prudence and success with which the Scotch banking companies had been conducted induced the directors to select a Scotch manager. One of the first resolutions the directors adopted, was to give deposit receipts for sums of ten pounds and upwards, for the purpose of encouraging the working classes in habits of providence and thrift. Mr. Sikes, being somewhat of a favourite with the manager, often heard from his lips most interesting accounts of the provident habits of the Scotch peasantry, and was informed by him of the fact that one of the banks at Perth paid not less than twenty thousand pounds a year as interest on deposits varying from ten to two hundred pounds each.

In 1837, Mr. Sikes became one of the cashiers of the company. This brought him into direct contact and intercourse with the very class which, from the direction his mind was taking, he so much wished to understand,—namely, the thrifty portion of the industrious classes. A considerable number of them had sums lying at interest. As years rolled on, Mr. Sikes often witnessed the depositor commencing with ten or twenty pounds, then make permanent additions to his little store, until at length the amount would reach one, two, or, in a few instances, even three hundred pounds. Mr. Sikes would often imagine the marvellous improvement that would be effected on the condition of the working classes, if every one of them became influenced by the same frugality and forethought, which induced these exceptional operatives to deposit their savings at his bank.

About that time, trade was in a wretched condition. The handloom weavers were almost entirely without employment. Privation and suffering prevailed on every side, and these were often borne with silent and noble heroism. Various remedies were proposed for the existing evils. Socialism, chartism, and free trade, were the favourites. Theories of the wildest and most impracticable character abounded, and yet even in those dark days there were instances of men who had to some degree made the future predominate over the present, who could fall back upon their reserve in the Joint Stock or Savings Bank to tide them over into better times. Believing in the beneficent results of free trade, Mr. Sikes was equally convinced that national prosperity, as well as national adversity, might be attended with great evils, unless the masses were endowed with habits of providence and thrift, and prepared by previous education for the "good time coming" so eloquently predicted by the orators of the League.

Many discussions with working men, in his homeward evening walks, convinced Mr. Sikes that there were social problems with which legislation would be almost powerless to grapple, and of these the thriftlessness of the masses of the people was one. An employer of five hundred hand-loom weavers had told Mr. Sikes that in a previous period of prosperity, when work was abundant and wages were very high, he could not, had he begged on bended knee, have induced his men to save a single penny, or to lay by anything for a rainy day. The fancy waistcoating trade had uniformly had its cycles of alternate briskness and depression; but experience, however stern its teachings, could not teach unwilling learners. It was at this period that Mr. Sikes was reading the late Archbishop Sumner's "Records of Creation," and met with the following passage: "The only true secret of assisting the poor, is to make them agents in bettering their own condition."

Simple as are the words, they shed light into Mr. Sikes's mind, and became the keynote and the test to which he brought the various views and theories which he had previously met with. Doles and charities, though founded frequently on the most benevolent motives, were too often deteriorating to their recipients. On the other hand, if self-reliance and self-help—the columns of true majesty in man—could only be made characteristics of the working classes generally, nothing could retard their onward and upward progress. Mr. Sikes observed that until the working classes had more of the money power in their hands, they would still be periodically in poverty and distress. He saw that if provident habits could only he generally pursued by them, the face of society would immediately be transformed; and he resolved, in so far as lay in his power, to give every aid to this good work.

In 1850, Savings Banks were only open a very few hours in each week. In Huddersfield, where more than £400,000 a year was paid in wages, the savings bank, after having been established over thirty years, had only accumulated £74,332. In 1850, Mr. Sikes addressed an anonymous letter to the editors of the Leeds Mercury, to which, by their request, he afterwards attached his name. In that letter he recommended the formation of Penny Savings Banks in connection with Mechanics' and similar institutes. In simple words, but with many telling facts, he showed how the young men and the young women of the working classes were growing up deprived of almost every opportunity of forming habits of thrift, and of becoming depositors in savings hanks.

The letter was received with general approbation. The committee of the Yorkshire Union of Mechanics' Institutes gave their cordial sanction to it; and Penny Banks were established in connection with nearly every Mechanics' Institute in Yorkshire. Mr. Sikes personally conducted one at Huddersfield; and down to the present time, it has received and repaid about thirty thousand pounds. In fact, the working people of Huddersfield, doubtless owing in a great measure to the practical example of Mr. Sikes,—have become most provident and thrifty,—the deposits in their savings bank having increased from seventy-four thousand pounds in 1850, to three hundred and thirty thousand pounds in 1874.

In 1854, Mr. Sikes published his excellent pamphlet on "Good Times, or the Savings Bank and the Fireside," to which we have already referred. The success which it met with induced him to give his attention to the subject of savings banks generally. He was surprised to find that they were so utterly inadequate to meet the requirements of the country. He sought an interview with Sir Cornewall Lewis, then Chancellor of the Exchequer, and brought the subject under his consideration. The Chancellor requested Mr. Sikes to embody his views in a letter, and in the course of a few months there appeared a pamphlet addressed to Sir Cornewall Lewis, entitled "Savings Banks Reforms." Mr. Sikes insisted on the Government guarantee being given for deposits made in Savings Banks; but this was refused.

Mr. Sikes next proceeded to ventilate the question of Post Office Savings Banks. He was disappointed that no measure for the improvement of Savings Banks had been adopted by Parliament. The day appeared very distant when his cherished wish would be realized,—that the Savings Bank should really become the Bank of the People. But the darkest hour precedes the dawn. When he had almost given up the notion of improving the existing Savings Banks, the idea suddenly struck him that in the money-order office there was the very organization which might be made the basis of a popular Savings Bank.

He communicated his plan in a letter to his friend Mr. Baines, then member for Leeds. The plan was submitted to Sir Rowland Hill, who approved of the suggestions, and considered the scheme "practicable so far as the Post Office was concerned." The plan was then brought under the notice of Mr. Gladstone, who afterwards carried the Bill through Parliament for the establishment of Post Office Savings Banks throughout the country.

To use the words of Mr. Sikes himself,—when predicting at the Social Science Association the success of the Post Office Savings Banks,— "Should the plan be carried out, it will soon be doing a glorious work. Wherever a Bank is opened and deposits received, self-reliance will to some extent be aroused, and, with many, a nobler life will be begun. They will gradually discern how ruthless an enemy is improvidence to working men; and how truly his friends are economy and forethought. Under their guidance, household purchases could be made on the most favourable terms—for cash; any wished-for house taken at the lowest rent for punctual payment; and the home enriched with comforts until it is enjoyed and prized by all. From such firesides go forth those inheriting the right spirit,—loving industry, loving thrift, and loving home. Emulous of a good example, they in their day and generation would nobly endeavour to lay by a portion of their income. Many a hard winter and many a slack time would be comfortably got over by drawing on the little fund, to be again replenished in better days. And if the plan were adopted, remembering that it would virtually bring the Savings Bank within less than an hour's walk of the fireside of every working man in the United Kingdom, I trust that it is not taking too sanguine a view to anticipate that it would render aid in ultimately winning over the rank and file of the industrial classes of the kingdom to those habits of forethought and self-denial which bring enduring reward to the individual, and materially add to the safety of the State."

The working classes have not yet, however, taken full advantage of the facilities for saving afforded them by the Post Office Savings Banks. Take Birmingham for instance, where the artizans are among the best-paid workmen of the town. In the list of depositors in the Post Office Savings Banks, we find that the artizans rank after the domestic servants, after the married and unmarried women, and after the miners. They only constitute about one-tenth of the entire depositors, though it is possible that they may deposit their savings in some other investments.

Then take the returns for the entire United Kingdom. Out of every ten thousand depositors in the Post Office Savings Banks, we find that the domestic servants are again the first; next, the women, married and single; next, persons of "no occupation" and "occupations not given;" next, the artizans, and after them, the labourers, miners, tradesmen, soldiers and sailors, clerks, milliners and dressmakers, professional men, and public officials, in the order stated. We must, however, regard the institution as still too young to have fully taken root. We believe that the living generation must pass away before the full fruits of the Post Office Savings Banks can be gathered in.

The inhabitants of Preston have exhibited a strong disposition to save their earnings during the last few years,—more especially since the conclusion of the last great strike. There is no town in England, excepting perhaps Huddersfield, where the people have proved themselves so provident and so thrifty. Fifty years ago, only one person in thirty of the population of Preston deposited money in the Savings Bank; twenty years ago, the depositors increased to one in eleven; and last year they had increased to one in five. In 1834, the sum of a hundred and sixty-five thousand pounds had been accumulated in the Savings Bank by 5,942 depositors; and in 1874, four hundred and seventy-two thousand pounds had been accumulated by 14,792 depositors, out of a total population of 85,428. Is there any other town or city that can show a more satisfactory result of the teaching, the experience, and the prosperity of the last twenty years?

Chapter 9

Little Things

"The sober comfort, all the peace which springs from the large aggregate of little things; on these small cares of daughter, wife, or friend, the almost sacred joys of Home depend."—Hannah More.

"Know when to spend and when to spare, and when to buy, and thou shalt ne'er be bare."

"He that despiseth little things, shall perish by little and little."—Ecclesiasticus.

Neglect of small things is the rock on which the great majority of the human race have split. Human life consists of a succession of small events, each of which is comparatively unimportant, and yet the happiness and success of every man depends upon the manner in which these small events are dealt with. Character is built up on little things,—little things well and honourably transacted. The success of a man in business depends on his attention to little things. The comfort of a household is the result of small things well arranged and duly provided for. Good government can only be accomplished in the same way,—by well-regulated provisions for the doing of little things.

Accumulations of knowledge and experience of the most valuable kind are the result of little bits of knowledge and experience carefully treasured up. Those who learn nothing or accumulate nothing in life, are set down as failures,—because they have neglected little things. They may themselves consider that the world has gone against them; but in fact they have been their own enemies. There has long been a popular belief in "good luck;" but, like many other popular notions, it is gradually giving way. The conviction is extending that diligence is the mother of good luck; in other words, that a man's success in life will be proportionate to his efforts, to his industry, to his attention to small things. Your negligent, shiftless, loose fellows never meet with luck; because the results of industry are denied to those who will not use the proper efforts to secure them.

It is not luck, but labour, that makes men. Luck, says an American writer, is ever waiting for something to turn up; Labour, with keen eye and strong will, always turns up something. Luck lies in bed and wishes the postman would bring him news of a legacy; Labour turns out at six, and with busy pen or ringing hammer lays the foundation of a competence. Luck whines; Labour whistles. Luck relies on chance; Labour on character. Luck slips downwards to self-indulgence; Labour strides upward, and aspires to independence.

There are many little things in the household, attention to which is indispensable to health and happiness. Cleanliness consists in attention to a number of apparent trifles—the scrubbing of a floor, the dusting of a chair, the cleansing of a teacup,—but the general result of the whole is an atmosphere of moral and physical well-being,—a condition favourable to the highest growth of human character. The kind of air which circulates in a house may seem a small matter,—for we cannot see the air, and few people know anything about it. Yet if we do not provide a regular supply of pure air within our houses, we shall inevitably suffer for our neglect. A few specks of dirt may seem neither here nor there, and a closed door or window would appear to make little difference; but it may make the difference of a life destroyed by fever; and therefore the little dirt and the little bad air are really very serious matters. The whole of the household regulations are, taken by themselves, trifles—but trifles tending to an important result.

A pin is a very little thing in an article of dress, but the way in which it is put into the dress often reveals to you the character of the wearer. A shrewd fellow was once looking out for a wife, and was on a visit to a family of daughters with this object. The fair one, of whom he was partially enamoured, one day entered the room in which he was seated with her dress partially unpinned, and her hair untidy: he never went back. You may say, such a fellow was "not worth a pin;" but he was really a shrewd fellow, and afterwards made a good husband. He judged of women as of men—by little things; and he was right.

A druggist advertised for an assistant, and he had applications from a score of young man. He invited them all to come to his shop at the same time, and set them each to make up a pennyworth of salts into a packet. He selected the one that did this little thing in the neatest and most expert manner. He inferred their general practical ability from their performance of this smallest bit of business.

Neglect of little things has ruined many fortunes and marred the best of enterprises. The ship which bore home the merchant's treasure was lost because it was allowed to leave the port from which it sailed with a very little hole in the bottom. For want of a nail the shoe of the aide-de-camp's horse was lost; for want of the shoe, the horse was lost; for want of the horse, the aide-de-camp himself was lost, for the enemy took him and killed him; and for want of the aide-de camp's intelligence, the army of his general was lost: and all because a little nail had not been properly fixed in a horse's shoe!

"It will do!" is the common phrase of those who neglect little things. "It will do!" has blighted many a character, blasted many a fortune, sunk many a ship, burnt down many a house, and irretrievably ruined thousands of hopeful projects of human good. It always means stopping short of the right thing. It is a makeshift. It is a failure and defeat. Not what "will do," but what is the best possible thing to do,—is the point to be aimed at! Let a man once adopt the maxim of "It will do," and he is given over to the enemy,—he is on the side of incompetency and defeat,—and we give him up as a hopeless subject!

M. Say, the French political economist, has related the following illustration of the neglect of little things. Once, at a farm in the country, there was a gate enclosing the cattle and poultry, which was constantly swinging open for want of a proper latch. The expenditure of a penny or two, and a few minutes' time, would have made all right. It was on the swing every time a person went out, and not being in a state to shut readily, many of the poultry were from time to time lost. One day a fine young porker made his escape, and the whole family, with the gardener, cook, and milkmaid, turned out in quest of the fugitive. The gardener was the first to discover the pig, and in leaping a ditch to cut off his escape, got a sprain that kept him to his bed for a fortnight. The cook, on her return to the farm-house, found the linen burnt that she had hung up before the fire to dry; and the milkmaid, having forgotten in her haste to tie up the cattle in the cow-house, one of the loose cows had broken the leg of a colt that happened to be kept in the same shed. The linen burnt and the gardener's work lost were worth full five pounds, and the colt worth nearly double that money: so that here was a loss in a few minutes of a large sum, purely for want of a little latch which might have been supplied for a few halfpence. Life is full of illustrations of a similar kind. When small things are habitually neglected, ruin is not far off. It is the hand of the diligent that maketh rich; and the diligent man or woman is attentive to small things as well as great. The things may appear very little and insignificant, yet attention to them is as necessary as to matters of greater moment.

Take, for instance, the humblest of coins—a penny. What is the use of that little piece of copper—a solitary penny? What can it buy? Of what use is it? It is half the price of a glass of beer. It is the price of a box of matches. It is only fit for giving to a beggar. And yet how much of human happiness depends upon the spending of the penny well.

A man may work hard, and earn high wages; but if he allows the pennies, which are the result of hard work, to slip out of his fingers—some going to the beershop, some this way, and some that,—he will find that his life of hard work is little raised above a life of animal drudgery. On the other hand, if he take care of the pennies—putting some weekly into a benefit society or an insurance fund, others into a savings bank, and confides the rest to his wife to be carefully laid out, with a view to the comfortable maintenance and culture of his family,—he will soon find that his attention to small matters will abundantly repay him, in increasing means, in comfort at home, and in a mind comparatively free from fears as to the future.

All savings are made up of little things. "Many a little makes a mickle." Many a penny makes a pound. A penny saved is the seed of pounds saved. And pounds saved mean comfort, plenty, wealth, and independence. But the penny must be earned honestly. It is said that a penny earned honestly is better than a shilling given. A Scotch proverb says, "The gear that is gifted is never sae sweet as the gear that is won." What though the penny be black? "The smith and his penny are both black." But the penny earned by the smith is an honest one.

If a man does not know how to save his pennies or his pounds, his nose will always be kept to the grindstone. Want may come upon him any day, "like an armed man." Careful saving acts like magic: once begun, it grows into habit. It gives a man a feeling of satisfaction, of strength, of security. The pennies he has put aside in his savings box, or in the savings bank, give him an assurance of comfort in sickness, or of rest in old age. The man who saves has something to weather-fend him against want; while the man who saves not has nothing between him and bitter, biting poverty.

A man may be disposed to save money, and lay it by for sickness or for other purposes; but he cannot do this unless his wife lets him, or helps him. A prudent, frugal, thrifty woman is a crown of glory to her husband. She helps him in all his good resolutions; she may, by quiet and gentle encouragement, bring out his better qualities; and by her example she may implant in him noble principles, which are the seeds of the highest practical virtues.

The Rev. Mr. Owen, formerly of Bilston,—a good friend and adviser of working people,—used to tell a story of a man who was not an economist, but was enabled to become so by the example of his wife. The man was a calico-printer at Manchester, and he was persuaded by his wife, on their wedding-day, to allow her two half-pints of ale a day, as her share. He rather winced at the bargain, for, though a drinker himself, he would have preferred a perfectly sober wife. They both worked hard; and he, poor man, was seldom out of the public-house as soon as the factory was closed.

She had her daily pint, and he, perhaps, had his two or three quarts, and neither interfered with the other? except that, at odd times, she succeeded, by dint of one little gentle artifice or another, to win him home an hour or two earlier at night; and now and then to spend an entire evening in his own house. They had been married a year, and on the morning of their wedding anniversary, the husband looked askance at her neat and comely person, with some shade of remorse, as he said, "Mary, we've had no holiday since we were wed; and, only that I have not a penny in the world, we'd take a jaunt down to the village, to see thee mother."

"Would'st like to go, John? "said she, softly, between a smile and a tear, so glad to hear him speak so kindly,—so like old times. "If thee'd like to go, John, I'll stand treat."

"Thou stand treat!" said he, with half a sneer: "Has't got a fortun,' wench?"

"Nay," said she, "but I've gotten the pint o' ale."

"Gotten what?" said he.

"The pint o' ale!" said she.

John still didn't understand her, till the faithful creature reached down an old stocking from under a loose brick up the chimney, and counted out her daily pint of ale in the shape of three hundred and sixty-five threepences, i.e., £4 11s. 3d., and put them into his hand, exclaiming, "Thou shalt have thee holiday, John!"

John was ashamed, astonished, conscience-stricken, charmed, and wouldn't touch it. "Hasn't thee had thy share? Then I'll ha' no more! "he said. He kept his word. They kept their wedding-day with mother,—and the wife's little capital was the nucleus of a series of frugal investments, that ultimately swelled out into a shop, a factory, warehouses, a country seat, carriage, and, perhaps, a Liverpool Mayor.

In the same way, a workman of even the humblest sort, whose prosperity and regularity of conduct show to his fellow-workmen what industry, temperance, manly tenderness, and superiority to low and sensual temptation can effect, in endearing a home which is bright even amidst the gloom of poverty—such a man does good as well as the most eloquent writer that ever wrote. If there were a few patriarchs of the people such as this, their beneficial influence would soon be sensibly felt by society at large. A life well spent is worth any number of speeches. For example is a language far more eloquent than words: it is instruction in action—wisdom at work.

A man's daily life is the best test of his moral and social state. Take two men, for instance, both working at the same trade and earning the same money; yet how different they may be as respects their actual condition. The one looks a free man; the other a slave. The one lives in a snug cottage; the other in a mud hovel. The one has always a decent coat to his back; the other is in rags. The children of the one are clean, well dressed, and at school; the children of the other are dirty, filthy, and often in the gutter. The one possesses the ordinary comforts of life, as well as many of its pleasures and conveniences—perhaps a well-chosen library; the other has few of the comforts of life, certainly no pleasures, enjoyments, nor books. And yet these two men earn the same wages. What is the cause of the difference between them?

It is in this. The one man is intelligent and prudent; the other is the reverse. The one denies himself for the benefit of his wife, his family, and his home; the other denies himself nothing, but lives under the tyranny of evil habits. The one is a sober man, and takes pleasure in making his home attractive and his family comfortable; the other cares nothing for his home and family, but spends the greater part of his earnings in the gin-shop or the public-house. The one man looks up; the other looks down. The standard of enjoyment of the one is high; and of the other low. The one man likes books, which instruct and elevate his mind; the other likes drink, which tends to lower and brutalize him. The one saves his money; the other wastes it.

Little Things

"I say, mate," said one workman to another, as they went home one evening from their work, "will you tell me how it is that you contrive to get on? how it is that you manage to feed and clothe your family as you do, and put money in the Penny Bank besides; whilst I, who have as good wages as you, and fewer children, can barely make the ends meet?"

"Well, I will tell you; it only consists in this—in taking care of the pennies!"

"What! Is that all, Ransom?"

"Yes, and a good 'all' too. Not one in fifty knows the secret. For instance, Jack, you don't."

"How! I? Let's see how you make that out."

"Now you have asked my secret, I'll tell you all about it. But you must not be offended if I speak plain. First, I pay nothing for my drink."

"Nothing? Then you don't pay your shot, but sponge upon your neighbours."

"Never! I drink water, which costs nothing. Drunken days have all their tomorrows, as the old proverb says. I spare myself sore heads and shaky hands, and save my pennies. Drinking water neither makes a man sick nor in debt, nor his wife a widow. And that, let me tell you, makes a considerable difference in our out-go. It may amount to about half-a-crown a week, or seven pounds a year. That seven pounds will clothe myself and children, while you are out at elbows and your children go barefoot."

"Come, come, that's going too far. I don't drink at that rate. I may take an odd half-pint now and then; but half-a-crown a week! Pooh! pooh!"

"Well, then, how much did you spend on drink last Saturday night? Out with it."

"Let me see: I had a pint with Jones; I think I had another with Davis, who is just going to Australia; and then I went to the lodge."

"Well, how many glasses had you there?"

"How can I tell? I forget. But it's all stuff and nonsense, Bill!"

"Oh, you can't tell: you don't know what you spent? I believe you. But that's the way your pennies go, my lad."

"And that's all your secret?"

"Yes; take care of the penny—that's all. Because I save, I have, when you want. It's very simple, isn't it?"

"Simple, oh yes; but there's nothing in it."

"Yes! there's this in it,—that it has made you ask me the question, how I manage to keep my family so comfortably, and put money in the Penny

Bank, while you, with the same wages, can barely make the ends meet. Money is independence, and money is made by putting pennies together. Besides, I work so hard for mine,—and so do you,—that I can't find it in my heart to waste a penny on drink, when I can put it beside a few other hard-earned pennies in the bank. It's something for a sore foot or a rainy day. There's that in it, Jack; and there's comfort also in the thought that, whatever may happen to me, I needn't beg nor go to the workhouse. The saving of the penny makes me feel a free man. The man always in debt, or without a penny beforehand, is little better than a slave."

"But if we had our rights, the poor would not be so hardly dealt with as they now are."

"Why, Jack, if you had your rights tomorrow, would they put your money back into your pocket after you had spent it?—would your rights give your children shoes and stockings when you had chosen to waste on beer what would have bought them? Would your rights make you or your wife, thriftier, or your hearthstone cleaner? Would rights wash your children's faces, and mend the holes in your clothes? No, no, friend! Give us our rights by all means, but rights are not habits, and it's habits we want—good habits. With these we can be free men and independent men now, if we but determine to be so. Good night, Jack, and mind my secret,—it's nothing but taking care of the pennies, and the pounds will take care of themselves."

"Good-night!" And Jack turned off at the lane-end towards his humble and dirty cottage in Main's Court. I might introduce you to his home,—but "home" it could scarcely be called. It was full of squalor and untidiness, confusion and dirty children, where a slattern-looking woman was scolding. Ransom's cottage, on the contrary, was a home. It was snug, trig, and neat; the hearthstone was fresh sanded; the wife, though her hands were full of work, was clean and tidy; and her husband, his day's work over, could sit down with his children about him, in peace and comfort.

The chief secret was now revealed. Ransom's secret, about the penny, was a very good one, so far as it went. But he had not really told the whole truth. He could not venture to tell his less fortunate comrade that the root of all domestic prosperity, the mainstay of all domestic comfort, is the wife; and Ransom's wife was all that a working man could desire. There can be no thrift, nor economy, nor comfort at home, unless the wife helps;—and a working man's wife, more than any other man's; for she is wife, housekeeper, nurse, and servant, all in one. If she be thriftless, putting money into her hands is like pouring water through a sieve. Let her be frugal, and she will make her home a place of comfort, and she will also make her husband's life happy,—if she do not lay the foundation of his prosperity and fortune.

One would scarcely expect that for a penny a day it would be possible to obtain anything valuable. And yet it may be easily shown how much a penny a day, carefully expended, might do towards securing a man's independence, and providing his wife and family against the future pressure of poverty and want.

Take up a prospectus and tables of a Provident Society, intended for the use of those classes who have a penny a day to spend,—that is, nearly all the working classes of the country. It is not necessary to specify any particular society, because the best all proceed upon the same data,—the results of extensive observations and experience of health and sickness;— and their tables of rates, certified by public actuaries, are very nearly the same. Now, looking at the tables of these Life and Sickness Assurance Societies, let us see what a penny a day can do.

1. For a penny a day, a man or woman of twenty-six years of age may secure the sum of ten shillings a week payable during the time of sickness, for the whole of life.

2. For a penny a day (payments ceasing at sixty years of age), a man or woman of thirty-one years of age may secure the sum of £50 payable at death, whenever that event may happen, even though it should be during the week or the month after the assurance has been effected.

3. For a penny a day, a young man or woman of fifteen may secure a sum of £100, the payment of the penny a day continuing during the whole of life, but the £100 being payable whenever death may occur.

4. For a penny a day, a young man or woman of twenty may secure an annuity of £26 per annum, or of 10s. per week for the whole of life, after reaching the age of sixty-five.

5. For a penny a day,—the payment commencing from the birth of any child,—a parent may secure the sum of £20, payable on such child reaching the age of fourteen years.

6. For a penny a day, continued until the child readies the age of twenty-one years, the sum of £45 may be secured, to enable him or her to begin business, or start housekeeping.

7. For a penny a day, a young man or woman of twenty-four may secure the sum of £100, payable on reaching the age of sixty, with the right of withdrawing four-fifths of the amount paid in, at any time; the

whole of the payments being paid back in event of death occurring before the age of sixty.

Such is the power of a penny a day! Who would have thought it? Yet it is true, as any one can prove by looking at the tables of the best assurance offices. Put the penny a day in the bank, and it accumulates slowly. Even there, however, it is very useful. But with the assurance office it immediately assumes a vast power. A penny a day paid in by the man of thirty-one, is worth £60 to his wife and family, in the event of his dying next month or next year! It is the combining of small savings for purposes of mutual assurance, by a large number of persons, that gives to the penny its enormous power.

The effecting of a life assurance by a working man, for the benefit of his wife and children, is an eminently unselfish act. It is a moral as well as a religious transaction. It is "providing for those of his own household." It is taking the right step towards securing the independence of his family, after he, the bread-winner, has been called away. This right investment of the pennies is the best proof of practical virtue, and of the honest forethought and integrity of a true man.

The late Joseph Baxendale was the constant friend of the working people who co-operated with him in the labours of his life. He was a man of strong common sense, and might have been styled the Franklin of Business. He was full of proverbial wisdom, and also full of practical help. He was constantly urging his servants to lay by something for a rainy day, or for their support in old age. He also used to pension off his old servants after they had ceased to be able to work.

He posted up Texts along his warehouses, so that those who ran might read. "Never despair," "Nothing without labour," "He who spends all he gets, is on the way to beggary," "Time lost cannot be regained," "Let industry, temperance, and economy be the habits of your lives." These texts were printed in large type, so that every passer-by might read them; while many were able to lay them to heart, and to practise the advices which they enjoined.

On other occasions Mr. Baxendale would distribute amongst his workpeople, or desire to be set up in his warehouses and places of business, longer and more general maxims. He would desire these printed documents to be put up in the offices of the clerks, or in places where men are disposed to linger, or to take their meals, or to assemble preparatory to work. They were always full of valuable advice. We copy one of them, on the Importance of Punctuality:—

"Method is the hinge of business; and there is no method without Punctuality. Punctuality is important, because it subserves the Peace and Good Temper of a family. The want of it not only infringes on necessary Duty, but sometimes excludes this duty. The calmness of mind which it produces is another advantage of Punctuality. A disorderly man is always in a hurry. He has no time to speak to you, because he is going elsewhere; and when he gets there, he is too late for his business, or he must hurry away to another before he can finish it. Punctuality gives weight to character. 'Such a man has made an appointment; then I know he will keep it.' And this generates Punctuality in you; for, like other virtues, it propagates itself. Servants and children must be punctual, when their Leader is so. Appointments, indeed, become debts. I owe you Punctuality, if I have made an appointment with you, and have no right to throw away your time, if I do my own."

Some may inquire, "Who was Joseph Baxendale?" He was, in fact, Pickford and Co., the name of a firm known all over England, as well as throughout the Continent. Mr. Baxendale was the son of a physician at Lancaster. He received a good education, went into the cotton trade, and came up to London to represent the firm with which he was connected. A period of commercial pressure having occurred, he desired to leave the cotton trade and to enter upon some other business. Mr. Pickford had already begun the business of a Carrier, but he was hampered by want of money. Mr. Baxendale helped him with capital, and for a time remained a sleeping partner; but finding that the business made no progress, principally for want of management, he eventually determined to take the active part in working and managing the concern.

He threw his whole energies into the firm of Pickford and Co. He reorganized the agencies, and extended them throughout the kingdom. He put flying vans upon the road, equal to our express trains; and slow vans, equal to our goods trains. He utilized the canals to a large extent, putting on flying boats between all the larger towns. Indeed the roads of the country were then so bad, that in certain seasons it was almost impossible to convey merchandize from one part of the country to another.

The carrying on of such an important and extensive business required much capital, great energy, and first-rate business management. The horses necessary to carry on the traffic were increased from about fifty, which they were in the time of Pickford, to more than a thousand; for relays of horses were necessary at all the stopping-places on the line of traffic, between London and Manchester, between London and Exeter, and between London and Edinburgh. A ship-building yard was established, where all the boats, flying and slow, required to carry on the business, were constructed at Mr. Baxendale's expense.

The carrying business required a great deal of personal supervision. Only a man of determined spirit and indomitable energy could have done it. He had a flying boat in which he rapidly passed along the canals, seeing that the men were at their posts, that the agents were at work, and the traffic duly provided for. He did this by night as well as by day. At other times, he would fly along the roads in his special travelling carriage,—always paying the highest prices to the innkeepers, in order that he might secure the best horses, and avoid delay and loss of time. He would overtake his vans, and see that his men were sober, and that they were well forward at the stations along the road; that their blunderbusses were loaded (for highway robbery was then one of the risks of travelling by road), that the agents were doing their duty, and that everything was in proper order.

Besides overtaking the vans, he would sometimes travel by a by-road—for he knew nearly every road in the country—push on, and then double back upon his drivers, who never knew whether he was before or behind them; and thus general vigilance became the rule of all. By these and various other means the business of the concern was admirably done, and the carrying trade of the country was brought to as high a state of perfection as was compatible with the then state of the roads and canals.

When all this had been accomplished, the disturbing influence of railways began. "I see mischief in these confounded iron roads," said the Duke of Bridgewater. But the time for railways had arrived, and they could not be postponed. The first railroads were used for the conveyance of coals from the pits to the seaside, where they were shipped for London. Then it was proposed that they should be laid for the conveyance of goods from town to town; and the largest traffic being in Lancashire, one of the first railways was constructed between Liverpool and Manchester, from which towns they were afterwards constructed in all directions throughout the country.

Had Mr. Baxendale resisted the new means of conveyance, he would, before long, have been driven off the road. But he clearly foresaw the ultimate triumph of the railway system; and he went with it, instead of against it. He relieved the Liverpool and Manchester Company of a great deal of trouble, by undertaking to manage their goods' traffic and by collecting and delivering it at both towns. Then, when the railways from Warrington to Birmingham and from Birmingham to London were projected, he gave evidence before the committees of Parliament, in proof of the estimated traffic. And when the lines were made, he transferred the goods from his carrying vans to the railway. He thus became a great railway carrier, collecting and delivering goods in all the cities and towns served by the railways which had by that time become established.

He also became a large shareholder in railways. His status in the South-Eastern line was so great, that he was invited to become chairman of the company. He was instrumental, in conjunction with the late Sir William Cubitt, in pushing on the line to Dover. But the Dover Harbour Board being found too stingy in giving accommodation to the traffic, and too grasping in their charges for harbour dues, Mr. Baxendale at once proceeded, on his own responsibility, to purchase Folkestone Harbour as the port of the South-Eastern Company. He next proceeded to get up the Boulogne and Amiens Railway, which was for the most part constructed with English capital; and the direct line from London to Paris was thus completed.

His arduous labours in connection with his own business, as well as with railway extension, having thrown him into ill-health, he went abroad for repose. While absent, a faction was got up in Liverpool for the purpose of appointing another chairman in his stead; and though he was unseated by a trick, he himself accepted his dismissal with pleasure. His sons were now able to help him in the conduct of his business, though he continued to the close of his life to take an interest in everything that was going on. He was never weary of well-doing; he never rested in giving his good advice, the results of his large experience, to the assistants, clerks, and working men employed in his various offices. We conclude our brief notice of his life by giving another of his "Run-and-Read Sermons," which he distributed plentifully among his employés, and had affixed in various portions of his warehouses. It was entitled "Good Maxims and Advice."

"An old servant of the concern observed, a short time ago, that he began life in the employ of Pickford, upon low wages, and that by frugality and industry he had gained a competency. His maxim was, never to spend more than ninepence out of every shilling. Although this may appear a trifle, recollect that it is five shillings in twenty, ten pounds in forty.

"Suppose a young man to pursue this system: Let him obtain the first twenty pounds, add each year ten pounds, he will at the end of six years be possessed of upwards of one hundred pounds. If in early life the opportunity is suffered to pass, it rarely happens that one can save money when more advanced in years.

"The concern in which we are engaged has been defrauded by those who have for thirty years received salaries, the savings from which, had they followed the plan that is recommended, would have placed them in situations of comparative affluence; and we should now have seen them respectable members of society.

"Upon industry and frugality our well-doing depends. It is not great talents, but steady application, that is required. There are none of us that may not obtain stations of respectability. 'God helps them that help themselves.' 'He that follows pleasure instead of business will shortly have no business to follow.'

"I frequently complain of what may be called trifles, but from these arising frequently, we are at length lost. Let each attend to his respective duties; keep the appointed hours; and never defer till tomorrow what may be done today.

"If business is more pressing than usual, give additional time, that your own accounts may not fall into confusion, and that you may not be the means of causing delay and trouble to others. It often happens that the negligence of individuals throws additional labour upon those who are anxious for regularity.

"Hiding or screening the faults or errors of others, is a system that has prevailed and caused much loss and injury,—frequently to the offending party, always to the employer.

"Late occurrences lead me to draw your attention to this subject: it is important in every sense, both as regards your public and private stations. There is nothing more worthy of a man than truth: nothing makes him feel himself so despicable as a lie. Recollect that men act lies without speaking them, and that all false appearances are lies. "He, therefore, who, seeing his employer injured, neglects to make it known, is equally guilty—with this addition, that he is practising a lie. Want of punctuality is a lie.

"Speak and act openly on all occasions. Errors will be fewer, and labour will be decreased.

"It seldom happens that we can do any important services, but small services are always in use. Take, therefore, every opportunity of assisting each other,—you are then most effectually serving your employers, as well as keeping up a spirit of cordiality and goodwill amongst yourselves.

Little Things

"A good Christian must be a good servant. Whatever your lot in life may be above all things remember that 'The fear of God is the beginning of wisdom.'"

Chapter 10

Masters and Men

"The sweat of industry would dry, and die, but for the end it works to."—Shakespeare.

"Man is a shop of rules, a well-trussed pack, Whose every parcel underwrites a law."—George Herbert.

"Care preserves what Industry gains. He who attends to his business diligently but not carefully, throws away with one hand what he gathers with the other."—Colton.

"The acquisition of property, the accumulation of capital, is already in the power of the better-paid working class; and legislation has but few further facilities to give, or obstacles to remove. Their savings are now so large that only soberer habits and rounder sense are needed to make them independent capitalists in less than half a lifetime."—W.R. Greg.

Employers can do a great deal towards promoting habits of thrift, prudence, and sobriety amongst their workpeople. Though the working man does not like to be patronized, he has no objections to be helped. We have already seen that individuals can do much; they can cultivate habits of economy, and lay by a certain portion of their earnings for help in time of need. But they want encouragement and assistance. They want sympathy; they want help.

If masters fully understood the immense amount of influence which they possess, they would extend their sympathy and confidence to their workmen,—which Would cost them so very little, and profit them so very much. We know of no instance where an employer has displayed a concern for the social well-being and improvement of his workmen, in which he has not been repaid by their increased respect and zeal on his behalf. He may, for instance, arrange that wages shall not be paid so as to drive them into the market late on Saturday nights, when they are often under the necessity of making their weekly purchases at a great disadvantage. Of course, workmen who possess a little store of savings, might make their purchases at greater advantage at any other time. The employer might also avoid paying wages in public-houses, and thus keep his workmen out of the way of incurring an expenditure upon drink, that might prove so hurtful.

But masters can do more than this. They can actively aid their workmen in the formation of prudent habits, by establishing savings banks for men and women, and penny banks for boys and girls; by encouraging the formation of provident clubs and building societies, of provision and clothing clubs, and in many other ways. They might also distribute among them, without any officious interference, good counsel as to the manner in which they might make the best use of their wages. Many large employers have already accomplished much practical good, by encouraging the formation of provident institutions,—in which they have never failed to secure the respect, and generally the co-operation, of their workmen.

At the same time there is much want of sympathy between masters and men. In fact, want of sympathy pervades all classes—the poorer, the working, the middle, and the upper classes. There are many social gaps between them, which cannot yet be crossed, which cannot yet be united. "If I were to be asked," said Judge Talfourd, on whom Death was at the moment laying his hand, "what is the great want of English society—to mingle class with class—I would say, in one word, the want is the want of sympathy." A great truth, but not yet appreciated. It is the old truth, on which Christianity is based, of "Love one another"—simple saying, but containing within it a gospel sufficient to renovate the world. But where men are so split and divided into classes, and are so far removed that they can scarcely be said to know one another, they cannot have a due social regard and consideration, much less a genuine sympathy and affection, for each other?

Charity cannot remedy the evil. Giving money, blankets, coals, and such-like, to the poor—where the spirit of sympathy is wanting,—does not amount to much. The charity of most of the Lord and Lady Bountifuls begins with money, and ends there. The fellow-feeling is absent. The poor are not dealt with as if they belonged to the same common family of man, or as if the same human heart beat in their breasts.

Masters and servants live in the same unsympathetic state. "Each for himself" is their motto. "I don't care who sinks, so that I swim." A man at an inn was roused from his slumber; "There is a fire at the bottom of the street," said the waiter. "Don't disturb me" said the traveller, "until the next house is burning." An employer said to his hands, "You try to get all you can out of me; and I try to get all I can out of you." But this will never do. The man who has any sympathy in him cannot allow such considerations to overrule his better nature. He must see the brighter side of humanity ever turned towards him. "Always to think the worst," said Lord Bolingbroke, "I have ever found the mark of a mean spirit and a base soul."

On the other hand, the operative class consider their interests to be quite distinct from those of the master class. They want to get as much for their labour as possible. They want labour to be dear that they may secure high wages. Thus, there being no mutual sympathy nor friendly feeling between the two classes,—but only money considerations,—collisions are frequent, and strikes occur. Both classes—backed by their fellows determined to "fight it out," and hence we have such destructive strikes as those of Preston, Newcastle, London, and South Wales.

The great end of both is gain, worldly gain, which sometimes involves a terrible final loss. A general suspicion of each other spreads, and society becomes cankered to the core. The remedy is only to be found in the cherishment of a larger Christian sympathy and more genuine benevolence. Thus only can the breath of society be sweetened and purified. Money gifts avail nothing, as between rich and poor. Unless there is a soul of goodness, and a real human fellowship between them, the mischief and the curse which the excellent Judge Talfourd lamented with his dying breath will never be overcome.

Some allege that this want of sympathy arises, for the most part, from the evils of Competition. It is "heartless," "selfish," "mischievous," "ruinous," and so on. It is said to produce misery and poverty to the million. It is charged with lowering prices, or almost in the same breath with raising them. Competition has a broad back, and can bear any amount of burdens.

And yet there is something to be said for competition, as well as against it. It is a struggle,—that must be admitted. All life is a struggle. Amongst workmen, competition is a struggle to advance towards higher wages. Amongst masters, to make the highest profits. Amongst writers, preachers, and politicians, it is a struggle to succeed,—to gain glory, reputation, or income. Like everything human, it has a mixture of evil in it. If one man prospers more than others, or if some classes of men prosper more than others, they leave other classes of men behind them. Not that they leave those others worse, but that they themselves advance.

Put a stop to competition, and you merely check the progress of individuals and of classes. You preserve a dead uniform level. You stereotype society, and its several orders and conditions. The motive for emulation is taken away, and Caste, with all its mischiefs, is perpetuated. Stop competition, and you stop the struggle of individualism. You also stop the advancement of individualism, and through that of society at large.

Under competition, the lazy man is put under the necessity of exerting himself; and if he will not exert himself, he must fall behind. If he do not work, neither shall he eat. My lazy friend, you must not look to me to do my share of the world's work, and yours too! You must do your own fair share of work, save your own money, and not look to me and to others to keep you out of the poor-house. There is enough for all; but do your own share of work you must.

Success grows out of struggles to overcome difficulties. If there were no difficulties, there would be no success. If there were nothing to struggle or compete for, there would be nothing achieved. It is well, therefore, that men should be under the necessity of exerting themselves. In this necessity for exertion, we find the chief source of human advancement— the advancement of individuals as of nations. It has led to most of the splendid mechanical inventions and improvements of the age. It has stimulated the shipbuilder, the merchant, the manufacturer, the machinist, the tradesman, the skilled workman. In all departments of productive industry, it has been the moving power. Is has developed the resources of this and of other countries,—the resources of the soil, and the character and qualities of the men who dwell upon it. It seems to be absolutely necessary for the purpose of stimulating the growth and culture of every individual. It is deeply rooted in man, leading him ever to seek after, and endeavour to realize, something better and higher than he has yet attained.

Of course, man is much more than a competing being. That is only one of his characteristics, and not the highest or noblest. He has sensibilities, sympathies, and aspirations, which should induce him to unite and cooperate with others in works for the common good. With unfettered individualism, there may, and there ought to be, beneficent cooperation for the general happiness. Men may unite to labour, to produce, and to share with each other the fruits of their corporate industry. But under any circumstances, there will be the instinct of competition, the opportunities for competition, and, though mixed with necessary evil, there will be the ultimate advantages of competition.

One of the results of industry and thrift is the accumulation of Capital. Capital represents the self-denial, the providence, and the enterprise of the past. The most successful accumulators of capital have in all times risen from the ranks of labour itself; they are working men who have shot ahead of their fellows, and who now give employment instead of receiving it. These persons,—who are not the less working men because they have ceased to be manual labourers,—by creating and extending the sphere of productive industry, must be regarded as amongst the most effective benefactors of the people, as they unquestionably are among the principal sources of the power and wealth of any nation. Without the capital accumulated by their thrift during many generations, the lot of the artizan would be most precarious.

There is not a mechanic but has the use of the money of the master who employs him. When the unskilled labourer lays down his spade, he leaves idle a capital worth eighteen-pence; but when a skilled artizan or mechanic leaves his mill or his workshop, he leaves idle a capital of from a hundred to two hundred pounds per man. Nor does the skilled workman run any risk whatever as regards the sums invested, though he virtually shares the profits in the shape of the wages paid for his labour. The profit which remains is the master's return for his management and his risks. It is well known, however, that the risks are not always covered, as the Gazette in bad times abundantly demonstrates.

The workman in good employment is not liable to losses by bad debts; he has no obsolete machinery from time to time left useless on his hands; and he has no anxiety about finding a market for his goods, nor fears respecting fluctuations in the price of the raw material. These are important advantages in his favour, which he does not usually take into account. It is true he suffers if trade is bad, but he earns high wages if it be good: he can then save money if he chooses to do so. He may be said to participate in the adversity or prosperity of his firm, but without incurring any of the liabilities of partnership.

Mr. Carlyle has given a curious account of the great English manufacturer. "Plugson, of St. Dolly Undershot, buccaneer-like, says to his men, 'Noble spinners, this is the hundred thousand we have gained, wherein I mean to dwell and plant my vineyards. The hundred thousand is mine, the three-and-sixpence daily was yours. Adieu, noble spinners! drink my health with this groat each, which I give you over and above!'"

This account of the manufacturing buccaneer is a picture drawn by a man of genius from his imagination. There are probably many readers who believe the picture to be drawn from fact. There may, of course, be masters who are buccaneers; but there are also masters who are not buccaneers. There are dishonest manufacturers, as there are dishonest literary men, dishonest publicans, dishonest tradesmen. But we must believe that in all occupations honesty is the rule, and dishonesty the exception. At all events, it is better that we should know what the manufacturers really are,—from fact rather than from fiction.

Let us first take a large manufacturing firm, or rather series of firms, well known in South Lancashire. We mean the cotton-spinning mills of the Messrs. Ashworth at Egerton and New Eagley. They have been in existence for more than seventy years. They have been repeatedly enlarged, and increasing numbers of workpeople have been employed at the uniform wages paid throughout the district. Workmen earn from seventeen shillings to two pounds a week. Women-weavers can earn as much as twenty-one shillings a week. Where the parents have children, the united earnings of families amount to as much as from £150 to £200 a year.

Then, as to what the Ashworths have done for the benefit of their workpeople. Schooling, by means of mutual instruction classes, was in operation from the first; but about the year 1825, when the works were greatly enlarged, and the population was considerably increased, a day school was opened for children, which was used as an evening school for young men, as well as for a Sunday-school. The continued extension of the works led to an enlargement of the school accommodation; and while this was being provided, arrangements were made for a news-room, library, and for the performance of divine worship on Sundays. A cricket-ground was also provided for the use of young people.

Misgivings were not unfrequently expressed that the zeal and expenditure incurred by the Messrs. Ashworth might one day be turned against them, to their annoyance and pecuniary loss. The prediction was realized in only a single instance. A young man of considerable talent, who when a child had been removed to the factory from a neighbouring workhouse, made very rapid progress at school, especially in arithmetic; and when a strike of the workpeople occurred in 1830, one of the great strike years, he became very officious as a leader. The strike was defeated by the employment of new hands, and it was attributed to the influence of this young man that the employed were brutally assailed by an infuriated mob, and that the windows of the schoolroom were smashed, and other works of destruction committed.

The employers, nevertheless, pursued their original design. They repaired the school-house, and endeavoured to increase the efficacy of the teaching. They believed that nothing was better calculated to remove ignorant infatuation than increased schooling. In a great many instances, the heads of the families had previously been engaged as hand-loom weavers, or in some pastoral pursuit; and it became evident that in course of time the exercise of their minds in the details of a new pursuit awakened their intelligence, and their general demeanour indicated marks of a higher cultivation.

The New Eagley Mills being situated in a narrow valley, several miles from Bolton, and the property being in the possession of the owners, they forbade the opening of any tavern or beerhouse on the estate; so that the district became distinguished for the order and sobriety of the inhabitants. A man of intemperate habits has little chance of remaining in the Ashworth villages. He is expelled, not by the employers, but by the men themselves. He must conform to the sober habits of the place, or decamp to some larger town, where his vices may be hidden in the crowd. Many of the parents have expressed how much gratification they have felt, that by reason of the isolated situation they enjoyed as a community, they had become so completely separated from the corrupt influences of music saloons and drink-shops.

The masters have added to their other obligations to the workpeople, the erection of comfortable cottages for their accommodation. They are built of stone, and are two-storied; some have two upper bedrooms, and others have three. On the ground floor there is a sitting-room, a living-room, and a scullery, with a walled courtyard enclosing the whole premises. The proprietor pays the poor-rates and other local charges, and the rentals of the houses vary from 2s. 4d. to 4s. 3d. a week.

The regularity of their employment, accompanied with the payment of wages on Friday night, doubtless promoted their local attachment to the place. Many of the descendants of the first comers remain on the spot; their social relations have been promoted; intermarriages have been frequent; and during the whole period there has not been a single prosecution for theft. The working people have also thriven as well as their masters. Great numbers of them are known to possess reserved funds in savings banks and other depositories for savings; and there are others of them who have invested their money in cottage buildings, and in various other ways.

But have not the men risen above their lot of labouring spinners? They have. Such of them as possessed skill, ability, and the faculty of organization, have been promoted from the ranks of labourers, and have become mill managers. "About thirty of these," says Mr. Henry Ashworth, "have been reckoned on the spur of the moment, and ten of them have become business partners or proprietors of mills.... Many manufacturers," adds Mr. Ashworth, "are to be found who have done a great deal to ameliorate the condition of those they have employed; and no one will doubt that they have been prompted, not by hopes of gain, but by emotions of goodwill."[1]

Manufacturers such as these do not, like Plugson of St. Dolly Undershot, gather up their fortunes and run away, leaving a groat each to their workpeople to drink their healths. They remain with them from generation to generation. The best and the noblest amongst them—the Ashworths of Turton, the Strutts of Derby, the Marshalls of Leeds, the Akroyds of Halifax, the Brooks of Huddersfield, and many others,—have continued to superintend their works for several generations. The Strutts were the partners of Arkwright, who was almost the beginner of English manufacture. In fact, it is only since Arkwright took out his patent for the spinning machine, and Watt took out his patent for the steam engine, that England has become a manufacturing country.

Where would England have been now, but for the energy, enterprise, and public spirit of our manufacturers? Could agriculture have supported the continuous increase of population? Is it not more probable that this country would have become overrun by beggars,—or that property would have been assailed and the constitution upset, as was the case in France,—but for the extensive and remunerative employment afforded to the labouring classes in the manufacturing districts? The steam engine has indeed proved the safety-valve of England. It enabled the kingdom to hold its ground firmly during the continental wars; and but for it, and the industries which it has established, England would probably by this time have sunk to the condition of a third or fourth-rate power.

It is true, the great manufacturers have become wealthy. But it would certainly have been singular if, with their industry, energy, and powers

---

1. The greater part of the above information is contained in the statement by Mr. Henry Ashworth, in the Reports on the Paris Universal Exhibition, 1867, vol. vi., pp. 161–163.

of organization, they had become poor! Men of the stamp of the Strutts, Ashworths, Marshalls, and others, do not work for wealth merely, though wealth comes to them. They have not become great because they were rich, but they have become rich because they were great. Accumulations of wealth are the result of exceptional industry, organization, and thrift, rather than of exceptional gain. Adam Smith has said: "It seldom happens that great fortunes are made by any one regularly-established and well-known branch of business, but in consequence of a long life of industry, frugality, and attention."

But it is not always so. For instance, Mr. Lister, of Bradford, after inventing the combing machine,—or at least combining the inventions of others into a complete combing machine of his own,—proceeded to invent a machine for using up silk waste (then cast away as useless), spinning it into silk of the finest kind, and by means of the power-loom to weave it into velvet of the best quality. The attempt had never before been made by any inventor; and it seemed to be of insuperable difficulty. Mr. Lister had already made a fortune by the success of his combing machine, such as to enable him to retire from business, and live in comfort for the rest of his life. But, urged by the irrepressible spirit of the inventor, he went onward with his silk machine. As he himself said, at a recent meeting at Bradford,[2]—"They might judge how hard he had worked to conquer the difficulties which beset him, when he told them that for twenty years he had never been in bed at half-past five in the morning; in fact, he did not think there was a man in England who had worked harder than he had." The most remarkable thing was, that he threw away an immense fortune before there was any probability of his succeeding. "He had almost brought himself to ruin, for he was £360,000 out of pocket before he even made a shilling by his machine; indeed, he wrote off a quarter of a million as entirely lost, before he began to make up his books again. Since then, his patent for the manufacture of silk had turned out one of the most successful of the day."

In the Park presented by Mr. Lister to the people of Bradford, a statue was recently erected by public subscription. It was unveiled by the Right Hon. W.E. Forster, who, in closing his speech, observed: "I doubt, after all, whether we are come here to do honour to Mr. Lister, so much as to do honour to ourselves. We wish to do honour to those working faculties

---

2. The meeting was held to receive the transfer of Mr. Lister's fine Park at Manningham, which he had presented to the Corporation of Bradford, "to be a People's Park for ever."

which have made our country of England a practical, and therefore a great and prosperous, and a powerful country. It is this untiring, unresting industry which Mr. Lister possesses, this practical understanding, this determination to carry out any object which he is convinced ought to be carried out, and his determination to fear no opposition and to care for no obstacle—it is these practical faculties that have made England what she is. What is it especially that we are honouring? It is the pluck which this man has shown; it is the feeling that, having to do with the worsted trade, he said to himself, 'Here is something which ought to be done; I will not rest until I have found out how it can be done; and having found out how it can be done, where is the man who shall stop my doing it?' Now it was upon that principle that he fought his long struggle; and so when we read the story of his struggles, ever since 1842, in those two great inventions, we raise this statue to the man who has successfully fought the battle, and hope that our sons and the sons of all, rich and poor together, will come in after-days to admire it, not merely because it gives them the form and features of a rich and successful man, but because it gives them the form and features of a man who was endowed with industry, with intellect, with energy, with courage, with perseverance,—who spared himself no pains in first ascertaining the conditions of the problems he had to solve,—and then whose heart never fainted, whose will never relaxed, in determining to carry out those conditions."

Great men are wise savers and wise spenders. Montesquieu has said of Alexander: "He found the first means of his prosperity and power in the greatness of his genius; the second, in his frugality and private economy; and the third, in his immense liberality to accomplish great objects. He spent but little on himself; but for public purposes his hand was always open." It was also said of the first Napoleon, that he was economical like Charlemagne, because he was great like Charlemagne. Napoleon was by no means a spendthrift, except in war; but he spent largely in accomplishing great public undertakings. In cases such as these, economy and generosity are well combined. And so it is in the cases of all men possessed of energy, industry, and great powers of organization.

It may seem out of keeping to compare great producers with great commanders. Yet the manufacturer often requires as much courage, as much genius, as much organizing power, as the warrior. The one considers how he shall keep his operatives in working order; the other how he shall keep his soldiers in fighting order. Both must be men of enterprize, of boldness, of keen observation, and close attention to details. And the manufacturer, from his position, needs to be the most benevolent man of the two. Viewed in this light, we regard Sir Titus Salt not only as a Captain of Industry, but as a Field-Marshal of Industry. He has been called the Prince of Manufacturers.

Titus Salt is a son of a Yorkshire wool-stapler. In the early part of his life he was a farmer near Bradford, and his inclination for agricultural pursuits was such, that it was thought he would continue to pursue this vocation. Being, however, a partner with his father in the wool business, and observing that manufactures were rapidly extending in the neighbourhood, he withdrew from the partnership, and commenced business at Bradford as a wool-spinner. He was one of the first to observe the uses of Alpaca wool. Large quantities of that material were stored at Liverpool,—imported from the Brazils. But the wool found no purchasers, until at length Mr. Salt bought a quantity, and spun it into an entirely new fabric. He then proceeded to buy up all the Alpaca that was to be found at Liverpool; made arrangements for purchasing all that came into the market; went on spinning Alpaca; and eventually established the manufacture. This was the foundation of Mr. Salt's fortune.

At length, after about twenty years' labour as a manufacturer, Mr. Salt thought of retiring from business, and again betaking himself to his favourite agricultural pursuits. He intended to retire on his fiftieth birthday, but before that time had arrived (having five sons to provide for) he reversed his decision, and resolved to continue in business a little longer, and to remain at the head of the firm. Having come to this determination, he made up his mind to leave Bradford. The borough was already overcrowded, and he did not like to be a party to increasing the population. He looked about for a site suitable for a manufacturing establishment, and at length fixed upon a large piece of ground in the beautiful valley of the Aire. An extension of the Leeds and Bradford Railway was in front, and the Leeds and Liverpool Canal behind it, so that there was every convenience for bringing up the raw materials, and of sending away the manufactured goods. On that spot Saltaire was erected—a noble monument of private enterprise, liberality, and wisdom.

It is not necessary to describe Saltaire. The buildings connected with the new works cover six and a half acres. The principal room is five hundred and fifty feet long. The weaving shed covers two acres. The combing shed occupies one acre. Everything is large, roomy, and substantial. The cost of constructing the factory, and the dwellings for the workpeople, amounted to more than a hundred and forty thousand pounds.

On the opening day, Mr. Salt dined three thousand five hundred persons in the combing shed. At the dinner, he said: "I cannot look around me, and see this vast assemblage of friends and workpeople, without being moved. I feel greatly honoured by the presence of the nobleman at my side. I am especially delighted at the presence of my workpeople. . . . I hope to draw around me a population that will enjoy the beauties of this neighbourhood,—a population of well-paid, contented, happy operatives. I have given instructions to my architects that nothing is to be spared to render the dwellings of the operatives a pattern to the country; and if my life is spared by Divine Providence, I hope to see satisfaction, contentment, and happiness around me."

This promise has been amply fulfilled. Mr. Salt has been influenced throughout by his sense of duty and responsibility. When he was applied to by the French Government for information as to his factory, he replied: "What has been attempted at Saltaire arose from my own private feeling and judgment, without the most remote idea that it would be made the subject of public interest and inquiry." With respect to the factory itself, little need be said. The object of its construction is to save time in the process of production. Not a minute is lost in pushing the material from one department to another. Every horse-power of steam is made to do its utmost, every moment of time is economized, and the productive capabilities of the factory are thus greatly increased.

We prefer to speak of the immense improvement which Mr. Salt, or rather Sir Titus Salt, has effected in the physical and moral condition of his workpeople. The plan of the works shows that Saltaire has been provided with a church, a Wesleyan chapel, and a Literary and Philosophical Institution. Large schools have been provided for boys, girls, and infants, with abundance of play-ground. For young men as well as old, there is a cricket-ground, bowling-green, and croquet-lawn, surrounded by pleasure-grounds. There is also a large dining-hall, baths and washhouses, a dispensary, and almshouses for pensioners.

About three thousand persons are employed in the works; and seven hundred and fifty-six houses have been erected for their accommodation. The rents run from two and fourpence to seven and sixpence a week, according to the accommodation. Some of the houses are used as boarding-houses. The rents include rates and water supply, and gas is sold at a low price. The cottages are built of stone, lined with brickwork. They contain a parlour or long room, a kitchen or scullery, a pantry and cellar, and three bedrooms. Each house has a separate yard, with the usual offices. The workpeople are well able to pay the rents. Single workmen earn from twenty-four to thirty-five shillings a week. A family, consisting of a father and six children, earn four pounds four shillings a week, or equal to a united income of over two hundred and twenty pounds a year.

The comfortable houses provided for the workpeople have awakened in them that home feeling which has led them to decorate their dwellings neatly and tastefully,—a sure sign of social happiness. Every visitor among the poor knows how such things combine to prevent vice and disease, to elevate the moral tone of working people, and to develop their intellectual powers. A man in a dirty house, says Mr. Rhind, the medical attendant at Saltaire, is like a beggar in miserable clothing. He soon ceases to have self-respect, and when that is gone there is but little hope.

Great attention is paid in Saltaire to education, even of the higher sort. There are day schools, night schools, mutual improvement classes, lectures, and discussions. Music—one of the most humanizing of pleasures—is one of the most favourite studies. "In almost every house in the town some form of musical instrument is found; and indeed, the choral and glee societies, together with the bands, have become household names." There is one full brass band for men, and another drum-and-fife band for boys; and concerts, vocal and instrumental, are regularly given by the workpeople in the dining-hall. The bands have instructors provided by the firm.

Besides taking part in the musical performances, a large number of the skilled workmen devote their leisure hours to various scientific amusements,—such as natural history, taxidermy, the making of philosophical instruments, such as air-pumps, models of working machinery, steam-engines, and articles of domestic comfort,—while some have even manufactured organs and other musical instruments.

There is no drinking-house in Saltaire, so that the vices and diseases associated with drunkenness are excluded from the locality. The diseases peculiar to poverty are also unknown in Saltaire. Everything is attended to—drainage, cleansing, and ventilation. There are baths of all kinds—plunge baths, warm baths, Turkish baths, and douche baths; and the wash-house, to enable the women to wash their clothes away from their cottages, is a great accommodation,—inasmuch as indoor washing is most pernicious, and a fruitful source of disease, especially to the young.

The workpeople are also thrifty. They invest their savings in the Penny Bank and Saving's Bank; whilst others invest in various building societies, gas companies, and other lucrative undertakings. In fact, they seem to be among the most favoured of human beings. With every convenience and necessity, as well as every proper pleasure provided for them,—with comfortable homes, and every inducement to stay at home,—with fishing clubs, boating clubs, and cricket clubs,—with schoolrooms, literary institutions, lecture-hall, museum, and class-rooms, established in their midst; and to crown all, with a beautiful temple for the worship of God,—there is no wonder that Saltaire has obtained a name, and that Sir Titus Salt has established a reputation among his fellow-men.

There are large numbers of employers who treat their workpeople quite as generously, though not in such a princely manner, as Sir Titus Salt. They pay the uniform rate of wages; help and encourage the employed to economize their surplus earnings; establish Savings Banks and Penny Banks for their use; assist them in the formation of co-operative associations for the purchase of pure food at a cheaper rate; build healthy cottages for their accommodation; erect schools for the education of their children; and assist them in every method that is calculated to promote their moral and, social improvement.

Mr. Edward Akroyd, formerly M.P. for Halifax, is another manufacturer who has exercised great influence throughout Yorkshire, by his encouragement of habits of thrift amongst working people. In his own district, at Copley and Haley Hill, near Halifax, he has built numerous excellent cottages for his workmen, and encouraged them to build their own houses by investing their spare earnings in building clubs. He has established co-operative clubs, to enable the men to purchase food and clothing at cost price. He has built excellent schools at his own expense, and provided them with a paid staff of teachers. He has built and endowed the very fine church of "All Souls" (Sir Gilbert Scott, architect), to which a large district, inclusive of the works, has been assigned. He has provided for his workpeople, both at Haley Hill and Copley, a Literary and Scientific Society, a Mutual Improvement Society, a Working Men's Library (to which he has presented more than five thousand books), a Working Men's Club and Newsroom, a Choral Society, supplied with an excellent library of music; a Recreation Club, provided with a bowling green; and a cricket ground, with quoits, and gymnastic apparatus, Mr. Akroyd has also allotted a large field to his workmen, dividing it into small gardens varying from a hundred to two hundred and forty square yards each. The small rent charged for each plot is distributed in prizes given at an annual flower-show held in his grounds, for the best growers of flowers, plants, and vegetables. Hence the Haley Hill Horticultural and Floral Society, one of the most thriving institutions of the kind in the neighbourhood. In short, Mr. Akroyd has done everything that a wise and conscientious master could have done, for the purpose of promoting the moral and spiritual welfare of the four thousand persons employed in his manufactories, who have been virtually committed to his charge.

But although Mr. Akroyd has done so much as a master for the men and women employed by him, he has perhaps done still more as a public benefactor by establishing the Yorkshire Penny Bank for Savings. As early as the year 1852, Mr. Akroyd instituted a Savings Bank to enable his workpeople to deposit sums of from one penny upwards. The system was found to work so well, and to have such a beneficial effect in making people provident, that he conceived the idea of extending its operations throughout the West Riding of Yorkshire. Having obtained the co-operation of several influential gentlemen, the scheme was started in 1856, and an Act of Parliament was obtained for constituting the Yorkshire Penny Savings Bank as it now exists.

Mr. Akroyd has recently furnished an Introduction to the narrative of the Yorkshire Penny Bank, from which we extract the following passage:—

"The way by which thoughts, or chance suggestions, enter into the minds of men, is sometimes passing strange! They may be the offspring of wayward fancy; or they may be the whisperings from a higher source. To the latter cause I am willing to attribute the idea which flashed across my mind during the present year to give to the public something beyond the bare outline of the scheme, in which, for years, many of them have taken a warm personal interest.

"It occurred in this wise. When in town, I occasionally attended, during Lent, the services at Whitehall Chapel, for the sake of hearing a Lenten sermon preached by one of Her Majesty's chaplains. One remarkable sermon of the series was delivered by the Rev. Charles Kingsley, on the 12th of March, on behalf of the Supplemental Ladies' Association of the London Society of Parochial Mission Women. In the sketch which the preacher gave of this excellent institution, he referred to a book entitled 'East and West,' in which the benefits derived by the London poor from the association are clearly set forth; but he dwelt chiefly on the wide separation which divides rich from poor, class from class, in London; and on the dangers which threaten Society from this cause, as was recently exemplified in France. Such was the impression made upon me by the sermon, that, before many days had elapsed, I had purchased 'East and West,' and given the book a careful perusal.

"From previous observation I had been struck with the sad contrast between the luxurious lives of those who reside at the West End of London, and the struggle for a hard, wretched existence which the crowded poor at the East, or in close purlieus elsewhere, are obliged to maintain until death closes the scene. How to bridge over the wide chasm intervening between the extremes of high and low in society, without injury to self-respect on either side, was the puzzling question, the problem to be solved. Yet, from the admirable introduction to this most useful little work, by the Countess Spencer, it appeared that a lady of high rank, and her noble-minded associates, had in some measure solved the problem, and bridged over the chasm.

"Hence I was led to reflect how much easier it is to discharge our duty to our neighbours, and to fulfil the leading object of the Parochial Mission Women Association, to 'help the poor to help themselves,' in provincial towns and in the country, where we are personally acquainted with each other, than in London, where we do not know our next-door neighbour. To help the poor to help themselves is the cardinal principle of the Yorkshire Penny Bank."[3]

The business of the bank commenced on the 1st of May, 1859. At the end of the year, when the bank had been in operation seven months, twenty-four branches had been opened. It went on increasing in the number of branches and depositors, and in the amounts deposited. In 1874, about two hundred and fifty branches had been established, and the amount of investments in the names of trustees had reached nearly four hundred thousand pounds.

The Yorkshire Penny Bank does not interfere with the Post Office Savings Bank. It has a special function, that of teaching the young of either sex the habit of saving. It is also convenient to the adult worker as a convenient receptacle for his savings. Many have been induced to save, in consequence of the banks having been brought almost to their very doors. One of the most remarkable facts connected with the history of Penny Banks is the sympathetic influence of juvenile thrift upon paternal recklessness and intemperance. The fact is well worthy the consideration of Temperance advocates, who would probably effect much greater practical good by enabling working people to save their

---

3. e Yorkshire Penny Bank, a Narrative; with an Introduction by Edward Akroyd, M.P.

money in the Penny Banks, than by any speech-making agency. Take, for instance, the following illustrations from Mr. Akroyd's narrative:—

An actuary says: "All the juvenile depositors seem inclined to take care of their pence by depositing them in the bank; and the grown-up people have become of the same turn of mind,—rather than carry their loose money to the public-house, or spend it foolishly. Some factory operatives have saved sufficient to buy stock and commence farming."

Another actuary says: "A drunken father being shamed out of his drunkenness by the deposits of his children, now deposits half-a-crown a week in the bank. A notoriously bad man, a collier, became a regular depositor himself, as well as depositing money in the name of his child; all his spare money having previously been spent in drink. From the date of his beginning to save, a perceptible improvement took place in his conduct and character. In another case, two boys prevailed upon their father, also a collier, to allow them to deposit a shilling a week, until they had saved sufficient to buy themselves each a suit of new clothes. Before then, all their father's earnings, as well as their own, had been spent in drink."

An actuary of another branch says he has seen fathers and mothers, who have been drunkards, send their children with money to the bank, He says: "My heart was made to rejoice when I saw a boy, who never had a suit of new clothes in his life, draw out his money, and in less than two hours return well clad, to take his place in the school to practise singing for Good Friday. At the meeting of the Band of Hope on Good Friday, he asked the parents and children to signify by holding up their hands whether or not the bank had been beneficial to them; when many hands were instantly raised,—one poor mother exclaiming, 'I will put up both my hands for my two bairns!'"

"A miner, the father of a family, reclaimed from drunkenness, saved his money in the bank until, with the aid of a loan from a building society, he built two houses at a cost of four hundred pounds. The bank has been to many people what the hive is to the bee—a kind of repository; and when the wintry days of sickness or adversity befall them, they have then the bank to flee to for succour."

A missionary says: "I met a man and his wife about two years ago—both drunk. I got them to sign the pledge, and since then to invest their money in our bank. The pawnbroker had got the greater part of their goods; but I am happy to say that they have got all the articles out of pawn, and can bring a little money almost every week to the bank; and when putting in the money, the man says that it is better than taking it to the public-house. Their home is now a very comfortable one."

A drunkard one night came to the bank, and flinging down a shilling for a start, said, "There! that is the price of six pints of beer; but I promise the landlords that they shan't have as much of my money as they have had." This man has become sober; and continues a regular depositor.

In another bank, a man who had been a reckless and desperate fellow was induced by his wife to deposit a few coppers in the bank. He did so, and his weekly deposits increased; while at the same time his visits to the public-house decreased. In the course of a short time he had a respectable balance to his credit; and this induced him to take a share in a building society, and then a second share. After continuing to pay upon these shares for some time, he purchased a piece of land, upon which he built two houses. One of these he occupies himself, and the other he lets. Besides this, he is now a respectable tradesman, having two or three journeymen and an apprentice working for him. He is sober and steady, and much respected by his friends and neighbours.

Many other cases of the same kind might be mentioned. In one case a boy saved sufficient money to buy a suit of clothes for his father, who had spent all his earnings in drink, and reduced himself and his family to poverty; in other cases, sons and daughters maintain their infirm parents without resorting to the parochial Board for assistance. Some save for one thing; some for another. Some save to emigrate; some to buy clothes; some to buy a watch; but in all cases frugality is trained, until saving becomes habitual.

One of the Yorkshire actuaries of the Penny Bank tells the following anecdote as conveying a lesson of perseverance and encouragement to branch managers. "Mr. Smith was one of our first managers, but after attending two or three times he left us, saying it was 'childish work.' My answer was, 'It is with children we have to do.' A short time after, I met him, and in the course of conversation I observed that I sometimes got down in the mouth, and did not know whether we were doing any good, and felt disposed to give up the bank; on which he warmly replied, 'For God's sake, you must not let such an idea get into your head; you little know the good you are doing; we have not a man about our place but either himself or some members of his family are depositors.'" The actuary adds, "If Colonel Akroyd ever despairs, I give him the above answer."

Savings banks have thus been the means of doing an immense amount of good. They have brought peace, happiness, and comfort into many thousands of families. The example of Mr. Akroyd should be largely imitated, and there ought not to be a county in the kingdom without its organized system of Penny Banks.

Chapter 11

The Crossleys—Masters and Men (Continued)

"The sense to enjoy riches, with the art t'enjoy them, and the virtue to impart."—Pope.

"My ventures are not in one bottom trusted, nor to one place; nor is my whole estate upon the fortune o' this present year."—Shakespeare.

"The roughest road often leads to the smoothest fortune."—Franklin.

"Who can find a virtuous woman? for her price is far above rubies. The heart of her husband doth safely trust in her, so that he shall have no need of spoil. . . . She seeketh wool and flax, and worketh willingly with her hands. . . . She layeth her hands to the spindle, and her hands hold the distaff. She stretcheth out her hand to the poor; yea, she reacheth forth her hands to the needy. . . . Strength and honour are her clothing; and she shall rejoice in time to come. . . . Her children arise up, and call her blessed; her husband also, and he praiseth her."—Proverbs of Solomon.

There are several large employers who have endeavoured to combine the principle of co-operation with the business of manufacturing; and to furnish to the men who have contributed to their past prosperity the opportunity of sharing in their future profits. The object of these masters has been to obviate the antagonism between capital and labour, and to spread the spirit of contentment among the operatives. Workmen who have saved their earnings, and stored them in savings banks, are in this manner enabled to become partners in the concerns in which they have formerly employed their labour.

The two principal manufacturing concerns of Halifax, those of James Akroyd and Son, and John Crossley and Sons, have thus become converted into joint stock companies. They have been so converted with the primary design of receiving the co-operation of the managers, workmen, and others associated with them; and with that view the directors have in all cases given them the priority in the allotment of the shares.

We have already referred to the philanthropic work accomplished by Edward Akroyd in the county of York. We have now to refer to the Crossley firm, whose carpets are known throughout the world. We refer to them with the greater pleasure, as their history contains a story which may possibly add to the interest of this book,—which, however useful, some readers may consider to be rather dull to read.

The founder of this firm was John Crossley. He belonged to an old Yorkshire family. His grandfather, who lived at King's Cross, near Halifax, was born of respectable parents, and had a good education, yet he was by no means fond of business. In fact, he spent the greater part of his time in hunting and shooting. His wife was, however, of a very different character. She was industrious, energetic, and an excellent household manager. She not only maintained herself, but her husband and her family. She did this by means of a boarding school which she kept,—one of the best in the neighbourhood of Halifax.

One of her sons, the father of John Crossley, was brought up to carpet-weaving. He learnt his business with Mr. Webster, of Clay-pits, one of whose daughters he afterwards married. John Crossley himself also became a carpet-weaver with his uncle; and when his apprenticeship was finished, he went to weave for Mr. Currer, a large carpet manufacturer at Luddenden Foot. While working at this factory, his master built a large fine house to live in. He thought he had money enough saved for the purpose, but circumstances proved that he had not. Mr. Currer told his foreman that he had kept an account of its cost until he had spent £4,000, and then he became so disgusted that he burnt the memorandum book, although the house was not nearly finished. He said "he had done all that to please a woman,"—meaning his wife. Although Mr. Currer was an excellent man of business, his wife was too fond of show, and the large fine house in which she was to live proved her husband's ruin. He died shortly after it was finished, and then the whole of his establishment was broken up.

After leaving Mr. Currer, John Crossley removed to Halifax to take the management of Mr. Job Lees' carpet manufactory in Lower George Yard, Halifax. He began to look out for a wife, and the history of his courtship is curious as well as interesting. The Crossleys seem to have had the good

The Crossleys—Masters and Men (Continued)

fortune to fall in with excellent wives; and the prosperity of the family is quite as much due to the Crossley women as to the Crossley men.

Martha Crossley, the future wife of John Crossley, was born at Folly Hall, near the Ambler Thorn Bar. Her great-grandfather, Thomas Turner, was a farmer. He lived at the Upper Scout Hall, Shibden, and the farmhouse which he occupied, at the head of the Shibden Valley, is still in existence. The eldest son was brought up to his father's business. The youngest son, Abraham, was brought up to farming, weaving, and combing. He married, and had three children—Abraham, Thomas, and Martha. Abraham, the eldest, was father of Mrs. John Crossley, née Turner.

Abraham was also brought up to farming and manufacturing; but it must be remembered that manufacturing was in those days conducted on a very much smaller scale than it is now. He afterwards went into partnership with his brother Thomas, to make worsted goods, but after his marriage the partnership was dissolved. He then became the proprietor of the Scout Farm, and there brought up his family.

Although Abraham Turner was a landed proprietor, he did not think it beneath him to allow his daughter Martha to go out to service. When about fifteen years old she went as a servant to Miss Oldfield at Warley. In that service, in her own person, she did the work of kitchenmaid, housemaid, and cook, and in addition to that, she milked four or five cows night and morning. She remained about ten years with Miss Oldfield. Her wages were at first fifteen-pence a week; after two years, they were increased to eighteen-pence; and after nine years' service, they were increased to six guineas a year. Yet during that time Martha Turner saved thirty pounds by sheer thrift.

John Crossley, the founder of the Crossley firm, and the husband of Martha Turner, was originally a carpet-weaver. One night, when working at the loom, he was taking his "drinking," and on laying down his black bottle it fell and broke. In trying to catch the bottle, he cut his arm so severely that it was thought he would have bled to death. He could not work at the loom any longer, and he was going about with his arm in a sling, when his employer, Mr. Currer, said to him, "John, do you think you could tie up a loom, as you cannot now weave?" John replied that he thought he could. He tried, and proved so expert that his master would not allow him to go back to the loom. John Crossley used to regard the accident to his arm as the turning-point in his life.

In the meantime he was going on with the business of courtship, though it was very much against the wish of the proud farmer—the

The Crossleys—Masters and Men (Continued)

father of Martha Turner. He declared that he would never allow his daughter to marry a weaver, or even a foreman of weavers. Perhaps the story of their courtship is best told in Martha's own words.

"When I went to the gate one evening, there was a young man standing there, who asked me if I wanted a sweetheart. I answered, 'Not I, marry! I want no sweethearts.' I then went into the house, and left him. I saw the same young man frequently about, but did not speak to him for years after. His name was John Crossley. When my mistress ascertained his object, she did all she could to set me against him. She told me that when she was a girl, she had gone to a boarding-school kept by a Mrs. Crossley,—that her husband's name was Tom Crossley, the grandfather of this very man that was courting me,—and that a wilder, idler scapegrace she never knew. She always said, when she saw him coming, 'There's young Crossley come again.'

"One day I received a love-letter from him, which I could now repeat word for word. I had several other suitors, but none were so persevering as John Crossley. He pressed me very much to have him. At last he sent me a letter to say that a house was vacant in Lower George Yard, close to the works he was managing, and that it was a great chance to meet with one so convenient. I told him that I was going home to spend the 5th of November, and would pass that way and look at the house, which I did. When I got home I asked my parents for their consent. They did not object much to it at the time; but I had not been at Miss Oldfield's more than a day or two, before they sent over my sister Grace to say that they would not give their consent to the match, and that if I insisted on being married to John Crossley, they would never look me in the face again.

"So soon as my sister was gone, I retired in a most distressed state of feeling to my bedroom, and opened my book that was the preparation for the sacrament, and the first place at which I opened I read these words: 'When thy father and thy mother forsake thee, then the Lord will take thee up.' This comforted me very much. I felt that the Lord was with me in this matter, and I could no longer doubt which was the path of duty. . . . I decided to accept John Crossley's offer, and we were married on the 28th day of January, 1800."

Mr. Crossley never did a better day's work than in marrying his excellent and noble wife. From that day forward she was his helper, his co-worker, his consoler. She assisted her husband in all his struggles, and in a certain sense she was the backbone of the Crossley family.

After the death of Mr. Job Lees, whose carpet manufactory he had managed, Mr. Crossley entered into partnership with two other persons, to take the plant and carry on the business. Some difference having occurred with the partners, he left the firm, and took a lease of Dean Clough Mill, where he entered into another partnership with his brother Thomas, and James Travers. There they carried on the business of worsted spinning. At the same time, John Crossley continued to spin and dye the yarns and to manage the looms of the firm which he had left. In fact, the dyeing and spinning for the old firm formed a considerable part of the business of the new one. Then came a crisis. The old firm took away their work: they sent the wool to be spun and the yarn to be dyed elsewhere. This was a great blow; but eventually it was got over by extra diligence, energy, and thrift,—Mrs. Crossley herself taking a full share in the labours and responsibility of her husband.

"In addition to the carpet making," she says in the Manuscript Memoir of her life, "we carried on the manufacture of shalloons and plainbacks, the whole of which I managed myself, so far as putting out the warps and weft, and taking in from the weavers. We had at one time as many as a hundred and sixty hand weavers on these goods. We sold the principal part of them in London. We had also about four looms making brace webs and body belts. The produce of these looms I sold principally to the Irish, who made them up into braces and hawked them about the country. I also made and stitched, with assistance, all the carpets that we sold retail. I used to get up to work by four o'clock in the morning, and being very diligent, I have usually earned two shillings before breakfast, by the time that my neighbours were coming downstairs."

The partnership of Crossley, Travers, and Crossley, lasted for twenty years. When the term had expired, the partners shared their savings; they amounted to £4,200, or fourteen hundred pounds to each. This was not a very large sum to make during twenty years' hard work; but Dean Clough Mill was then but a small concern, and each partner did his own share of handiwork in spinning, dyeing, and weaving. Mrs. Crossley says that "the fourteen hundred pounds came in very useful." In fact, it was only a beginning. John Crossley eventually bought the Dean Clough Mills out and out. He had a family of eight children to provide for; and he put his sons for the most part into his business. They followed the example of their parents, and became thrifty, useful, and honourable men.

John Crossley, the founder of the firm, has observed, that in the course of his life he was a keen observer of men and things. He says he noticed many of the failures of his neighbours in bringing up their children. Some fathers were so strict with their children, keeping them so constantly at home, and letting them see so little of the world in which they lived, that when the fathers died and the children were removed from all restraint, they came forth into the world like calves, and found everything entirely different from what they expected. Such unguided young persons, Mr. Crossley found, soon became wild, lost, and ruined. Then he observed the opposite extreme,—where the fathers indulged their children so much, that they became quite unfitted to endure the hardships of the world,—and, like a vessel that is sent to sea without a helm, they soon became stranded on the shores of life.

Hence Mr. Crossley endeavoured to steer clear of both extremes, and to give to his sons as much knowledge and experience of life as possible. When at home, he always had one of his sons near him; or when he went from home, he always took one of them with him. Thus they gained a great deal of practical knowledge of life, and knew something of the good and evil in the world; and as they grew older, they were all the better able to turn their own lives to the best account.

It is not necessary to follow the history of the Crossley family further. John Crossley died in 1837, after which the firm was conducted by John, Joseph, and Sir Francis Crossley, Bart. The latter represented the West Riding of the county of York at the time of his death, a few years ago. In 1857 he purchased a splendid piece of ground, which he presented to the Corporation of Halifax, to be used as a People's Park for ever. In the speech which he made on the occasion of presenting it, he said, amongst other things, that he had often discussed with his friend the Mayor the philosophy of money. "I recollect very well," he said, "once entering into the question with him, when I was twenty years younger than I am now, and saying that I saw a great deal of emptiness about this money-getting; that many were striving for that which they thought would make them happy, but that it was like a bubble upon the water—no sooner caught than burst.... Had I," he afterwards said, "been of noble birth, or traced my origin (like some in this room) to those who came in with William the Conqueror, however true it might be, it would not have been good, it would even be boastful to have done so.[1] But since I am of humble

---

1. Those who "came in with William the Conqueror" are not the oldest but the youngest of British families. They are the most recent occupiers of British soil. The Angles and Saxons, whose lands the Normans divided amongst themselves, occupied Britain many hundred years before the arrival of the Conqueror. In the remote dales of Yorkshire and Lancashire, the ancient race still exists. And thus the Crossley family may have a much longer pedigree, could they but trace it, than any of those who "came in with William the

The Crossleys—Masters and Men (Continued)

birth, perhaps it will be allowed me to say a little of those who ought to share the honour which is heaped upon me. My mother was the daughter of a farmer who lived upon his own estate, and although it was not large, it had been in the family for many generations. Her father made the same mistake that Jacob made,—Jacob made too much of Joseph, and her father made too much of Mary. My mother was seventeen, and quick in disposition. She said that right was not done to her at home, and she was determined to make her own way in the world, whatever the consequences might be. She went out to service, contrary to the wish of her father. I am honoured today with the presence of one who has descended from the family who engaged her as servant: I mean Mr. Oldfield, of Stock Lane, vice-chairman of the Halifax Board of Guardians. In that service, in her own person, she did the work of kitchenmaid, of housemaid, and of cook; and in addition to that she regularly milked six cows every night and morning. Besides which, she kept the house, which was as clean as a little palace. But this was not enough to employ her willing hands. Her mistress took in wool or tops to spin, and she could do what scarcely any in Warley could have done,—she spun that wool to thirty-six hanks in the pound, and thus earned many a guinea for her mistress, besides doing all her other work."[2]

Sir Francis went on to relate the history of his father (as given above from his own manuscript), until the time when he took the Dean Clough Mill. "My mother," he says, "went thither with her usual energy. As she was going down the yard at four o'clock in the morning, she made this vow: 'If the Lord does bless us at this place, the poor shall taste of it.' It is to this vow, given with so much faithfulness, and kept with so much fidelity, that I attribute the great success which my father had in business. My mother was always looking how she could best keep this vow. In the days that are gone by, when it was a dreary thing to give employment to a large number of people, the advice that she gave to her sons was, 'Do not sell your goods for less than they cost, for it would ruin you without permanently benefiting any one; but if you can go on giving employment

---

Conqueror." The latter are able to trace their origin because their numbers are so small, their possessions so large, and their introduction as English proprietors comparatively so recent.

2. In these snobbish days, when rich people are so often ashamed of their fathers and grandfathers, and vainly endeavour to make out their ancient 'nobility,' it was honest and manly on the part of Sir Francis Crossley thus publicly to relate these facts; and to share with his mother the honour of conferring his splendid present of the People's Park on the townsmen of Halifax.

during the winter, do so, for it is a bad thing for a working man to go home and hear his children cry for bread, when he has none to give them."'

And now with respect to the manner in which Sir Francis Crossley fulfilled the vow of his mother. "On the 10th of September, 1855," he said, "I left Quebec early in the morning, for the White Mountains in the United States. I remember passing through some of the most glorious scenery I had ever seen. On reaching the hotel at the White Mountains, I went out alone for an evening walk. It was a beautiful spot. The sun was just declining behind Mount Washington, amidst all the glorious drapery of an American sunset. I felt as if I was walking with God. 'What,' said I, 'shall I render for all His benefits to me? Lord, what wilt Thou have me to do?' The answer came immediately. It was this: 'It is true thou canst not bring the many thousands thou has left behind thee in thy native country, to see this beautiful scenery, but thou canst take such scenery to them. It is possible so to arrange art and nature that they shall be within the reach of every working man in Halifax; that he shall go and take his evening walk there, after his day's toil has been done.' Well, that seemed to me a glorious thought! I walked home, and my prayer that night was, that in the morning I might feel that my thought was justified, and that I might be spared to put it in execution. I slept soundly that night, and when I awoke my impression was confirmed. On the 10th of September, when I left Quebec for the White Mountains, I had no more idea of making a park than any one here has of building a city. On the day I reached home, I felt as convinced that I should carry out my thought, as I was of my own existence. And from that day to this I have never flinched from the undertaking, whatever difficulties might arise. It is a happy day for me that I have been permitted to see the result, in the People's Park that has been opened today."

The Park was opened in August, 1857.[3] Three years later, a fine statue of Sir Francis Crossley (by Mr. Joseph Durham) was placed in the Park, so that all comers, while beholding the princely gift, might also see the form and features of the giver. The cost of the statue was defrayed by public subscription, in which persons of all political parties joined. The preparation of the statue was delayed by the revolution in Italy, which placed Victor Emanuel on the Italian throne. While the quarrymen at

---

3. The Park is situated in the centre of the borough of Halifax, and covers twelve acres and a half of ground. It cost Sir Francis Crossley £35,000, who also gave to the Corporation £6,300 to be invested for its maintenance.

The Crossleys—Masters and Men (Continued)

Carrara were digging out the block of marble of which the figure was to be sculptured, they were roused by shouts of "Liberty," coupled with the name of Garibaldi, and they left their work to join the banner of that victorious leader. In front of the statue is the following inscription: "This statue of Frank Crossley, Esq., M.P. for the West Riding of the county of York, donor of the People's Park, was erected August 14, 1860, by the inhabitants of Halifax, his native town, as a tribute of gratitude and respect to one whose public benefactions and private virtues deserve to be remembered."

But the vow of Martha Crossley was not yet entirely fulfilled: "If the Lord does bless us at this place, the poor shall taste of it." That was what she promised on her husband's entering into possession of Dean Clough Mills; and her sons have nobly fulfilled her promise. In 1864, the extensive business of John Crossley and Sons, with all its mills, machinery, plant, warehouses and stock-in-trade—at Halifax, Kidderminster, Manchester, and London,—was converted into a joint-stock company. The company was formed with the primary design of receiving the co-operation of all parties associated with the business, and with the object of securing a spirit of harmony and the material well-being and profit of the workpeople, clerks, managers, and others interested in the concern. In order to enable the workpeople to join in the business, a large sum of money was lent to them for the purpose of taking up returned shares in the company; and the workpeople took them up to a large extent. A preference was always given to the managers and operatives; and the amount of shares applied for by them was invariably allotted in full.

The results of this system have proved entirely satisfactory; the directors reporting that "the active energies of all parties necessary to ensure success have been fully enlisted. They claim originality, in their method of securing the direct interest of the employés, and they rejoice in being able to report that the system has more than realized their highest expectations."[4] At the present time, the employés hold shares in the company, of the value of about thirty thousand pounds; and the deposit bank, founded for the use of the workpeople exclusively, contains money-savings amounting to more than sixteen thousand pounds! And thus the vow of Martha Crossley, that the poor should taste of the prosperity of John Crossley and Sons, has been amply and nobly fulfilled!

---

4. Reports of the Paris Universal Exhibition, 1867, vol. vi., pp. 119—141.

The Crossleys—Masters and Men (Continued)

One of the most promising of co-operative undertakings established by employers for the benefit of their workpeople, was that of the Messrs. Briggs and Son, of Whitwood collieries, near Wakefield. The collieries were converted into a limited company in 1865. The working colliers were made partners in the prosperity of the concern to this extent,—that whenever the divisible profits accruing from the business in any year, after making allowance for depreciation, exceeded ten per cent, on the capital embarked, all those employed by the company were to receive one-half of such excess profit as a bonus, to be distributed amongst them in proportion to their respective earnings during the year. The object of the owners was to put an end to strikes, which had sometimes placed them in peril of their lives, and also to enable them to live on better terms with their workpeople. The colliers were invited to become shareholders, and thus to take a personal interest in the prosperity of the concern.

The project was received with great favour by the friends of co-operation. Mr. John Stuart Mill, in his Principles of Political Economy, announced that "the Messrs. Briggs had taken the first step; and that it was highly honourable on the part of those employers of labour to have initiated a system so full of benefit both to the operatives employed and to the general interests of social improvement." Mr. Hughes, M.P., after visiting the collieries, expressed his surprise at the great success achieved in the first year of working the collieries as a partnership of industry. "I believe," he said to the owners, "that in taking this step you have done a great work for England, and one which will be gratefully recognized before long by the country." The promoters also claimed a reward from the Paris Universal Exhibition, for having been "the first large employers in England who have allowed all their workpeople, whether co-shareholders with them or not, to participate in all divisible profits beyond a fixed percentage on the paid-up capital of the company."

Only a few years have passed, and already this promising partnership of industry has come to an end. It has not been brought to an end by the masters, but by the men. The masters were satisfied with the profits made during the recent high prices of coal; but the men were not satisfied with the wages. Had they been as free as the Welsh colliers, they would have insisted on being paid as highly; but it would have been, as it was in Wales, ruinous to the masters. The system of industrial partnership had at length to be abandoned, and the men now work for wages instead of for part-profits. The truth is, the colliers were not sufficiently educated to appreciate the advantages of the industrial scheme. Though some of the

The Crossleys—Masters and Men (Continued)

Whitwood workmen have been stimulated by thrift, to build and furnish houses of their own, the greater number of them, during the recent flush of prosperity, squandered their wages on frivolity, extravagance, and intemperance.

The attempt was also made by several firms engaged in the iron trade, to embody the principle of co-operation in their respective concerns. Amongst these were the firms of Greening and Co., Manchester, and Fox, Head, and Co., Middlesborough.

The experiments were to a certain extent brought to an end by the greed or laziness of the colliers, who have for a time destroyed the prosperity of the iron trade. Messrs. Greening and Co. started with great enthusiasm; and the results were very successful as regards the workpeople. Nothing could have been better than the spirit of goodwill, and even devotion, which was displayed by many of them. But, unhappily, contracts were taken by the management, which resulted in a series of losses; and the scheme ended in liquidation. Mr. Greening states that "the Distribution Societies have as yet been much more successful than the Production Societies;" but he hopes "to see the latter crown the edifice by making workers everywhere no longer servants, but co-partners with capital."

The firm of Fox, Head, and Co. also admitted their workmen to a partnership of profits. They had for some time been much annoyed by strikes. Their works had stood idle for about a fourth of the whole time that had elapsed since their commencement. The system of co-operation was adopted in 1866, at the close of a long strike. One of the conditions of the scheme was that Fox, Head, and Co. should not be members of any association of employers, and that the workmen should not be members of any trades union. The original intention was to pay the workmen a bonus according to profits. They eventually adopted the practice of the Messrs. Briggs and Co., which was, to divide the profits over ten per cent. into two parts: the one to belong to the capitalists as their profit, and the other to be divided amongst all those who had received wages or salaries during the year, in proportion to the amount received by them. An opportunity was also afforded to the workmen of depositing their savings with the firm; but as there was only one instance, during three years, of a workman applying to invest his savings, this clause was withdrawn.

In consequence of the depressed state of the iron trade, there were no profits to be divided during the first two years. The men were, however,

The Crossleys—Masters and Men (Continued)

paid the current rate of wages, and were saved the expenses of Union levies. The co-operative store, which had been founded by the workmen, was in a very prosperous condition. In the third year of the co-operative scheme, a bonus of two and a half per cent, was divided between the employers and the employed. The workmen also received an advance of five per cent. in wages. In the fourth year the wages of the workmen were further increased ten per cent., and this took the cream off the bowl. However, a bonus of four per cent. was paid on the wages and salaries received by the employés during that year. At the meeting held to communicate the result of the year's business, Mr. Head said:—

"There may be some who think the tendency of our policy has been too sentimental. I don't believe in doing business on sentimental principles. But I contend that mere money-making is not the sole end of existence. We have been associated with many of you for several years, and we cannot help feeling a considerable interest in you. After all, life is not so very long. Another twenty or thirty years will see us all under ground, and there will be other employers and other workmen carrying on business at Newport Rolling Mills. It would indeed be strange if we did not take some interest in those with whom we are so much associated. And so, without in the least relaxing discipline, or sacrificing any true principle of business, we hold it to be our duty as employers, as well as your duties as employés, to consider each other's interests, and to do all that each of us can in the way of true and hearty co-operation."

The coal famine began to tell upon the iron-workers. The furnaces were often laid off for want of coal. The principal causes of the bad supply of coal arose from shorter hours of labour, and higher wages for less work. Yet a bonus of three and a quarter per cent, was allowed on the wages and salaries received by the employés during the year 1871. The co-operative stores continued to be very productive, and many of the members saved considerable sums of money. In the next year, a bonus of three and a half per cent, was divided. But difficulties were in store. The coal famine continued. The employers of labour held meetings to resist the successive advances of wages, and to counteract the operations of the trades unions.

Mr. Head strongly urged the men to hold together: "Cease to be deluded," he said, "by these trades unions. Save all you can, and with your savings provide against the day of sickness—a day which is sure to come sooner or later. Provide for old age; read good books,—you have every chance now, with a free library in the town. Give credit to others for wishing to be straightforward and honest as well as yourselves; and in every way I would ask you to act as reasonable, straightforward, sensible English workmen ought to do. Show that you can appreciate being well used, that you can appreciate those who put themselves to trouble that they may do you good; and beware lest, by want of sympathy, you drive the best of the employers out of the business, and retain those alone who are despotic and tyrannical. Cease to follow those who are actuated by self-interest, or by blind impulse; who do not care a bit if they get you into trouble, provided only they serve their own selfish ends. Such men are but blind leaders of the blind, and if you follow them you will eventually find yourselves deserted, and lying hopelessly and helplessly in the last ditch."

It was of no use. The men's wages went up twenty per cent.; and there was an end of the bonuses. The coal famine continued. The masters, instead of making profits, made immense losses. The price of iron went down. The mills stood idle for two months. The result was, that when the masters next met the workmen in public meeting, Mr. Waterhouse, the auditor, reported that "while the gross earnings of the year have exceeded the expenditure on materials, wages, and trade charges, they have been insufficient to cover the full amounts to be provided under the co-operative scheme for interest on capital, depreciation, and the reserve for bad debts; and that consequently it was his duty to declare that no amount was at present payable as bonus either to employers or employed." No further report was issued in 1875, excepting an announcement that there was no dividend, and that the firm did not intend to continue the co-operative scheme any longer. During the time that it lasted, the employés had received about eight thousand pounds in bonuses.

Since then, Sir Joseph Whitworth has announced his intention of giving his workmen a bonus upon his profits; but the principle of the division has not yet been announced. On hearing of his intention, Mr. Carlyle wrote the following letter to Sir Joseph:—

"Would to heaven that all the captains of industry in England had a soul in them such as yours. The look of England is to me at this moment abundantly ominous, the question of capital and labour growing ever more anarchic, insoluble altogether by the notions hitherto applied to it— pretty sure to issue in petroleum one day, unless some other gospel than that of the 'Dismal Science' come to illuminate it. Two things are pretty sure to me. The first is that capital and labour never can or will agree together till they both first of all decide on doing their work faithfully throughout, and like men of conscience and honour, whose highest aim is to behave like faithful citizens of this universe, and obey the eternal commandments of Almighty God, who made them. The second thing is, that a sadder object than even that of the coal strike, or any other conceivable strike, is the fact that—loosely speaking—we may say all England has decided that the profitablest way is to do its work ill, slurily, swiftly, and mendaciously. What a contrast between now and say only a hundred years ago! At the latter date all England awoke to its work—to an invocation to the Eternal Maker to bless them in their day's labour, and help them to do it well. Now, all England—shopkeepers, workmen, all manner of competing labourers—awaken as with an unspoken but heartfelt prayer to Beelzebub,—'Oh, help us, thou great Lord of Shoddy, Adulteration, and Malfeasance, to do our work with the maximum of sluriness, swiftness, profit, and mendacity, for the devil's sake. Amen.'"

Fortunately, there is not a great deal of truth in this letter, nor in the "heartfelt prayer" to Shoddy. The Right Hon. Mr. Forster ought to know something of labour and capital, and at a recent meeting of the Cobden Club he stated that "they were often told that they had a war within their borders between labour and capital; but as an employer of labour ever since he came to manhood, he would only say that he never knew a time in which employer and employed were on better terms."

The late Sir Francis Crossley observed that there was a good deal of unreasonable feeling abroad. It was held by some that it was wrong for working men to sell their labour at the best price; but it must be remembered that their labour was the only thing they had to sell; and the best thing to do was to leave those matters to take their natural course. It was a great mistake, on the part of employers, to suppose that the lowest-priced labour was always the cheapest. If there was not so much desire to run down the price of labour, and the masters showed a more conciliatory spirit, there would be fewer strikes and outrages.

"What a contrast between now and say only a hundred years ago!" Certainly there is a very great contrast. England was not a manufacturing country a hundred years ago. We imported nearly everything, except corn, wool, and flax. We imported the greatest part of our iron from Spain, Sweden, Germany, and Russia. We imported our pottery from Holland, our hats from Flanders, our silk from France, our cloth and carpets from Belgium. Our cotton manufactures, our woollen and flax manufactures, our machine manufactures, could scarcely be said to exist.

The Crossleys—Masters and Men (Continued)

Coal could scarcely be had, for the coal-pits could not be kept clear of water.

A hundred years ago, we could not build a steam-engine; we could scarcely build a bridge. Look at the churches built a hundred years ago, and behold the condition of our architecture. A hundred years ago, we had fallen to almost the lowest condition as a nation. We had not a harbour; we had not a dock. The most extensive system of robbery prevailed on the River Thames. The roads, such as they were, swarmed with highwaymen; and black-mail was levied by the Highlanders upon the Lowland farmers, down to the middle of last century.

A hundred years ago, our ships were rotten; they were manned by prisoners taken from the hulks, or by working men pressed in the streets in open day. When James Watt was learning his trade of an instrument maker in London, a hundred years ago, he durst scarcely walk abroad lest he should be seized and sent to India or the American plantations. Less than a hundred years ago, the colliers and salters of Scotland were slaves. It is not forty years since women and children worked in coalpits. Surely we are not to go down upon our knees and pray for a restoration of the horrible things that existed a hundred years ago.

A hundred years ago, Ireland was treated like a conquered country; and hangings and shootings of rebels were frequent. The fleet at the Nore mutinied; and the mutiny was put down by bloodshed and executions. Towns and cities swarmed with ruffians; and brutal sports and brutal language existed to a frightful degree. Criminals were hanged, five or six together, at Tyburn. Gibbets existed at all the cross-roads throughout the country. The people were grossly ignorant, and altogether neglected. Scepticism and irreligion prevailed, until Wesley and Whitfield sprang up to protest against formalism and atheism. They were pelted with rotten eggs, sticks, and stones. A Methodist preacher was whipped out of Gloucester.

A hundred years ago, literature was at a very low ebb. The press was in a miserable state. William Whitehead was Poet Laureate! Who knows of him now? Gibbon had not written his "Decline and Fall." Junius was the popular writer. Political corruption was scarified in his letters. The upper classes were coarse, drunken, and ill-mannered. Bribery and corruption on the grossest scale were the principal means for getting into Parliament. Mr. Dowdeswell, M.P. for Worcestershire, said to the Commons, "You have turned out a member for impiety and obscenity. What halfdozen members of this House ever meet over a convivial bottle, that their discourse is entirely free from obscenity, impiety, or abuse of Government?"

Though drunkenness is bad enough now, it was infinitely worse a hundred years ago. The publican's signboards announced, "You may here get drunk for a penny, dead-drunk for twopence, and have clean straw for nothing." Drunkenness was considered a manly vice. To drink deep was the fashion of the day. Six-bottle men were common. Even drunken clergymen were not unknown.

What were the popular amusements of the people a hundred years ago? They consisted principally of man-fighting, dog-fighting, cock-fighting, bull baiting, badger-drawing, the pillory, public whipping, and public executions. Mr. Wyndham vindicated the ruffianism of the Ring in his place in Parliament, and held it up as a school in which Englishmen learnt pluck and "the manly art of self-defence." Bull-baiting was perhaps more brutal than prize-fighting, though Wyndham defended it as "calculated to stimulate the noble courage of Englishmen." The bull was secured to a stake in the market-place or the bull-ring (the name still survives in many towns), and there the animal was baited by the rabble dogs of the neighbourhood. One can scarcely imagine the savageness of the sport—the animal mutilations, the imprecations of ruffians worse than brutes, the ferociousness and drunkenness, the blasphemy and unspeakable horrors of the exhibition. The public mind of this day absolutely revolts at such brutality. Yet, less than a hundred years ago—on the 24th of May, 1802,—a Bill for the abolition of bull-baiting was lost in the House of Commons by sixty-four to fifty-one,—Mr. Wyndham contending that horse-racing and hunting were more cruel than bull-baiting or prize-fighting!

The pillory was one of our time-honoured institutions fifty years ago, and men and women used to be placed there for offences, such as a wise legislature would have endeavoured to conceal from public consideration. The horrid scenes which then took place, when men, women, and children collected in crowds to pelt the offenders with missiles, were so disgusting, that they cannot be described. Not more seemly were the public whippings then administered to women in common with the coarsest male offenders. The public abominations and obscenities of the "good old times" would almost have disgraced the days of Nero.

But bull-baiting, cock-fighting, and other ferocious amusements, have now departed. Even the village stocks have rotted out. Drunkenness has become disreputable. The "good old times" have departed, we hope

The Crossleys—Masters and Men (Continued)

never to return. The labourer has now other resources beside the public-house. There are exhibitions and people's parks, steamboats and railways, reading-rooms and coffee-rooms, museums, gardens, and cheap concerts. In place of the disgusting old amusements, there has come a healthier, sounder life, greater enlightenment, more general sobriety, and a humaner spirit. We have in a hundred years outgrown many of our savage tendencies. We are not less brave as a people, though less brutal. We are quite as manly, though much less gross. Manners are more refined, yet as a people we have not lost our pluck, energy, and endurance. We respect ourselves more, and as a nation we have become more respected. We now think with shame of the manners of a hundred years ago.

The achievements of which England has most reason to be proud, have been accomplished during the last hundred years. English slaves have been emancipated, both at home and abroad. Impressment has been done away with. Parliamentary representation has been conferred upon all classes of the people. The Corn Laws have been abolished. Free trade has been established. Our ports are now open to the whole world.

And then, see what our inventors have accomplished! James Watt invented the steam-engine, which in a few years created a large number of new industries, and gave employment to immense numbers of people. Henry Cort invented the puddling-process, and enabled England to rely upon its own stores of iron, instead of depending upon foreign and perhaps hostile countries. All the docks and harbours round the English coast have been formed during the present century. The steamboat, the railway, and the telegraph have only been invented and applied during the last fifty years.

With respect to the charge made against the English workman as to the "sluriness, swiftness, and mendacity" of his work, it is simply impossible that this should be so. Our ports are free and open to the world; and if Frenchmen, Germans, Belgians, or Americans could execute better work than Englishmen, we should not only cease to export, but also lose our home trade. The foreigner is now free to undersell us, if he can, in our own markets.

It was in the perfect confidence that Englishmen were the best and most honest workers in the world, that free trade was established. Should we ever become a shoddy manufacturing people, free trade will probably be abolished; and we shall then impose prohibitory duties upon foreign manufactures. But is it not the fact that every year sees an increase in the exports of English goods,—that English workmanship is not considered

The Crossleys—Masters and Men (Continued)

the worst, but the best, in the general markets of the world,—and that numerous foreign makers place an English mark upon their productions in order to ensure their sale?

It is by means of English workmen and English tools and machines that continental manufactories themselves have been established; and yet, notwithstanding their cheaper labour, we should command the foreign market, but for the prohibitory duties which foreigners impose upon English manufactures. Mr. Brassey, in his book on Work and Wages, says, "It may be affirmed that as practical mechanics the English are unsurpassed. The presence of the English engineer, the solitary representative, among a crew of foreigners, of the mechanical genius of his country, is a familiar recollection to all who have travelled much in the steamers of the Mediterranean. Consul Lever says that in the vast establishment of the Austrian Lloyds at Trieste, a number of English mechanical engineers are employed, not only in the workshops, but as navigating engineers in the company's fleet. Although there is no difficulty in substituting for these men Germans or Swiss, at lower rates of payment, the uniform accuracy of the English, their intelligence, their consummate mastery of all the details of their art, and their resources in every case of difficulty, have entirely established their superiority."[5]

The English are also the best miners, the best tool-makers, the best instrument-makers, the best "navvies," the best ship-builders, the best spinners and weavers. Mr. Brassey says that during the construction of the Paris and Rouen Railway, the Frenchman, Irishman, and Englishman were employed side by side. In the same quarry at Bounierés, the Frenchman received three francs, the Irishman four, and the Englishman six; and the last was found to be the most advantageous workman of the three. The superiority of the English workman over persons of other nations was equally remarkable whenever there was an opportunity of employing him side by side with them.

There is no doubt about the "swiftness" of English Workmanship. But this is one of the merits of English mechanism. M. Jules Simon observes that heretofore the manual labourer has been an intelligent force, but by means of machinery he is converted into an intelligent director of force. It is by the speed of the English machinery, and the intelligent quickness of the workmen, that his master makes a profit, and himself such high wages as compared with continental workmen. In France, one person

---

5. Work and Wages, p. 114.

The Crossleys—Masters and Men (Continued)

is employed to mind fourteen spindles; in Russia, one to twenty-eight; in Prussia, one to thirty-seven; and in Great Britain, one to seventy-four spindles. It is by means of the swiftness of our machinery that we are enabled to bring cotton from India, manufacture it in Manchester, return the manufactured article to the place from which it was taken, and sell it at a lower price than the native-made calico.

Mr. Chadwick mentions the following case. "A lady, the wife of an eminent cotton manufacturer, went to him one day rejoicing, with a fine piece of muslin, as the produce of India, which she had bought in London, and showing it to him, said, if he produced a fabric like that, he would really be doing something meritorious in textile art. He examined it, and found that it was the produce of his own looms, near Manchester, made for the Indian market exclusively, bought there, and re-sold in England as rare Indian manufacture!"[6]

An annual report is furnished to the Government, by our foreign consuls, with reference to the character and condition of the working classes in most parts of the civilized world. Mr. Walter, M.P., in a recent address to an assembly of workmen, referred to one of these reports. He said, "There is one remark, in particular, that occurs with lamentable frequency throughout the report,—that, with few exceptions, the foreign workman does not appear 'to take pride in his work,' nor (to use a significant expression) to 'put his character into it.' A remarkable instance of this is mentioned of a country which generally constitutes an honourable exception to this unhappy rule. Switzerland is a country famous for its education and its watches; yet the following passage from the report will show that neither knowledge nor skill will suffice without the exercise of that higher quality on which I have been dwelling. 'As a rule,' it says, 'Swiss workmen are competent in their several trades, and take an interest in their work; for, thanks to their superior education, they fully appreciate the pecuniary advantages to their masters, and indirectly to themselves, of adhering strictly to this course. A striking instance of the impolicy of acting otherwise has lately happened at St. Imier, in the Bernese Jura, and produced a deep impression. In this district, for some years past, a great falling off in the quality of the watches manufactured has taken place, owing to the inhabitants finding it much more profitable to increase the production at the cost of the workmanship than to abide

---

6. Address on Economy and Free Trade. By Edwin Chadwick, C.B., at the Association for the Promotion of Social Science at York, 1861.

by the old rules of the trade. They prospered beyond all expectation for a considerable time, but finally their watches got such a bad name that they became unsaleable, and the result is a general bankruptcy of nearly all the watchmakers of this particular district."

One thing, however, remains to be said of foreign workmen generally. Although they do not work so hard as the English, they take much better care of their earnings. They are exceedingly frugal and economical. Frenchmen are much soberer than Englishmen, and much better mannered. They are, on the whole, greatly more provident than English workmen. Mr. Brassey states that when the Paris and Rouen Railway works were commenced, the contractors endeavoured to introduce a system by which the workmen were to be paid once a fortnight; but very soon after the operations had begun, the Frenchmen requested that the pay might take place only once a month.

Mr. Reid, managing director of the line, told the House of Commons Committee on Railway Labourers, that a French labourer is a much more independent person than an Englishman, and much more respectable. He stated, in support of his opinion, this remarkable circumstance, that whereas a French labourer desired to be paid only once a month, the English labourer desired to be paid every Saturday night,—and by the following Wednesday he wanted something on account of the week's work. "Nothing could be a greater test," said Mr. Reid, "of the respectability of a working man than being able to go without his pay for a month."[7]

Although the French workman has nothing like the same facilities for saving as the English, the Journal des Débats alleges that he saves ten times as much as his rival. There are only about a thousand savings banks and branches established in France, and yet two millions of persons belonging to the lower ranks last year had invested in them about twenty-eight millions sterling. But the Frenchman of the city prefers investing in Government Rentes; and the Frenchman of the country prefers investing in land. All, however, are thrifty, saving, and frugal; because they are educated in economy from their earliest years.

---

7. Thomas Brassey, M.P., On Work and Wages.

Chapter 12

Living Beyond the Means

"By no means run in debt: take thine own measure. Who cannot live on twenty pounds a year, Cannot on forty: he's a man of pleasure, A kind of thing that's for itself too dear."—George Herbert.

"But what will Mrs. Grundy say?"—Old Play.

"Yes and No are, for good or evil, the Giants of Life."—Jerrold.

"A hundred years of vexation will not pay a farthing of debt."—From the French.

"Respectability is all very well for folks who can have it for ready money: but to be obliged to run into debt for it—it's enough to break the heart of an angel."—Jerrold.

Extravagance is the pervading sin of modern society. It is not confined to the rich and moneyed classes, but extends also to the middle and working classes.

There never was such a burning desire to be rich, or to seem to be rich. People are no longer satisfied with the earnings of honest industry; but they must aim at becoming suddenly rich,—by speculation, gambling, betting, swindling, or cheating.

General extravagance is to be seen everywhere. It is especially the characteristic of town life. You see it in the streets, in the parks, in the churches. The extravagance of dress is only one of its signs. There is a general prodigality in social display. People live in a style beyond their means; and the results are observed in commercial failures, in lists of

Living Beyond the Means

bankrupts, and in criminal courts, where business men are so often convicted of dishonesty and fraud.

Appearances must be kept up. Men must seem to be rich. Hypocrites can easily impose upon those who are willing to be convinced. People must now live in a certain style, inhabit handsome houses, give good dinners, drink fine wines, and have a handsome equipage. Perhaps they are only able to accomplish this by overreaching or by dishonesty. Everybody wondered at the generosity and style of Redpath and Robson; but there are hundreds, if not thousands, of Redpaths and Robsons now.

There is another class of people, not fraudulent, but extravagant; though perhaps on the brink of becoming fraudulent. They live up to their means, and often beyond them. They desire to be considered "respectable people." They live according to the pernicious adage, "One must do as others do." They do not consider whether they can afford to live up to or beyond their means; but they think it necessary to secure the "respect" of others. In doing so, they usually sacrifice their own self-respect. They regard their dress, their establishments, their manner of living, and their observance of fashion, as the sole tests of respectability and rank. They make an appearance in the eyes of the world; though it may be entirely hypocritical and false.

But they must not seem poor! They must hide their poverty by every effort. They spend their money before it is earned,—run into debt at the grocer's, the baker's, the milliner's, and the butcher's. They must entertain their fashionable "friends," at the expense of the shopkeepers. And yet, when misfortunes overtake them, and when their debts have become overwhelming, what becomes of the "friends"? They fly away, and shun the man who is up to his ears in debt!

Yet poverty is more than half disarmed by those who have the moral courage to say. "I can't afford it." Fair-weather friends are of no use whatever, except as an indication of the depth of snobbery to which human beings can descend. What is "a visiting connection"? It is not at all calculated to elevate one in social, or even in business life. Success mainly depends upon character, and the general esteem in which a person is held. And if the attempt is made to snatch the reward of success before it is earned, the half-formed footing may at once give way, and the aspirant will fall, unlamented, into the open-mouthed dragon of debt.

"Mrs. Grundy," in the play, is but an impersonation of the conventionalism of the world. Custom, habit, fashion, use and wont, are all represented in her. She may be a very vulgar and commonplace person, but her power is nevertheless prodigious. We copy and imitate her in all things. We are pinned to her apron-string. We are obedient at her bidding. We are indolent and complaisant, and fear to provoke her ill-word. "What will Mrs. Grundy say?" quells many a noble impulse, hinders many a self-denying act.

There seems to be a general, though unconscious conspiracy existing, against each other's individuality and manhood. We discourage self-reliance, and demand conformity. Each must see with others' eyes, and think through others' minds. We are idolaters of customs and observances, looking behind, not forwards and upwards. Pinned down and held back by ignorance and weakness, we are afraid of standing alone, or of thinking and acting for ourselves. Conventionalism rules all. We fear stepping out into the free air of independent thought and action. We refuse to plant ourselves upon our instincts, and to vindicate our spiritual freedom. We are content to bear others' fruit, not our own.

In private affairs, the same spirit is alike deleterious. We live as society directs, each according to the standard of our class. We have a superstitious reverence for custom. We dress, and eat, and live, in conformity with the Grundy law. So long as we do this, we are "respectable," according to class notions. Thus many rush open-eyed upon misery, for no better excuse than a foolish fear of "the world." They are afraid of "what others will say of them;" and, in nine cases out of ten, those who might probably raise the voice of censure, are not the wise or the far-seeing, but much oftener the foolish, the vain, and the short-sighted.

Sir William Temple has said, that "a restlessness in men's minds to be something that they are not, and to have something that they have not, is the root of all immorality." The statement is strictly correct. It has been attested by universal experience.

Keeping up appearances is one of the greatest social evils of the age. There is a general effort, more particularly amongst the middle and upper classes, at seeming to be something that they are not. They put on appearances, live a life of sham, and endeavour to look something superior to what they really are.

"Respectability" is one of the chief aims. Respectability, regarded in its true sense, is a desirable thing. To be respected, on right grounds, is an object which every man and woman is justified in obtaining. But modern respectability consists of external appearances. It means wearing fine clothes, dwelling in fine houses, and living in fine style. It looks to the outside,—to sound, show, externals. It listens to the chink of gold in the pocket. Moral worth or goodness forms no part of modern respectability. A man in these days may be perfectly "respectable," and yet altogether despicable.

This false and demoralizing habit arises from the overweening estimate which is formed of two things, well enough in their place,—rank and wealth. Everybody struggles to rise into some superior class. The spirit of caste is found as keenly at work among the humblest as among the highest ranks. At Birmingham, there was a club of workmen with tails to their coats, and another without tails: the one looked down upon the other. Cobbett, so felicitous in his nicknames, called his political opponent, Mr. Sadler, "a linendraper." But the linendraper also has plenty of people beneath him. The linendraper looks down on the huckster, the huckster on the mechanic, and the mechanic on the day labourer. The flunkey who exhibits his calves behind a baron, holds his head considerably higher than the flunkey who serves a brewer.

It matters not at what class you begin, or however low in the social scale, you will find that every man has somebody beneath him. Among the middling ranks, this sort of exclusiveness is very marked. Each circle would think it a degradation to mix on familiar terms with the members of the circle beneath it. In small towns and villages, you will find distinct coteries holding aloof from each other, perhaps despising each other, and very often pelting each other with hard words. The cathedral towns, generally, have at least six of such distinct classes, ranking one beneath the other.

And while each has his or her own exclusive circle, which all of supposed inferior rank are precluded from entering, they are at the same time struggling to pass over the line of social demarcation which has been drawn by those above them. They are eager to overleap it, and thus gain admission into a circle still more exclusive than their own.

There is also a desperate scramble for front places, and many are the mean shifts employed to gain them. We must possess the homage of society! And for this purpose we must be rich, or at least seem to be so. Hence the struggles after style—the efforts made to put on the appearances of wealth—the dash, the glitter, and the show of middle and upper class life;—and hence, too, the motley train of palled and vitiated tastes—of shrunken hearts and stunted intellects—of folly, frivolity, and madness.

One of the most demoralizing practices of modern refinement is the "large party" system. People cram their houses with respectable mobs;

thus conforming to a ridiculous custom. Rousseau, with all his aberrations of mind, said, "I had rather have my house too small for a day, than too large for a twelvemonth." Fashion exactly reverses the maxim; and domestic mischief is often begun with a large dwelling and suitable accommodations. The misfortune consists in this,—that we never look below our level for an example, but always above it.

It is not so much, however, in the mere appearances kept up, as in the means taken to keep them up, that the fruitful cause of immorality is to be found. A man having assumed a class status, runs all risks to keep it up. It is thought to be a descent in the world, to abridge oneself of a superfluity. The seeming-rich man, who drives his close carriage and drinks champagne, will not tolerate a descent to a gig and plain beer; and the respectable man, who keeps his gig, would think it a degradation to have to travel afoot or in a 'bus, between his country house and his town office. They will descend to immorality rather than descend in apparent rank; they will yield to dishonesty rather than yield up the mock applause and hollow respect of that big fool, "the world."

Everybody can call to mind hundreds of cases of men—"respectable men"—who, from one extravagance have gone on to another—wantonly squandering wealth which was not theirs—in order to keep up a worldly reputation, and cut a figure before their admiring fellows;—all ending in a sudden smash, a frightful downfall, an utter bankruptcy—to the ruin, perhaps, of thousands. They have finished up with paying a respectable dividend of sixpence in the pound! Indeed it is not too much to say, that five-sixths of the fraud and swindling that disgrace commercial transactions, have had their origin in the diseased morality of "keeping up appearances."

To be "respectable," in the false sense of the word,—what is not sacrificed? Peace, honesty, truth, virtue,—all to keep up appearances. We must cheat, and scrub, and deceive, and defraud, that "the world" may not see behind our mask! We must torment and enslave ourselves, because we must extort "the world's" applause, or at least obtain "the world's" good opinion!

How often is suicide traceable to this false sentiment! Vain men will give up their lives, rather than their class notions of respectability. They will cut the thread of existence, rather than cut fashionable life. Very few suicides are committed from real want. "We never hear," says Joel Barlow, "of a man committing suicide for want of a loaf of bread, but it is often done for want of a coach."

Of this mean and miserable spirit of class and caste, women are the especial victims. They are generally brought up with false notions of life, and are taught to estimate men and things rather by their external appearances than by their intrinsic worth. Their education is conducted mainly with the view of pleasing and attracting the admiration of others, rather than of improving and developing their qualities of mind and heart. They are imbued with notions of exclusiveness, fashion, and gentility. A respectable position in society is held up to them as the mark to be aimed at. To be criminal or vicious is virtually represented to them as far less horrible than to be "vulgar." Immured within the bastile of exclusivism, woman is held captive to all the paltry shifts and expediencies of convention, fashion, gentility, and so forth. The genuine benevolence of her nature is perverted; her heart becomes contracted; and the very highest sources of happiness—those which consist in a kindly sympathy with humanity in all ranks of life—are as a well shut up and a fountain sealed.

Is it not a fact, that in what is called "fashionable society," a fine outside appearance is regarded almost in the light of a virtue?—that to be rich, or to have the appearance of riches, is esteemed as a merit of a high order;—whereas, to be poor, or to seem so, ranks as something like an unpardonable offence? Nay, such is the heartlessness of this class spirit, that a young woman, belonging to the better class, who, by misfortune or family reverses, has been thrown upon her own resources, and who endeavours, by her own honest hands, to earn her honest bread, immediately loses caste, and is virtually expelled from "respectable" society. The resolution to be independent—the most invigorating resolution which can take possession of the human mind—is scouted in such circles as a degrading thing; and those who have been brought up within the influence of fashion, will submit to the most severe privations, rather than submit to the loss of their class and caste respectability!

Thus brought up, it is no wonder that woman has been the co-partner with man in upholding the general extravagance of the age. There never was such a rage for dress and finery amongst English women as there is now. It rivals the corrupt and debauched age of Louis XV. of France. A delirium of fashion exists. Women are ranked by what they wear, not by what they are. Extravagance of dress, and almost indecency of dress, has taken the place of simple womanly beauty. Wordsworth once described the "perfect woman nobly planned." Where will you find the perfect woman now? Not in the parti-coloured, over-dressed creature—the thing of shreds and patches—with false hair, false colour, false eyebrows, false everything. "Some of nature's journeymen have made them, and not made them well, they imitate humanity so abominably."

The evil does not stop with the moneyed classes. It descends to those who have nothing but their salary to live upon. It descends to the wives of clerks and shopmen. They, too, dress for respectability. They live beyond their means. They must live in gimcrack suburban villas, and "give parties." They must see what is going on at the theatres. Every farthing is spent so soon as earned,—sometimes before. The husband does not insure his life, and the wife runs into debt. If the man died tomorrow, he would leave his wife and children paupers. The money he ought to have saved during his life of toil, is spent on "respectability;" and if he leaves a few pounds behind him, they are usually spent in giving the thriftless husband a respectable funeral.

"Is that dress paid for?" asked a husband. "No." "Then you are allowing yourself to be clothed at another man's expense!" No woman is justified in running into debt for a dress, without her husband's knowledge and consent. If she do so, she is clothing herself at the expense of the draper. This is one of the things that worry a man who is trying to keep his head above water; and it is often sufficient to turn his heart against his wife and her extravagances. It is in this way that incomes are muddled away, and that life is rendered the scene of bitterness and discontent. This is especially the case when both husband and wife are alike spendthrifts.

By running into debt yourself, or by your allowing your wife to run into debt, you give another person power over your liberty. You cannot venture to look your creditor in the face. A double knock at the door frightens you: the postman may be delivering a lawyer's letter demanding the amount you owe. You are unable to pay it, and make a sneaking excuse. You invent some pretence for not paying. At length you are driven to downright lying. For "lying rides on debt's back."

What madness it is to run in debt for superfluities! We buy fine articles—finer than we can pay for. We are offered six months'—twelve months' credit! It is the shopkeeper's temptation; and we fall before it. We are too spiritless to live upon our own earnings; but must meanwhile live upon others.' The Romans regarded their servants as their enemies. One might almost regard modern shopkeepers in the same light. By giving credit, by pressing women to buy fine clothes, they place the strongest temptation before them. They inveigle the wives of men who are disposed to be honest into debt, and afterwards send in untruthful bills. They charge heavier prices, and their customers pay them,—sometimes doubly pay them; for it is impossible to keep a proper check upon long-due accounts.

Professor Newman's advice is worthy of being followed. "Heartily do I wish," he says, "that shop debts were pronounced after a certain day irrecoverable at law. The effect would be that no one would be able to ask credit at a shop except where he was well known, and for trifling sums. All prices would sink to the scale of cash prices. The dishonourable system of fashionable debtors, who always pay too late, if at all, and cast their deficiencies on other customers in the form of increased charges, would be at once annihilated. Shopkeepers would be rid of a great deal of care, which ruins the happiness of thousands."[1]

A perfect knowledge of human nature is in the prayer, "Lead us not into temptation." No man and no woman ever resists temptation after it has begun to be temptation. It is in the outworks of the habits that the defence must lie. The woman who hesitates to incur a debt which she ought not to incur, is lost. The clerk or apprentice who gloats over his master's gold, sooner or later appropriates it. He does so when he has got over the habitual feeling which made any approach to it an impossibility. Thus the habits which insinuate themselves into the thousand inconsiderable acts of life, constitute a very large part of man's moral conduct.

This running into debt is a great cause of dishonesty. It does not matter what the debt is, whether it be for bets unsettled, for losses by cards, for milliners' or drapers' bills unpaid. Men who have been well educated, well trained, and put in the way of earning money honestly, are often run away with by extravagances, by keeping up appearances, by betting, by speculation and gambling, and by the society of the dissolute of both sexes.

The writer of this book has had considerable experience of the manner in which young men have been led from the way of well-doing into that of vice and criminality. On one occasion his name was forged by a clerk, to enable him to obtain a sum of money to pay the debts incurred by him at a public-house. The criminal was originally a young man of good education, of reasonable ability, well-connected, and married to a respectable young lady. But all his relatives and friends were forgotten—wife and child and all—in his love for drink and card-playing. He was condemned, and sentenced to several years' imprisonment.

---

1. Lectures on Political Economy, p. 255.

In another case the defaulter was the son of a dissenting minister. He stole some valuable documents, which he converted into money. He escaped, and was tracked. He had given out that he was going to Australia, by Southampton. The Peninsular and Oriental steamer was searched, but no person answering to his description was discovered. Some time passed, when one of the Bank of England notes which he had carried away with him, was returned to the Bank from Dublin. A detective was put upon his track; he was found in the lowest company, brought back to London, tried, and sentenced to twelve months' imprisonment.

In another case, the criminal occupied a high position in a railway company,—so high that he was promoted from it to be Manager of the Royal Swedish Railway. He was one of the too numerous persons who are engaged in keeping up appearances, irrespective of honesty, morality, or virtue. He got deeply into debt, as most of such people do; and then he became dishonest. He became the associate of professional thieves. He abstracted a key from the office of which he was in charge, and handed it to a well-known thief. This was the key of the strong box in which gold and silver were conveyed by railway from London to Paris. A cast of the key was taken in wax, and it was copied in iron. It was by means of this key that "The Great Gold Robbery" was effected. After some time the thieves were apprehended, and the person who had stolen the key—the keeper-up of appearances, then Manager of the Royal Swedish Railway—was apprehended, convicted, and sentenced by Baron Martin to Transportation for Life.

The Rev. John Davis, the late Chaplain of Newgate, published the following among other accounts of the causes of crime among the convicted young men who came under his notice:—

"I knew a youth, the child of an officer in the navy, who had served his country with distinction, but whose premature death rendered his widow thankful To receive an official appointment for her delicate boy in a Government office. His income from the office was given faithfully to his mother; and it was a pleasure and a pride to him to gladden her heart by the thought that he was helping her. She had other children—two little girls, just rising from the cradle to womanhood. Her scanty pension and his salary made every one happy. But over this youth came a love of dress. He had not strength of mind to see how much more truly beautiful a pure mind is, than a finely decorated exterior. He took pleasure in helping his mother and sisters, but did not take greater pleasure in thinking that to do this kindness to them he must be contented for a time to dress a little worse than his fellow-clerks; his clothes might appear a little worn, but they were like the spot on the dress of a soldier arising from the discharge of duty; they were no marks of undue carelessness; necessity had wrought them; and while they indicated necessity, they marked also the path of honour, and without such spots duty must have been neglected. But this youth did not think of such great thoughts as these. He felt ashamed at his threadbare but clean coat. The smart, new-shining dress of other clerks mortified him.... He wanted to appear finer. In an evil hour he ordered a suit of clothes from a fashionable tailor. His situation and connections procured him a short credit. But tradesmen must be paid, and he was again and again importuned to defray his debt. To relieve himself of his creditor he stole a letter containing a £10 note. His tailor was paid, but the injured party knew the number of the note. It was traced to the tailor, by him to the thief, with the means and opportunity of stealing it, and in a few days he was transported. His handsome dress was exchanged for the dress of a convict. Better by far would it have been for him to have worn his poorer garb, with the marks of honest labour upon it. He formed only another example of the intense folly of love of dress, which, exists quite as much amongst foolish young men as amongst foolish young women."

When Sir Charles Napier left India, he issued an order to the Army, in which he reproved the officers for contracting debts without the prospect of paying them. The Commander-in-Chief found that he was subject to constant complaints against officers for non-payment of debts; and in some cases he found that the ruin of deserving and industrious tradesmen had been consequent on that cause. This growing vice he severely reprimanded, as being derogatory to the character of the gentleman, as a degrading thing, as entitling those who practised it to "group with the infamous, with those who are cheats, and whose society is contamination." He strongly urged them to stick to their duties, to reprobate extravagance and expense of all sorts, and to practise rigid economy; for "to drink unpaid-for champagne and unpaid-for beer, and to ride unpaid-for horses, is to be a cheat and not a gentleman."

The extravagance of these young "gentlemen" in India is, in too many respects, but a counterpart of the extravagance of our young "gentlemen" at home. The revelations of extravagances at Oxford and Cambridge point to the school in which they have learnt their manners. Many worthy parents have been ruined by the sons whom they had sent thither to be made scholars of; but who have learnt only to be "gentlemen" in the popular acceptation of the word. To be a "gentleman" nowadays, is to be a gambler, a horse-racer, a card-player, a dancer, a hunter, a roué,—or all combined. The "gentleman" lives fast, spends fast, drinks fast, dies fast. The old style of gentleman has degenerated into a "gent" and a "fast" man. "Gentleman" has become disreputable; and when it is now employed, it oftener signifies an idle spendthrift, than an accomplished, virtuous, laborious man.

Young men are growing quite shameless about being in debt; and the immorality extends throughout society. Tastes are becoming more extravagant and luxurious, without the corresponding increase of means to enable them to be gratified. But they are gratified, nevertheless; and debts are incurred, which afterwards weigh like a millstone round the neck. Extravagant habits, once formed and fostered, are very difficult to give up. The existing recklessness of running into debt without the prospect, often without even the intention, of paying the debt, saps the public morals, and spreads misery throughout the middle and upper classes of society. The tone of morality has sunk, and it will be long before it is fairly recovered again.

In the mean time, those who can, ought to set their faces against all expenditure where there are not sufficient means to justify it. The safest plan is, to run up no bills, and never to get into debt; and the next is, if one does get into debt, to get out of it again as quickly as possible. A man in debt is not his own master: he is at the mercy of the tradesmen he employs. He is the butt of lawyers, the byword of creditors, the scandal of neighbours; he is a slave in his own house; his moral character becomes degraded and defiled; and even his own household and family regard him with pity akin to contempt.

Montaigne said, "I always feel a pleasure in paying my debts, because I discharge my shoulders of a wearisome load and of an image of slavery." Johnson might well call Economy the mother of Liberty. No man can be free who is in debt. The inevitable effect of debt is not only to injure personal independence, but, in the long run, to inflict moral degradation. The debtor is exposed to constant humiliations. Men of honourable principles must be disgusted by borrowing money from persons to whom they cannot pay it back;—disgusted with drinking wine, wearing clothes, and keeping up appearances, with other people's money. The Earl of Dorset, like many other young nobles, became involved in debt, and borrowed money upon his property. He was cured of his prodigality by the impertinence of a city alderman, who haunted his antechamber for the purpose of dunning him for his debt. From that day the Earl determined to economize, to keep entirely out of everybody's debt,—and he kept his word.

Let every man have the fortitude to look his affairs in the face,—to keep an account of his items of income and debts, no matter how long or black the list may be. He must know how he stands from day to day, to be able to look the world fairly in the face. Let him also inform his wife, if he has one, how he stands with the world. If his wife be a prudent woman, she will help him to economize his expenditure, and enable him to live honourably and honestly. No good wife will ever consent to wear clothes and give dinners that belong not to her, but to her shopkeeper.

The knowledge of arithmetic is absolutely necessary to those who would live within their means. Women are especially ignorant of arithmetic; they are scarcely taught the simplest elements, for female teachers think the information useless. They prefer to teach languages, music, deportment, the use of the globes. All these may be important, but the first four rules of arithmetic are better than all. How can they compare their expenditure with their receipts, without the knowledge of addition and subtraction? How can they know precisely what to spend in rent, or clothing, or food, or for service, unless they know the value of figures? How can they check the accounts of their tradesmen or their servants? This want of knowledge of arithmetic is the cause, not only of great waste, but of great misery. Many a family of good position has fallen into destitution merely because of their ignorance of this branch of knowledge.

Young people often rush into marriage without reflection. A young man meets a pretty face in a ball-room, likes it, dances with it, flirts with it, and goes home to dream about it. At length he falls in love with it, courts it, marries it, and then he takes the pretty face home, and begins to know something more about it. All has as yet been "very jolly." The face has hitherto been charming, graceful, artless, and beautiful. It has now to enter upon another sphere of life. It has to be seen much closer; it has to be seen daily; and it has to begin housekeeping.

Most newly married people require some time to settle quietly down together. Even those whose married life has been the happiest, arrive at peace and repose through a period of little struggles and bewilderments. The husband does not all at once find his place, nor the wife hers. One of the very happiest women we know has told us, that the first year of her married life was the most uncomfortable of all. She had so much to learn—was so fearful of doing wrong—and had not yet found her proper position. But, feeling their way, kind and loving natures will have no difficulty in at last settling down comfortably and peacefully together.

It was not so with the supposed young man and his pretty "face." Both entered upon their new life without thinking; or perhaps with exaggerated expectations of its unalloyed happiness. They could not make allowances for lovers subsiding into husband and wife; nor were they prepared for the little ruffles and frettings of individual temper; and both felt disappointed. There was a relaxation of the little attentions which are so novel and charming to lovers. Then the pretty face, when neglected, found relief in tears.

There is nothing of which men tire sooner, especially when the tears are about trifles. Tears do not in such cases cause sympathy, but breed repulsion. They occasion sourness, both on the one side and the other. Tears are dangerous weapons to play with. Were women to try kindness and cheerfulness instead, how infinitely happier would they be. Many are the lives that are made miserable by an indulgence in fretting and carking, until the character is indelibly stamped, and the rational enjoyment of life becomes next to a moral impossibility.

Mental qualities are certainly admirable gifts in domestic life. But though they may dazzle and delight, they will not excite love and affection to anything like the same extent as a warm and happy heart. They do not wear half so well, and do not please half so much. And yet how little pains are taken to cultivate the beautiful quality of good temper and happy disposition! And how often is life, which otherwise might have been blessed, embittered and soured by the encouragement of peevish and fretful habits, so totally destructive of everything like social and domestic comfort! How often have we seen both men and women set themselves round about as if with bristles, so that no one dared to approach them without the fear of being pricked. For want of a little occasional command over one's temper, an amount of misery is occasioned in society which is positively frightful. Thus is enjoyment turned into bitterness, and life becomes like a journey barefooted, amongst prickles, and thorns, and briars.

In the instance we have cited, the pretty face soon became forgotten. But as the young man had merely bargained for the "face"—as it was that to which he had paid his attentions—that which he had vowed to love, honour, and protect.—when it ceased to be pretty, he began to find out that he had made a mistake. And if the home be not made attractive,—if the newly married man finds that it is only an indifferent boarding-house,—he will gradually absent himself from it. He will stay out in the evenings, and console himself with cigars, cards, politics, the theatre, the drinking club; and the poor pretty face will then become more and more disconsolate, hopeless, and miserable.

Perhaps children grow up; but neither husband nor wife know much about training them, or keeping them healthy. They are regarded as toys when babies, dolls when boys and girls, drudges when young men and women. There is scarcely a quiet, happy, hearty hour spent during the life of such a luckless couple. Where there is no comfort at home, there is only a succession of petty miseries to endure. Where there is no cheerfulness,—no disposition to accommodate, to oblige, to sympathize with one another,—affection gradually subsides on both sides.

It is said, that "When poverty comes in at the door, loves flies out at the window." But it is not from poor men's houses only that love flies. It flies quite as often from the homes of the rich, where there is a want of loving and cheerful hearts. This little home might have been snug enough; with no appearance of want about it; rooms well furnished; cleanliness pervading it; the table well supplied; the fire burning bright; and yet without cheerfulness. There wanted the happy faces, radiant with contentment and good humour. Physical comfort, after all, forms but a small part of the blessings of a happy home. As in all other concerns of life, it is the moral state which determines the weal or woe of the human condition.

Most young men think very little of what has to follow courtship and marriage. They think little of the seriousness of the step. They forget that when the pledge has once been given, there is no turning back, The knot cannot be untied. If a thoughtless mistake has been made, the inevitable results will nevertheless follow. The maxim is current, that "marriage is a lottery." It may be so if we abjure the teachings of prudence—if we refuse to examine, inquire, and think—if we are content to choose a husband or a wife, with less reflection than we bestow upon the hiring of a servant, whom we can discharge any day—if we merely regard attractions of face, of form, or of purse, and give way to temporary impulse or to greedy avarice—then, in such cases, marriage does resemble a lottery, in which you may draw a prize, though there are a hundred chances to one that you will only draw a blank.

But we deny that marriage has any necessary resemblance to a lottery. When girls are taught wisely how to love, and what qualities to esteem in a companion for life, instead of being left to gather their stock of information on the subject from the fictitious and generally false personations given to them in novels; and when young men accustom themselves to think of the virtues, graces, and solid acquirements requisite in a wife, with whom they are to spend their days, and on whose temper and good sense the whole happiness of their home is to depend, then it will be found that there is very little of the "lottery" in marriage; and that, like any concern of business or of life, the man or woman who judges and acts wisely, with proper foresight and discrimination, will reap the almost certain consequences in a happy and prosperous future. True, mistakes may be made, and will be made, as in all things human; but nothing like the grievous mistake of those who stake their happiness in the venture of a lottery.

Another great point is, to be able to say No on proper occasions. When enticements allure, or temptations assail, say No at once, resolutely and determinedly. "No; I can't afford it." Many have not the moral courage to adopt this course. They consider only their selfish gratification. They are unable to practise self-denial. They yield, give way, and "enjoy themselves." The end is often defalcation, fraud, and ruin. What is the verdict of society in such cases? "The man has been living beyond his means." Of those who may have been entertained by him, not one of them will thank him, not one of them will pity him, not one of them will help him.

Every one has heard of the man who couldn't say No. He was everybody's friend but his own. His worst enemy was himself. He ran rapidly through his means, and then called upon his friends for bonds, bails, and "promises to pay." After spending his last guinea, he died in the odour of harmless stupidity and folly.

His course in life seemed to be directed by the maxim of doing for everybody what everybody asked him to do. Whether it was that his heart beat responsive to every other heart, or that he did not like to give offence, could never be ascertained; but certain it is, that he was rarely asked to sign a requisition, to promise a vote, to lend money, or to endorse a bill, that he did not comply. He couldn't say "No;" and there were many who knew him well, who said he had not the moral courage to do so.

His father left him a snug little fortune, and he was at once beset by persons wanting a share of it. Now was the time to say "No," if he could; but he couldn't. His habit of yielding had been formed; he did not like to be bored; could not bear to refuse; could not stand importunity; and almost invariably yielded to the demands made upon his purse. While his money lasted, he had no end of friends. He was a universal referee—everybody's bondsman. "Just sign me this little bit of paper," was a request often made to him by particular friends, "What is it?" he would mildly ask; for, with all his simplicity, he prided himself upon his caution! Yet he never refused. Three months after, a bill for a rather heavy amount would fall due, and who should be called upon to make it good but everybody's friend—the man who couldn't say "No."

At last a maltster, for whom he was bondsman—a person with whom he had only a nodding acquaintance—suddenly came to a stand in his business, ruined by heavy speculations in funds and shares; when the man who couldn't say "No" was called upon to make good the heavy duties due to the Crown. It was a heavy stroke, and made him a poor man. But he never grew wise. He was a post against which every needy fellow came and rubbed himself; a tap, from which every thirsty soul could drink; a flitch, at which every hungry dog had a pull; an ass, on which every needy rogue must have his ride; a mill, that ground everybody's corn but his own; in short, a "good-hearted fellow," who couldn't for the life of him say "No."

It is of great importance to a man's peace and well-being that he should be able to say "No" at the right time. Many are ruined because they cannot or will not say it. Vice often gains a footing within us, because we will not summon up the courage to say "No." We offer ourselves too often as willing sacrifices to the fashion of the world, because we have not the honesty to pronounce the little word. The duellist dares not say "No," for he would be "cut." The beauty hesitates to say it, when a rich blockhead offers her his hand, because she has set her ambition on an "establishment." The courtier will not say it, for he must smile and promise to all.

When pleasure tempts with its seductions, have the courage to say "No" at once. The little monitor within will approve the decision; and virtue will become stronger by the act. When dissipation invites, and offers its secret pleasures, boldly say "No." If you do not, if you acquiesce and succumb, virtue will have gone from you, and your self-reliance will have received a fatal shock. The first time may require an effort; but strength will grow with use. It is the only way of meeting temptations to idleness, to self-indulgence, to folly, to bad custom, to meet it at once with an indignant "No." There is, indeed, great virtue in a "No," when pronounced at the right time.

Living Beyond the Means

A man may live beyond his means until he has nothing left. He may die in debt, and yet "society" does not quit its hold of him until he is laid in his grave. He must be buried as "society" is buried. He must have a fashionable funeral. He must, to the last, bear witness to the power of Mrs. Grundy. It is to please her, that the funeral cloaks, hatbands, scarves, mourning coaches, gilded hearses, and processions of mutes are hired. And yet, how worthless and extravagant is the mummery of the undertaker's grief; and the feigned woe of the mutes, saulies, and plume bearers, who are paid for their day's parade!

It is not so much among the wealthy upper classes that the mischiefs of this useless and expensive mummery are felt, as amongst the middle and working classes. An expensive funeral is held to be "respectable." Middle-class people, who are struggling for front places in society, make an effort to rise into the region of mutes and nodding plumes; and, like their "betters," they are victimised by the undertakers. These fix the fashion for the rest; "we must do as Others do;" and most people submit to pay the tax. They array themselves, friends, and servants, in mourning; and a respectable funeral is thus purchased.

The expenditure falls heavily upon a family, at a time when they are the least able to bear it. The bread-winner has been taken away, and everything is left to the undertaker. How is a wretched widow in the midst of her agony, or how are orphan children, deprived of the protecting hand of a parent, to higgle with a tradesman about the cheapening of mourning suits, black gloves, weepers, and the other miserable "trappings of woe"? It is at such a moment, when in thousands of cases every pound and every shilling is of consequence to the survivors, that the little ready money they can scrape together is lavished, without question, upon a vulgar and extravagant piece of pageantry. Would not the means which have been thus foolishly expended in paying an empty honour to the dead, be much better applied in being used for the comfort and maintenance of the living?

The same evil propagates itself downwards in society. The working classes suffer equally with the middle classes, in proportion to their means. The average cost of a tradesman's funeral in England is about fifty pounds; of a mechanic, or labourer, it ranges from five pounds to ten pounds. In Scotland funeral expenses are considerably lower. The desire to secure respectable interment for departed relatives, is a strong and widely-diffused feeling among the labouring population; and it does them honour. They will subscribe for this purpose, when they will for no other. The largest of the working-men's clubs are burial clubs. Ten pounds are usually allowed for the funeral of a husband, and five pounds for the funeral of a wife. As much as fifteen, twenty, thirty, and even forty pounds, are occasionally expended on a mechanic's funeral, in cases where the deceased has been a member of several clubs, on which occasions the undertakers meet and "settle" between them their several shares in the performance of the funeral. It is not unusual to insure a child's life in four or five of these burial clubs; and we have heard of a case where one man had insured payments in no fewer than nineteen different burial clubs in Manchester!

When the working-man, in whose family a death has occurred, does not happen to be a member of a burial club, he is still governed by their example, and has to tax himself seriously to comply with the usages of society, and give to his wife or child a respectable funeral. Where it is the father of the family himself who has died, the case is still harder. Perhaps all the savings of his life are spent in providing mourning for his wife and children at his death. Such an expense, at such a time, is ruinous, and altogether unjustifiable.

Does putting on garments of a certain colour constitute true mourning? Is it not the heart and the affections that mourn, rather than the outside raiment? Bingham, in speaking of the primitive Christians, says that "they did not condemn the notion of going into a mourning habit for the dead, nor yet much approve of it, but left it to all men's liberty as an indifferent thing, rather commending those that either omitted it wholly, or in short laid it aside again, as acting more according to the bravery and philosophy of a Christian."

John Wesley directed, in his will, that six poor men should have twenty shillings each for carrying his body to the grave,—"For," said he, "I particularly desire that there may be no hearse, no coach, no escutcheon, no pomp, except the tears of those that loved me, and are following me to Abraham's bosom. I solemnly adjure my executors, in the name of God, punctually to observe this."

It will be very difficult to alter the mourning customs of our time. We may anxiously desire to do so, but the usual question will occur—"What will people say?" "What will the world say?" We involuntarily shrink back, and play the coward like our neighbours. Still, common sense, repeatedly expressed, will have its influence; and, in course of time, it cannot fail to modify the fashions of society The last act of Queen Adelaide, by which she dispensed with the hired mummery of undertakers' grief,—and the equally characteristic request of Sir Robert Peel on his deathbed, that no ceremony, nor pomp, should attend his last obsequies,—cannot fail to have their due effect upon the fashionable world; and through them, the middle classes, who are so disposed to imitate them in all things, will in course of time benefit by their example. There is also, we believe, a growing disposition on the part of the people at large to avoid the unmeaning displays we refer to; and it only needs the repeated and decided expression of public opinion, to secure a large measure of beneficial reform in this direction.

Societies have already been established in the United States, the members of which undertake to disuse mourning themselves, and to discountenance the use of it by others. It is only, perhaps, by association and the power of numbers that this reform is to be accomplished; for individuals here and there could scarcely be expected to make way against the deeply-rooted prejudices of the community at large.

Chapter 13

Great Debtors

"What would life be without arithmetic, but a scene of horrors? You are going to Boulogne, the city of debts, peopled by men who never understood arithmetic."—Sydney Smith.

"Quand on doit et qu'on ne paye pas, c'est comme si on ne devait pas." ["When one has to pay and pays not, it's as if one does not have to pay."].— Araene Houssaye.

"Of what a hideous progeny is debt the father! What lies, what meanness, what invasions on self-respect, what cares, what double-dealing! How in due season it will carve the frank, open face into wrinkles: how like a knife, it will stab the houeat heart."—Douglas Jerrold.

"The human species, according to the best theory I can form of it, is composed of two distinct races, the men who borrow and the men who lend. To these two original diversities may be reduced all those impertinent classifications of Gothic and Celtic tribes, white men, black men, red men, and such-like."— Charles Lamb.

People do not know what troubles they are brewing for themselves when they run into debt. It does not matter for what the debt is incurred. It hangs like a millstone round a man's neck until he is relieved of it. It presses like a nightmare upon him. It hinders the well-being of his family. It destroys the happiness of his household.

Even those who are in the regular receipt of large incomes, feel crippled, often for years, by the incubus of debt. Weighed down by this, what can a man do to save—to economise with a view to the future of his wife and children? A man in debt is disabled from insuring his life, from insuring his house and goods, from putting money in the bank, from buying a house or a freehold. All his surplus gains must go towards the payment of his debt.

Even men of enormous property, great lords with vast landed estates, often feel themselves oppressed and made miserable by loads of debt. They or their forefathers having contracted extravagant habits—a taste for gambling, horseracing, or expensive living,—borrow money on their estates, and the burden of debt remains. Not, perhaps, in the case of strictly entailed estates—for the aristocracy have contrived so that their debts shall be wiped out at their death, and they can thus gratify their spendthrift tastes at the expense of the public—the estates going comparatively unburdened to the entailed heir. But comparatively few are in the position of the privileged classes. In the case of the majority, the debts are inherited with the estates, and often the debts are more than the estates are worth. Thus it happens that a large part of the lands of England are at this moment the property of mortgagees and money-lenders.

The greatest men have been in debt. It has even been alleged that greatness and debt have a certain relation to each other. Great men have great debts; they are trusted. So have great nations; they are respectable, and have credit. Spiritless men have no debts, neither have spiritless nations; nobody will trust them. Men as well as nations in debt secure a widely extended interest. Their names are written in many books; and many are the conjectures formed as to whether they will pay—or not. The man who has no debts slips through the world comparatively unnoticed; while he who is in everybody's books has all eyes fixed upon him. His health is enquired after with interest; and if he goes into foreign countries, his return is anxiously looked for.

The creditor is usually depicted as a severe man, with a hard visage; while the debtor is an open-handed generous man, ready to help and entertain everybody. He is the object of general sympathy. When Goldsmith was dunned for his milk-score and arrested for the rent of his apartments, who would think of pitying the milk-woman or the landlady? It is the man in debt who is the prominent feature of the piece, and all our sympathy is reserved for him. "What were you," asked Pantagruel of Panurge, "without your debts? God preserve me from ever being without them! Do you think there is anything divine in lending or in crediting others? No! To owe is the true heroic virtue!"

Yet, whatever may be said in praise of Debt, it has unquestionably a very seedy side. The man in debt is driven to resort to many sorry expedients to live. He is the victim of duns and sheriff's officers. Few can treat them with the indifference that Sheridan did, who put them into livery to wait upon his guests. The debtor starts and grows pale at every knock at his door. His friends grow cool, and his relatives shun him. He is ashamed to go abroad, and has no comfort at home. He becomes crabbed, morose, and querulous, losing all pleasure in life. He wants the passport to enjoyment and respect—money; he has only his debts, and these make him suspected, despised, and snubbed. He lives in the slough of despond. He feels degraded in others' eyes as well as in his own. He must submit to impertinent demands, which he can only put off by sham excuses. He has ceased to be his own master, and has lost the independent bearing of a man. He seeks to excite pity, and pleads for time. A sharp attorney pounces on him, and suddenly he feels himself in the vulture's gripe. He tries a friend or a relative, but all that he obtains is a civil leer, and a cool repulse. He tries a money-lender; and, if he succeeds, he is only out of the frying-pan into the fire. It is easy to see what the end will be,—a life of mean shifts and expedients, perhaps ending in the gaol or the workhouse.

Can a man keep out of debt? Is there a possibility of avoiding the moral degradation which accompanies it? Could not debt be dispensed with altogether, and man's independence preserved secure? There is only one way of doing this; by "living within the means." Unhappily, this is too little the practice in modern times. We incur debt, trusting to the future for the opportunity of defraying it. We cannot resist the temptation to spend money. One will have fine furniture and live in a high-rented house; another will have wines and a box at the opera; a third must give dinners and music-parties:—all good things in their way, but not to be indulged in if they cannot be paid for. Is it not a shabby thing to pretend to give dinners, if the real parties who provide them are the butcher, the poulterer, and the wine-merchant, whom you are in debt to, and cannot pay?

A man has no business to live in a style which his income cannot support, or to mortgage his earnings of next week or of next year, in order to live luxuriously today. The whole system of Debt, by means of which we forestall and anticipate the future, is wrong. They are almost as much to blame who give credit, and encourage customers to take credit, as those are who incur debts. A man knows what his actual position is, if he pays his way as he goes. He can keep within his means, and so apportion his expenditure as to reserve a fund of savings against a time of need. He is always balanced up; and if he buys nothing but what he pays for in cash, he cannot fail to be on the credit side of his household accounts at the year's end.

But once let him commence the practice of running up bills—one at the tailor's, another at the dressmaker's and milliner's, another at the butcher's, another at the grocer's, and so on,—and he never knows how he stands. He is deceived into debt; the road is made smooth and pleasant for him; things flow into the house, for which he does not seem to pay. But they are all set down against him; and at the year's end, when the bills come in, he is ready to lift up his hands in dismay. Then he finds that the sweet of the honey will not repay for the smart of the sting.

It is the same as respects the poorer classes. Not many years since, Parliament passed a law facilitating the establishment of Small Loan Societies, for the purpose of helping small tradesmen and poor people generally to raise money on an emergency. The law was at once pounced upon by the numerous race of Graballs, as a means of putting money in their purse. They gave the working classes facilities for running into debt, and for mortgaging their future industry. A few men, desirous of making money, would form themselves into a Loan Club, and offer sums of money ostensibly at five per cent, interest, repayable in weekly instalments. The labouring people eagerly availed themselves of the facility for getting into debt. One wanted money for a "spree," another wanted money for a suit of clothes, a third for an eight-day clock, and so on; and instead of saving the money beforehand, they preferred getting the money from the Club, keeping themselves in difficulties and poverty until the debt was paid off. Such a practice is worse than living from hand to mouth: it is living upon one's own vitals.

It is easy to understand how the partners in the Loan Club made money. Suppose that they advanced ten pounds for three months at five per cent. It is repayable in weekly instalments at ten shillings a week,—the repayments commencing the very first week after the advance has been made. But though ten shillings are repaid weekly until the debt is wiped off, interest at five per cent, is charged upon the whole amount until the last instalment is paid off. So that, though the nominal interest is five per cent., it goes on increasing until, during the last week, it reaches the enormous rate of one hundred per cent.! This is what is called "eating the calf in the cow's belly."

Men of genius are equally facile in running into debt. Genius has no necessary connection with prudence or self-restraint, nor does it exercise any influence over the common rules of arithmetic, which are rigid and inflexible. Men of genius are often superior to what Bacon calls "the wisdom of business." Yet Bacon himself did not follow his own advice, but was ruined by his improvidence. He was in straits and difficulties when a youth, and in still greater straits and difficulties when a man. His life was splendid; but his excessive expenditure involved him in debts which created a perpetual craving for money. One day, in passing out to his antechambers, where his followers waited for his appearance, he said, "Be seated, my masters; your rise has been my fall." To supply his wants, Bacon took bribes, and was thereupon beset by his enemies, convicted, degraded, and ruined.

Even men with a special genius for finance on a grand scale, may completely break down in the management of their own private affairs. Pitt managed the national finances during a period of unexampled difficulty, yet was himself always plunged in debt. Lord Carrington, the ex-banker, once or twice, at Mr. Pitt's request, examined his household accounts, and found the quantity of butcher's meat charged in the bills was one hundredweight a week. The charge for servants' wages, board wages, living, and household bills, exceeded £2,300 a year. At Pitt's death, the nation voted £40,000 to satisfy the demands of his creditors; yet his income had never been less than £6,000 a year; and at one time, with the Wardenship of the Cinque Ports, it was nearly £4,000 a year more. Macaulay truly says that "the character of Pitt would have stood higher if, with the disinterestedness of Pericles and De Witt, he had united their dignified frugality."

But Pitt by no means stood alone. Lord Melville was as unthrifty in the management of his own affairs, as he was of the money of the public. Fox was an enormous ower, his financial maxim being that a man need never want money if he was willing to pay enough for it. Fox called the outer room at Almack's, where he borrowed on occasions from Jew lenders at exorbitant premiums, his "Jerusalem Chamber." Passion for play was his great vice, and at a very early age it involved him in debt to an enormous amount. It is stated by Gibbon that on one occasion Fox sat playing at hazard for twenty hours in succession, losing £11,000. But deep play was the vice of high life in those days, and cheating was not unknown. Selwyn, alluding to Fox's losses at play, called him Charles the Martyr.

Sheridan was the hero of debt. He lived on it. Though he received large sums of money in one way or another, no one knew what became of it, for he paid nobody. It seemed to melt away in his hands like snow in summer. He spent his first wife's fortune of £1,600 in a six weeks' jaunt to Bath. Necessity drove him to literature, and perhaps to the stimulus of poverty we owe "The Rivals," and the dramas which succeeded it. With his second wife he obtained a fortune of £5,000, and with £15,000 which he realized by the sale of Drury Lane shares, he bought an estate in Surrey, from which he was driven by debt and duns. The remainder of his life was a series of shifts, sometimes brilliant, but oftener degrading, to raise money and evade creditors. Taylor, of the Opera-house, used to say that if he took off his hat to Sheridan in the street, it would cost him fifty pounds; but if he stopped to speak to him, it would cost a hundred.

One of Sheridan's creditors came for his money on horseback." That is a nice mare," said Sheridan. "Do you think so?" "Yes, indeed;—how does she trot?" The creditor, flattered, told him he should see, and immediately put the mare at full trotting pace, on which Sheridan took the opportunity of trotting round the nearest corner. His duns would come in numbers each morning, to catch him before he went out. They were shown into the rooms on each side of the entrance hall. When Sheridan had breakfasted, he would come down, and ask, "Are those doors all shut, John?" and on being assured that they were, he marched out deliberately between them.

He was in debt all round—to his milkman, his grocer, his baker, and his butcher. Sometimes Mrs. Sheridan would be kept waiting for an hour or more while the servants were beating up the neighbourhood for coffee, butter, eggs, and rolls. While Sheridan was Paymaster of the Navy, a butcher one day brought a leg of mutton to the kitchen. The cook took it and clapped it in the pot to boil, and went upstairs for the money; but not returning, the butcher coolly removed the pot lid, took out the mutton, and walked away with it in his tray.[1] Yet, while living in these straits, Sheridan, when invited with his son into the country, usually went in two chaises and four—he in one, and his son Tom following in the other.

The end of all was very sad. For some weeks before his death he was nearly destitute of the means of subsistence. His noble and royal friends had entirely deserted him. Executions for debt were in his house, and he passed his last days in the custody of sheriffs' officers, who abstained from conveying him to prison merely because they were assured that to remove him would cause his immediate death.[2]

---

1. Haydon—Autobiography, vol. ii., p. 104.
2. Memoirs of the Life of Sir S. Romilly, vol. iii., p. 262.

The Cardinal de Retz sold off everything to pay his debts, but he did not recover his liberty. He described the perpetual anguish of the debtor. He even preferred confinement in the Castle of Vincennes, to being exposed to the annoyances of his creditors. Mirabeau's life was one of perpetual debt; for he was a dreadful spendthrift. The only mode by which his father could keep him out of scrapes, was by obtaining a lettre de cachet, and having him safely imprisoned. Though Mirabeau wielded the powers of the State, when he died he was so poor, or had been so extravagant, that he was still indebted to the tailor for his wedding suit.

Lamartine ran through half-a-dozen fortunes, and at the end of his life was "sending round the hat." Lamartine boldly proclaimed that he hated arithmetic, "that negative of every noble thought." He was accordingly driven to very shabby shifts to live. The Cours de Litterature alone brought him in 200,000 francs a year, yet 'the money ran through his hands like quicksilver. His debts are said to have amounted to three millions of francs; yet his style of living remained unchanged. One of his enthusiastic admirers, having stinted himself in subscribing towards the repurchase of the Lamartine estates, went into a fishmonger's one day to purchase a piece of turbot. It was too dear for his means. A distinguished-looking personage entered, paused for a moment before the turbot, and without questioning the price, ordered the fish to be sent to his house. It was M. de Lamartine.

Webster, the American statesman, was afflicted with impecuniosity, arising from his carelessness about money matters, as well as from his extravagance. If we are to believe Theodore Parker, Webster, like Bacon, took bribes. "He contracted debts and did not settle, borrowed and yielded not again. Private money sometimes clove to his hands. . . . A senator of the United States, he was pensioned by the manufacturers of Boston. His later speeches smell of bribes." Monroe and Jefferson were always in want of money, and often in debt; though they were both honest men.

The life which public men lead nowadays, is often an incentive to excessive expenditure. They may be men of moderate means; they may even be poor; but not many of them moving in general society have the moral courage to seem to be so. To maintain their social position, they think it necessary to live as others do. They are thus drawn into the vortex of debt, and into all the troubles, annoyances, shabby shifts, and dishonesties, which debt involves.

Men of science are for the most part exempt from the necessity of shining in society; and hence they furnish but a small number of instances of illustrious debtors. Many of them have been poor, but they have usually lived within their means. Kepler's life was indeed a struggle with poverty and debt; arising principally from the circumstance of his salary, as principal mathematician to the Emperor of Germany, having been always in arrear. This drove him to casting nativities in order to earn a living. "I pass my time," he once wrote, "in begging at the doors of crown treasurers." At his death he left only twenty-two crowns, the dress he wore, two shirts, a few books, and many manuscripts. Leibnitz left behind him a large amount of debt; but this may have been caused by the fact that he was a politician as well as a philosopher, and had frequent occasion to visit foreign courts, and to mix on equal terms with the society of the great.

Spinoza was poor in means; yet inasmuch as what he earned by polishing glasses for the opticians was enough to supply his wants, he incurred no debts. He refused a professorship, and refused a pension, preferring to live and die independent. Dalton had a philosophical disregard for money. When his fellow-townsmen at Manchester once proposed to provide him with an independence, that he might devote the rest of his life to scientific investigation, he declined the offer, saying that "teaching was a kind of recreation to him, and that if richer he would probably not spend more time in his investigations than he was accustomed to do." Faraday's was another instance of moderate means and noble independence. Lagrange was accustomed to attribute his fame and happiness to the poverty of his father, the astronomer royal of Turin. "Had I been rich," he said, "probably I should not have become a mathematician."

The greatest debtor connected with science was John Hunter, who expended all his available means—and they were wholly earned by himself—in accumulating the splendid collection now known as the Hunterian Museum. All that he could collect in fees went to purchase new objects for preparation and dissection, or upon carpenters' and bricklayers' work for the erection of his gallery. Though his family were left in straitened circumstances at his death, the sale of the collection to the nation for £15,000 enabled all his debts to be paid, and at the same time left an enduring monument to his fame.

Great artists have nearly all struggled into celebrity through poverty, and some have never entirely emerged from it. This, however, has been mainly because of their improvidence. Jan Steen was always in distress, arising principally from the habit he had acquired of drinking his own beer; for he was first a brewer, and afterwards a tavern-keeper. He drank and painted alternately, sometimes transferring the drinking scenes of which he had been a witness to the canvas, even while himself in a state of intoxication. He died in debt, after which his pictures rose in value, until now they are worth their weight in gold.

Notwithstanding the large income of Vandyck, his style of living was so splendid and costly as to involve him in heavy debt. To repair his fortunes, he studied alchemy for a time, in the hope of discovering the philosopher's stone. But towards the end of his life he was enabled to retrieve his position, and to leave a comfortable competency to his widow. Rembrandt, on the other hand, involved himself in debt through his love of art. He was an insatiable collector of drawings, armour, and articles of vertu, and thus became involved in such difficulties that he was declared a bankrupt. His property remained under legal control for thirteen years, until his death.

The great Italian artists were for the most part temperate and moderate men, and lived within their means. Haydon, in his Autobiography, says, "Rafaelle, Michael Angelo, Zeuxis, Apelles, Rubens, Reynolds, Titian, were rich and happy. Why? Because with their genius they combined practical prudence." Haydon himself was an instance of the contrary practice. His life was a prolonged struggle with difficulty and debt. He was no sooner free from one obligation, than he was involved in another. His "Mock Election" was painted in the King's Bench prison, while he lay there for debt. There is a strange entry in his Journal: "I borrowed £10 today of my butterman, Webb, an old pupil of mine, recommended to me by Sir George Beaumont twenty-four years ago, but who wisely, after drawing hands, set up a butter shop, and was enabled to send his old master £10 in his necessity." Haydon's Autobiography is full of his contests with lawyers and sheriffs' officers. Creditors dogged and dunned him at every step. "Lazarus's head," he writes, "was painted just after an arrest; Eucles was finished from a man in possession; the beautiful face in Xenophon in the afternoon, after a morning spent in begging mercy of lawyers; and Cassandra's head was finished in agony not to be described, and her hand completed after a broker's man in possession, in an execution put in for taxes."[3]

Cowper used to say that he never knew a poet who was not thriftless; and he included himself. Notwithstanding his quiet, retired life, he was constantly outrunning the constable. "By the help of good management,"

---

3. Haydon—Autobiography, vol. ii., p. 400.

he once wrote, "and a clear notion of economical matters, I contrived in three months to spend the income of a twelvemonth." But though the number of thriftless poets may be great, it must not be forgotten that Shakespeare, who stands at the head of the list, was a prudent man. He economized his means, and left his family in comfort. His contemporaries were, however, for the most part indebted men. Ben Jonson was often embarrassed, and always poor, borrowing twenty shillings at a time from Henslowe; though he rarely denied himself another jolly night at the "Mermaid." Massinger was often so reduced in circumstances as not to be able to pay his score at the same tavern.

Greene, Peele, and Marlowe lived lives of dissipation, and died in poverty. Marlowe was killed in a drunken brawl. When Greene was on his deathbed, dying of the disease which his excesses had caused, he was haunted by the debt of ten pounds which he owed to the shoemaker who had lodged him. He then warned his friend Peele to amend his ways; but Peele, like him, died in distress and debt, one of the last letters he wrote being an imploring letter to Burleigh asking for relief,—"Long sickness," said he, "having so enfeebled me as maketh bashfulness almost impudency." Spenser died forsaken, and in want. Ben Jonson says of him that "he died for lack of bread in King Street, and refused twenty broad pieces sent to him by my lord of Essex," adding, "he was sorrie he had no time to spend them."

Of later poets and literary men, Milton died in obscurity, though not in debt. Lovelace died in a cellar. Butler, the author of "Hudibras," died of starvation in Rose Alley, the same place in which Dryden was beaten by hired ruffians. Otway was hunted by bailiffs to his last hiding-place on Tower Hill. His last act was to beg a shilling of a gentleman, who gave him a guinea; and buying a loaf to appease his hunger, he choked at the first mouthful. Wycherley lay seven years in gaol for debt, but lived to die in his bed at nearly eighty. Fielding's extravagance and dissipation in early life involved him in difficulties which he never entirely shook off, and his death was embittered by the poverty in which he left his widow and child in a foreign land.

Savage had a pension of fifty pounds a year, which he usually spent in a few days. It was then fashionable to wear scarlet cloaks trimmed with gold lace; and Johnson one day met him, just after he had got his pension, with one of these cloaks upon his back, while, at the same time, his naked toes were sticking through his shoes. After living a life of recklessness and dissipation, he died in prison, where he had lain six months for debt. In concluding his "Life of Savage," Johnson says: "This relation will not be wholly without its use, if those who, in confidence of superior capacities or attainments, disregard the common maxims of life, shall be reminded that nothing will supply the want of prudence, and that negligence and irregularity, long continued, will make knowledge useless, wit ridiculous, and genius contemptible."

Sterne died poor, if he did not die insolvent. At his death, a subscription was got up for the support of his wife and daughter. Churchill was imprisoned for debt, occasioned by his dissoluteness and extravagance,—Cowper characterizing him as "spendthrift alike of money and of wit." Chatterton, reduced to a state of starvation and despair, poisoned himself in his eighteenth year. Sir Richard Steele was rarely out of debt. In many respects he resembled Sheridan in temperament and character. He was full of speculation, and was always on the point of some grand stroke of luck, which was to make his fortune. He was perpetually haunted by duns and bailiffs; yet he did not stint himself of luxuries so long as he obtained credit. When appointed to the office of Commissioner of Stamps, with a moderate income, he set up a carriage with two and sometimes four horses; and he maintained two houses, one in London, the other at Hampton. His means being altogether inadequate to this style of living, he soon became drowned in greater debt than before. He was repeatedly impounded by lawyers, and locked up in sponging-houses. Executions were put into his houses; his furniture was sold off; his wife wanted the commonest necessaries of life; and still the pleasure-loving Steele maintained his equanimity and good temper. Something great was always on the point of turning up in his favour. One of his grandest schemes was that for bringing fish alive to the London market; "and then," said he to his wife, "you will be better provided for than any lady in England." But the good turn never came to Sir Richard; and he died out at elbows on his wife's little property in Wales.

Goldsmith was another of the happy-go-lucky debtors. He swam in debt. He was no sooner out of it, than he was plunged into it again, deeper than before. The first money he earned as a tutor—it was all the money he had—was spent in buying a horse. His relations raised £50, and sent him to the Temple to study law, but he got no farther than Dublin, where he spent or gambled away all the money. Then he went to Edinburgh to study medicine, and was forced to fly from it, having become surety for a friend. He started on the tour of Europe without any money in his pocket—with nothing but his flute; and he begged and played, until he came back to England, as poor as he went. He himself used afterwards to say that there was hardly a kingdom in Europe in which he was not a debtor.[4]

Even when Goldsmith began to earn money freely, he was still in debt. He gave away with one hand what he earned with the other. He was dunned for his milk-score, arrested for rent, threatened by lawyers, but never learnt the wisdom of economy. In the same month in which the second edition of his "Vicar of Wakefield" was published, his bill of fifteen guineas, drawn on Newbery, was returned dishonoured. When he was figuring at Boswell's dinner in Old Bond Street in the "ratteen suit lined with satin, and bloom-coloured silk breeches," the clothes belonged to his tailor, and remained unpaid till his death.

Prosperity increased his difficulties rather than diminished them; the more money he had, the more thoughtless and lavish was his expenditure. He could refuse no indulgence, either to himself or others. He would borrow a guinea and give it to a beggar. He would give the clothes off his back, and the blankets off his bed. He could refuse nobody. To meet his thoughtless expenditure, he raised money by promising to write books which he never began. He was perpetually discounting tomorrow, and mortgaging an estate already overburthened. Thus he died, as he had begun, poor, embarrassed, and in debt. At his death he owed over two thousand pounds: "Was ever poet," says Johnson, "so trusted before?"

The case of Goldsmith and others has been cited as instances of the harsh treatment of genius by the world, and in proof of the social disabilities of literary men and artists. It has been held that society should be more indulgent to its men of genius, and that Government should do something more for them than it now does. But nothing that society or Government could do for men of genius would be likely to prove of any service to them, unless they will do what other and less gifted men do,—exhibit self-respect and practise ordinary economy. We may pity poor Goldsmith, but we cannot fail to see that he was throughout his own enemy. His gains were large, amounting to about £8,000 in fourteen years; representing a much larger sum of money at the present day. For his "History of the Earth and Animated Nature" he received £850,—and the book was, at best, but a clever compilation. Johnson said of him that "if he can tell a horse from a cow, that is the extent of his knowledge of zoology." The representation of his "Good-natured Man" produced

---

4. Forster—Life of Goldsmith, ed. 1863, p. 41.

him £500. And so on with his other works. He was as successful as Johnson was; but then he had not Johnson's sobriety, self-restraint, and self-respect.

Yet Goldsmith, in his thoughtful moments, knew the right path, though he had not the courage to pursue it. In a letter to his brother Henry respecting the career of his son, Goldsmith wrote: "Teach, my dear sir, to your son, thrift and economy. Let his poor wandering uncle's example be placed before his eyes. I had learned from books to be disinterested and generous before I was taught from experience the necessity of being prudent. I had contracted the habits and notions of a philosopher, while I was exposing myself to the insidious approaches of cunning; and often by being, even with my narrow finances, charitable to excess, I forgot the rules of justice, and placed myself in the very situation of the wretch who thanked me for my bounty."

Byron had scarcely reached manhood when he became involved in debt. Writing to Mr. Becher, in his twentieth year, he said, "Entre nous, I am cursedly dipped; my debts, everything inclusive, will be nine or ten thousand before I am twenty-one." On his coming of age, the festivities at Newstead were celebrated by means supplied by money-lenders at enormously usurious rates of interest. His difficulties did not diminish, but only increased with time. It is said that his mother's death was occasioned by a fit of rage, brought on by reading the upholsterer's bills.[5] When the first canto of "Childe Harold" was published, Byron presented the copyright to Mr. Dallas, declaring that he would never receive money for his writings,—a resolution which he afterwards wisely abandoned. But his earnings by literature at that time could not have lightened the heavy load of debt under which he staggered. Newstead was sold, and still the load accumulated. Then he married, probably in the expectation that his wife's fortune would release him; but her money was locked up, and the step, instead of relieving him, brought only an accession of misery. Every one knows the sad result of the union; which was aggravated by the increasing assaults of duns and sheriffs' officers.

Byron was almost driven to sell the copyright of his books, but he was prevented from doing so by his publisher, who pressed upon him a sum of money to meet his temporary wants. During the first year of his marriage, his house was nine times in the possession of bailiffs, his door was almost daily beset by duns, and he was only saved from gaol by the

---

5. Moore—Life of Byron, ed. 1860. p. 127.

privileges of his rank. All this, to a sensitive nature such as his, must have been gall and bitterness; while his wife's separation from him, which shortly followed, could not fail to push him almost to the point of frenzy. Although he had declined to receive money for his first poems, Byron altered his views, and even learnt to drive a pretty hard bargain with his publisher.[6] But Moore does not, in his biography of the poet, inform us whether he ever got rid, except by death, of his grievous turmoil of debt.

There is the greatest difference in the manner in which men bear the burden of debt. Some feel it to be no burden at all; others bear it very lightly; whilst others look upon creditors in the light of persecutors, and themselves in the light of martyrs. But where the moral sense is a little more keen,—where men use the goods of others, without rendering the due equivalent of money—where they wear unpaid clothes, eat unpaid meat, drink unpaid wines, and entertain guests at the expense of the butcher, grocer, wine-merchant, and greengrocer,—they must necessarily feel that their conduct is of the essence, not only of shabbiness, but of dishonesty, and the burden must then bear very heavily indeed.

Of light-hearted debtors, the proportion is considerable. Thus Theophilus Cibber, when drowned in debt, begged the loan of a guinea, and spent it on a dish of ortolans. Thus Foote when his mother wrote to him—"Dear Sam, I am in prison for debt—come and help your loving mother,"—replied, "Dear Mother, so am I, which prevents his duty being paid to his loving mother by her affectionate son." Steele and Sheridan both bore the load lightly. When entertaining company, they put the bailiffs who were in possession in livery, and made them wait at table, passing them off as servants. Nothing disturbed Steele's equanimity; and when driven from London by debt, he carried his generosity into the country, giving prizes to the lads and lasses assembled at rural games and country dances. Sheridan also made very light of his debts, and had many a good joke over them. Some one asked him how it was that the O' was not prefixed to his name, when he replied that he was sure no family had a better right to it, "for in truth, we owe everybody." And when a creditor once apologized for the soiled and tattered state of a bill, which

---

6. "You offer 1,500 guineas for the new Canto [the fourth of 'Childe Harold']: I won't take it. I ask two thousand five hundred guineas for it, which you will either give or not as you think proper. . . . If Mr. Eustace was to have two thousand for a poem on Education; if Mr. Moore is to have three thousand for Lalla; if Mr. Campbell is to have three thousand for his prose or poetry.—I don't mean to disparage these gentlemen or their labours.—but I ask the aforesaid price for mine."—Lord Byron to Mr. Murray, Sept. 4th, 1817.

had been much worn by being so often presented, Sheridan advised him "as a friend, to take it home and write it upon parchment."

Very different was it in the case of poor Burns, who was almost driven distracted because he owed a debt of £7 4s. for a volunteer's uniform, which he could not pay. He sent to his friend Thomson, the publisher of his songs, imploring the loan of £5, promising full value in "song-genius."[7] His last poem was a "love song," in part payment of the loan, which he composed only a few days before his death.

Sydney Smith had a severe struggle with poverty in the early part of his life. He had a poor living, a wide parish, and a large family. His daughter says that his debts occasioned him many sleepless nights, and that she has seen him in an evening, when bill after bill has poured in (carefully examining them, and gradually paying them off), quite overcome by the feeling of the debt hanging over him, cover his face with his hands, and exclaim, "Ah! I see I shall end my old age in a gaol."[8] But he bore up bravely under the burden, labouring onward with a cheerful heart, eking out his slender means by writing articles for the Edinburgh, until at length promotion reached him, and he reaped the reward of his perseverance, his industry, and his independence.

De Foe's life was a long battle with difficulty and debt. He was constantly involved in broils, mostly of his own stirring up. He was a fierce pamphleteer from his youth up; and was never for a moment at rest, He was by turns a soldier with the Duke of Monmouth, a pantile maker, a projector, a poet, a political agent, a novelist, an essayist, a historian. He was familiar with the pillory, and spent much of his time in gaol. When reproached by one of his adversaries with mercenariness, he piteously declared how he had, "in the pursuit of peace, brought himself into innumerable broils;" how he had been "sued for other men's debts, and stripped naked by public opinion, of what should have enabled him to pay his own;" how, "with a numerous family, and with no helps but his own industry, he had forced his way, with undiscouraged diligence,

---

7. "After all my boasted independence," he said, "curst necessity compels me to implore you for five pounds. A cruel scoundrel of a haberdasher, to whom I owe an account, taking it into his head that I am dying, has commenced a process, and will infallibly put me in jail. Do, for God's sake, send me that sum, and by return of post. Forgive me this earnestness; but the horrors of a jail have made me half distracted. I do not ask all this gratuitously: for upon returning health I promise and engage to furnish you with five pounds' worth of the neatest song-genius you have seen."—Burns to Thomson. 12th July, 1796. Burns died on the 21st of the same month.

8. Lady Holland—Memoir of the Rev. Sydney Smith, vol. i, p. 206.

through a sea of debt and misfortune," and "in gaols, in retreats, and in all manner of extremities, supported himself without the assistance of friends and relations." Surely, there never was such a life of struggle and of difficulty as that of the indefatigable De Foe. Yet all his literary labours, and they were enormous, did not suffice to keep him clear of debt, for it is believed that he died insolvent.[9]

Southey was, in his own line, almost as laborious a writer as De Foe; though his was the closet life of the student, and not the aggressive life of the polemic. Though he knew debt, it never became his master; and from an early period in his career, he determined not to contract a debt that he was not able to discharge. He was not only enabled to do this, but to help his friends liberally—maintaining for a time the families of his brothers-in-law, Coleridge and Lovell—by simply not allowing himself any indulgences beyond his actual means, though these were often very straitened. The burthen he carried would have borne down a man less brave and resolute; but he worked, and studied, and wrote, and earned money enough for all his own wants, as well as the wants of those who had become dependent upon him. He held on his noble way without a murmur or complaint. He not only liberally helped his relatives, but his old schoolfellows, in distress. He took Coleridge's wife and family to live with him, at a time when Coleridge had abandoned himself to opium-drinking. To meet the numerous claims upon him, Southey merely imposed upon himself so much extra labour. He was always ready with good advice to young men who sought his help. Thus he encouraged Kirke White, Herbert Knowles, and Dusantoy, all of whom died young and full of promise. He not only helped them with advice and encouragement, but with money; and his timely assistance rescued the sister of Chatterton from absolute want. And thus he worked on nobly and unselfishly to the last—finding happiness and joy in the pursuit of letters—"not so learned as poor, not so poor as proud, not so proud as happy." These were his own words.

The most touching story in Sir Walter Scott's life, is the manner in which he conducted himself after the failure of the publishing house of Constable and Co., with which he had become deeply involved. He had built Abbotsford, become a laird, was sheriff of his county, and thought himself a rich man; when suddenly the Constable firm broke down, and he found himself indebted to the world more than a hundred thousand

---

9. George Chalmers—Life of De Foe, p. 92.

pounds. "It is very hard," he said, when the untoward news reached him, "thus to lose all the labour of a lifetime, and to be made a poor man at last. But if God grant me health and strength for a few years longer, I have no doubt that I shall redeem it all." Everybody thought him a ruined man, and he almost felt himself to be so. But his courage never gave way. When his creditors proposed to him a composition, his sense of honour forbade his listening to them. "No, gentlemen," he replied; "Time and I against any two." Though the debts had been contracted by others, he had made himself legally responsible for them; and, strong in his principle of integrity, he determined, if he could, to pay them off to the last farthing. And he set himself to do it: but it cost him his life.

He parted with his town house and furniture, delivered over his personal effects to be held in trust for his creditors, and bound himself to discharge a certain amount of his liabilities annually. This he did by undertaking new literary works, some of them of great magnitude, the execution of which, though they enabled him to discharge a large portion of his debt, added but little to his reputation. One of his first tasks was his "Life of Napoleon Buonaparte," in nine volumes, which he wrote, in the midst of pain, sorrow, and ruin, in about thirteen months,—receiving for it about fourteen thousand pounds. Even though struck by paralysis, he went on writing until in about four years he had discharged about two-thirds of the debt for which he was responsible,—an achievement probably unparalleled in the history of letters.

The sacrifices and efforts which he made during the last few years of his life, even while paralyzed and scarcely able to hold his pen, exhibit Scott in a truly heroic light. He bore up with unconquerable spirit to the last. When his doctor expostulated with him against his excessive brain-work, he replied, "If I were to be idle, I should go mad: in comparison to this, death is no risk to shrink from." Shortly before his last fatal attack, when sitting dozing in his chair on the grass in front of the house at Abbotsford, he suddenly roused himself, threw off the plaids which covered him, and exclaimed, "This is sad idleness. Take me to my own room, and fetch the keys of my desk." They wheeled him into his study, and put pens and paper before him. But he could not grasp the pen; he could not write; and the tears rolled down his cheeks. His spirit was not conquered, but his bodily powers were exhausted and shattered; and when at length he died, he fell asleep—like a child.

Scott felt, what every sensitive nature must feel, that poverty is a much lighter burden to bear than debt. There is nothing ignominious about poverty. It may even serve as a healthy stimulus to great spirits. "Under gold mountains and thrones," said Jean Paul, "lie buried many spiritual giants." Richter even held that poverty was to be welcomed, so that it came not too late in life. And doubtless Scott's burden was all the heavier to bear, because it came upon him in his declining years.

Shakespeare was originally a poor man: "It is a question," says Carlyle, "whether, had not want, discomfort, and distress warrants been busy at Stratford-on-Avon, Shakespeare had not lived killing calves or combing wool! "To Milton's and Dryden's narrow means we probably owe the best part of their works.

Johnson was a very poor man, and a very brave one. He never knew what wealth was. His mind was always greater than his fortune; and it is the mind that makes the man rich or poor, happy or miserable. Johnson's gruff and bluff exterior covered a manly and noble nature. He had early known poverty and debt, and wished himself clear of both. When at college, his feet appeared through his shoes, but he was too poor to buy new ones. His head was full of learning, but his pockets were empty. How he struggled through distress and difficulty during his first years in London the reader can learn from his "Life." He bedded and boarded for fourpence-halfpenny a day, and when too poor to pay for a bed, he wandered with Savage whole nights in the streets.[10] He struggled on manfully, never whining at his lot, but trying to make the best of it.

These early sorrows and struggles of Johnson left their scars upon his nature; but they also enlarged and enriched his experience, as well as widened his range of human sympathy. Even when in his greatest distress he had room in his heart for others whose necessities were greater than his own; and he was never wanting in his help to those who needed it, or were poorer than himself.

From his sad experience, no one could speak with greater authority on the subject of debt than Johnson. "Do not accustom yourself," he wrote to Boswell, "to consider debt only an inconvenience; you will find it a calamity. Let it be your first care not to be in any man's debt. Whatever you have, spend less. Frugality is not only the basis of quiet, but of

---

10. "He said a man might live in a garret at eighteen-pence a week; few people would inquire where he lodged; and if they did, it was easy to say, 'Sir, I am to be found at such a place.' By spending threepence in a coffee house, he might be for some hours every day in very good company; he might dine for sixpence, breakfast on bread and milk for a penny, and do without supper. On clean-shirt day he went abroad and paid visits." BOSWELL—Life of Johnson.

beneficence." To Simpson, the barrister, he wrote, "Small debts are like small shot; they are rattling on every side, and can scarcely be escaped without a wound: great debts are like cannon, of loud noise, but little danger. You must therefore be enabled to discharge petty debts, that you may have leisure, with security to struggle with the rest." "Sir," said he to the patient and receptive Boswell, "get as much peace of mind as you can, and keep within your income, and you won't go far wrong."

Men who live by their wits, their talents, or their genius, have, somehow or other, acquired the character of being improvident. Charles Nodier, writing about a distinguished genius, said of him—"In the life of intelligence and art, he was an angel; in the common practical life of every day, he was a child." The same might be said of many great writers and artists. The greatest of them have been so devoted—heart and soul—to their special work, that they have not cared to think how the efforts of their genius might be converted into pounds, shillings, and pence. Had they placed the money consideration first, probably the world would not have inherited the products of their genius. Milton would not have laboured for so many years at his "Paradise Lost," merely for the sake of the five pounds for which he sold the first edition to the publisher. Nor would Schiller have gone on toiling for twenty years up to the topmost pinnacles of thought, merely for the sake of the bare means of living which he earned by his work.

At the same time, men of genius should not disregard the common rules of arithmetic. If they spend more than they earn, they will run into debt. Nor will complaining of the harshness of the world keep them out of it. They have to stand or fall on their merits as men, and if they are not provident they will suffer the same consequences as others. Thackeray, in painting the character of Captain Shandon, in his "Pendennis," gave considerable offence to the literary profession; yet he only spoke the truth. "If a lawyer," said he, "or a soldier, or a parson, outruns his income, and does not pay his bills, he must go to gaol; and an author must go too."

Literary men are not neglected because they are literary men. But they have no right to expect that society will overlook their social offences because they are literary men. It is necessary for the world's sake, as well as for their own sake, that literary men and artists should take care to "provide against the evil day" like other people. "Imagination and art," says Madame de Staël, "have need to look after their own comfort and happiness in this world." The world ought to help them generously; all good men ought to help them; but what is better than all, they ought to help themselves.

Chapter 14

Riches and Charity

"Who—who—who's here I, Robert of Doncaster. That I spent, that I had; That I gave, that I have; That I left, that I lost." Epitaph, a.d. 1579.

"If thou art rich, thou art poor; for, like an ass, whose back with ingots bows, thou bear'st thy heavy riches but a journey and death unloads thee."—Shakespeare.

"Il est bon d'être charitable, mais envers qui? C'est là le point."["It is good to be charitable, but to whom? That's the point."]—La Fontaine.

"There are many idlers to whom a penny begged is sweeter than a shilling earned."—Douglas Jerrold.

"He stole a pig, and in God's name gave the trotters to the poor."—From the Spanish.

Man must be thrifty in order to be generous. Thrift does not end with itself, but extends its benefits to others. It founds hospitals, endows charities, establishes colleges, and extends educational influences. Benevolence springs from the best qualities of the mind and heart. Its divine spirit elevates the benefactors of the world—the Howards, Clarksons, and Naviers—to the highest pedestals of moral genius and of national worship.

The same feeling pervades our common humanity. The poorest man, the daily worker, the obscurest individual, shares the gift and the blessing of doing good—a blessing that imparts no less delight to him who gives than to him who receives.

"Man is dear to man; the poorest poor Long for some moments, in a weary life, When they can know and feel that they have been Themselves the fathers and the dealers-out Of some small blessings; have been kind to such As needed kindness, for this single cause, That we have all of us one human heart."

The duty of helping the helpless is one that speaks trumpet-tongued; but especially to those who profess love to God and goodwill to men. It is a duty that belongs to men as individuals, and as members of the social body. As individuals, because we are enjoined to help the widow and the fatherless in their affliction; and as members of the social body, because society claims of every man that he shall be a helper in the cause of progress and of social well-being.

It is not necessary that men should be rich, to be helpful to others. John Pounds was not a rich man; yet by his influence Ragged Schools were established. He was temperate, and saved enough from his earnings to buy food for his pupils. He attracted them by his kindness, sometimes by a "hot potato;" he taught them, and sent them out into the world, fortified by his good example, to work in it, and do their duty towards it. Nor was Robert Raikes, the founder of Sunday and other schools, a rich man; neither was Thomas Wright, the prison philanthropist. Nor were St. Vincent de Paul and Father Mathew—the promoters of education and temperance. Nor were the great men of science—Newton, Watt, and Faraday; nor the great missionaries—Xavier, Martyn, Carey, and Livingstone.

A fine instance of gentleness and generosity is recorded in Walton's memoir of Dr. Donne. When the latter, long straitened in his means, had entered upon the Deanery of St. Paul's, and was thereby provided with an income more than sufficient for all his wants, he felt that those means had been entrusted to him, for good uses, and to employ for human help and to the glory of the Giver thereof. At the foot of a private account, "to which God and His angels only were witnesses with him," Dr. Donne computed first his revenue, then what was given to the poor and other pious uses, and lastly, what rested for him and his; and having done that, he then blessed each year's poor remainder with a thankful prayer.

Dr. Donne did most of his good in secret, letting not his right hand know what his left hand did. He redeemed many poor from prison; helped many a poor scholar; and employed a trusty servant or a discreet friend to distribute his bounty where it was most needed. A friend whom he had known in days of affluence, having by a too liberal heart and carelessness become decayed in his estate and reduced to poverty, Donne sent him a hundred pounds. But the decayed gentleman returned it with thanks, saying that he wanted it not;—for, says Walton, in narrating the event, "as there be some spirits so generous as to labour to conceal and endure a sad poverty, rather than expose themselves to those blushes that attend the confession of it, so there be others to whom nature and grace have afforded such sweet and compassionate souls as to pity and prevent the distresses of mankind; which I have mentioned because of Dr. Donne's reply, whose answer was, 'I know you want not what will sustain nature, for a little will do that; but my desire is that you, who in the days of your plenty have cheered and raised the hearts of so many of your dejected friends, would now receive this from me, and use it as a cordial for the cheering of your own;'"—and upon these terms it was received.

The truth is, that we very much exaggerate the power of riches. Immense subscriptions are got up for the purpose of reforming men from their sinful courses, and turning them from evil to good. And yet subscriptions will not do it. It is character that can do the work; money never can. Great changes in society can never be effected through riches. To turn men from intemperance, improvidence, and irreligion, and to induce them to seek their happiness in the pursuit of proper and noble objects, requires earnest purpose, honest self-devotion, and hard work. Money may help in many respects; but money by itself can do nothing. The apostle Paul planted the knowledge of the Christian religion over half the Roman empire; yet he supported himself by tent-making, and not by collecting subscriptions. Men of anxious, earnest, honest hearts, are far more wanted than rich men—willing to give money in charity.

Nothing is so much over-estimated as the power of money. All the people who are looking out for front seats in "society," think it the one thing needful. They may be purse-liberal, but they are also purse-proud. The hypocritical professions of some people, with a view to elicit the good opinion of others, in the teeth of their daily life and practice, is nothing short of disgusting. "Oh, Geordie, jingling Geordie," said King James, in the novel, "it was grand to hear Baby Charles laying down the guilt of dissimulation, and Steenie lecturing on the turpitude of incontinence!"

Some people have an idolatrous worship of money. The Israelites had their golden Calf; the Greeks had their golden Jupiter. Old Bounderby valued the man who was worth a "hundred thousand pounds." Others do the same. The lowest human nature loves money, possessions, value. "What is he worth?" "What is his income?" are the usual questions. If you say, "There is a thoroughly good, benevolent, virtuous man!" nobody will notice him. But if you say, "There is a man worth a million of money," he will be stared at till out of sight. A crowd of people used to collect at Hyde Park Corner to see a rich man pass. "Here comes old Crockie!" and the crowd would separate to allow him to pass, amidst whispers of admiration. It was old Crockford, who made a large fortune by keeping a gambling-house.

"The very sound of millions," says Mrs. Gore,[1] "tickles the ear of an Englishman! He loves it so much, indeed, that it all but reconciles him to the National Debt; and when applied to private proprietorship, it secures deference for lowness of mind, birth, habits, and pursuits. . . . Ambition and money-love, if they tend to ennoble a country, reduce to insignificance the human particles of which the nation is composed. In their pursuit of riches, the English are gradually losing sight of higher characteristics; . . . our pursuit of railway bubbles and every other frantic speculation of the hour, affords sufficient evidence of the craving after capital superseding every better aspiration, whether for this world or the next."

The love of gold threatens to drive everything before it. The pursuit of money has become the settled custom of the country. Many are so absorbed by it, that every other kind of well-being is either lost sight of, or altogether undervalued. And then the lovers of money think to recover their moral tone by bestowing charity! Mountains of gold weigh heavily upon the heart and soul. The man who can withstand the weight of riches, and still be diligent, industrious, and strong in mind and heart, must be made of strong stuff. For, people who are rich, are almost invariably disposed to be idle, luxurious, and self-indulgent.

"If money," said the Rev. Mr. Griffiths, Rector of Merthyr, "did not make men forget men, one-half of the evil that is in the world would never occur. If masters drew nearer to the men, and men were permitted to draw nearer their masters, we should not be passing through this fiery ordeal. Let them do something to win the men out of the public-houses; let them spare more of their enormous gains to build places of amusement and recreation for the people; let them provide better houses to live in, better conveniences for decency, better streets; and if all these

---

1. Introduction to "Men of Capital."

things are done we shall have neither lock-outs nor strikes. We hear with pomp and triumph of the millions and millions that have been dug out of this old Welsh land of ours, but we hear nothing—and we see, indeed, less—of the public buildings, the people's parks, the public libraries and public institutions, and other civilizing agencies. Fifteen months ago, when we were in the highest tide of prosperity, I said all this, and no notice was taken of it. Why should any notice be taken of a preaching parson or a Christian minister of any kind, when sovereigns fly about like snowflakes in winter, or may be gathered like blackberries in summer?"[2]

Men go on toiling and moiling, eager to be richer; desperately struggling, as if against poverty, at the same time that they are surrounded with abundance. They scrape and scrape, add shilling to shilling, and sometimes do shabby things in order to make a little more profit; though they may have accumulated far more than they can actually enjoy. And still they go on, worrying themselves incessantly in the endeavour to grasp at an additional increase of superfluity. Perhaps such men have not enjoyed the advantages of education in early life. They have no literary pleasures to fall back upon; they have no taste for books; sometimes they can scarcely write their own names. They have nothing to think of but money,—and of what will make money. They have no faith, but in riches! They keep their children under restriction and bring them up with a servile education.

At length, an accumulation of money comes into the children's hands. They have before been restricted in their expenditure; now they become lavish. They have been educated in no better tastes. They spend extravagantly. They will not be drudges in business as their father was. They will be "gentlemen," and spend their money "like gentlemen." And very soon the money takes wings and flies away. Many are the instances in which families have been raised to wealth in the first generation, launched into ruinous expense in the second, and disappeared in the third,—being again reduced to poverty. Hence the Lancashire proverb, "Twice clogs, once boots." The first man wore clogs, and accumulated a "a power o' money;" his rich son spent it; and the third generation took up the clogs again. A candidate for parliamentary honours, when speaking from the hustings, was asked if he had plenty brass. "Plenty brass?" said he; "ay, I've lots o' brass!—I stink o' brass!"

The same social transformations are known in Scotland. The proverb there is, "The grandsire digs, the father bigs, the son thigs,"[3]—that is,

---

2. Sermon preached at Merthyr during the South Wales strike.
3. Dublin University Magazine.

the grandfather worked hard and made a fortune, the father built a fine house, and the son, "an unthrifty son of Linne," when land and goods were gone and spent, took to thieving. Merchants are sometimes princes today and beggars tomorrow; and so long as the genius for speculation is exercised by a mercantile family, the talent which gave them landed property may eventually deprive them of it.

To be happy in old age—at a time when men should leave for ever the toil, anxiety, and worry of money-making—they must, during youth and middle life, have kept their minds healthily active. They must familiarize themselves with knowledge, and take an interest in all that has been done, and is doing, to make the world wiser and better from age to age. There is enough leisure in most men's lives to enable them to interest themselves in biography and history. They may also acquire considerable knowledge of science, or of some ennobling pursuit different from that by which money is made. Mere amusement will not do. No man can grow happy upon amusement. The mere man of pleasure is a miserable creature,—especially in old age. The mere drudge in business is little better. Whereas the study of literature, philosophy, and science is full of tranquil pleasure, down to the end of life. If the rich old man has no enjoyment apart from money-making, his old age becomes miserable. He goes on grinding and grinding in the same rut, perhaps growing richer and richer. What matters it? He cannot eat his gold. He cannot spend it. His money, instead of being beneficial to him, becomes a curse. He is the slave of avarice, the meanest of sins. He is spoken of as a despicable creature. He becomes base, even in his own estimation.

What a miserable end was that of the rich man who, when dying, found no comfort save in plunging his hands into a pile of new sovereigns, which had been brought to him from the bank. As the world faded from him, he still clutched them; handled and fondled them one by one,—and then he passed away,—his last effort being to finger his gold! Elwes the miser died shrieking, "I will keep my money!—nobody shall deprive me of my property!" A ghastly and humiliating spectacle!

Rich men are more punished for their excess of economy, than poor men are for their want of it. They become miserly, think themselves daily growing poorer, and die the deaths of beggars. We have known several instances. One of the richest merchants in London, after living for some time in penury, went down into the country, to the parish where he was born, and applied to the overseers for poor's relief. Though possessing millions, he was horror-struck by the fear of becoming poor. Relief was granted him, and he positively died the death of a pauper. One of the richest merchants in the North died in the receipt of poor's relief. Of course, all that the parish authorities had doled out to these poor-rich men was duly repaid by their executors.

And what did these rich persons leave behind them? Only the reputation that they had died rich men. But riches do not constitute any claim to distinction. It is only the vulgar who admire riches as riches. Money is a drug in the market. Some of the most wealthy men living are mere nobodies. Many of them are comparatively ignorant. They are of no moral or social account. A short time since, a list was published of two hundred and twenty-four English millionaires. Some were known as screws; some were "smart men" in regard to speculations; some were large navvies, coal-miners, and manufacturers; some were almost unknown beyond their own local circle; some were very poor creatures; very few were men of distinction. All that one could say of them was, that they died rich men.

"All the rich and all the covetous men in the world," said Jeremy Taylor, "will perceive, and all the world will perceive for them, that it is but an ill recompense for all their cares, that by this time all that shall be left will be this, that the neighbours shall say, He died a rich man: and yet his wealth will not profit him in the grave, but hugely swell the sad accounts of his doomsday."

"One of the chief causes," says Mrs. Gore, "which render the pursuit of wealth a bitterer as well as more pardonable struggle in England than on the Continent, is the unequal and capricious distribution of family property. . . . Country gentlemen and professional men,—nay, men without the pretension of being gentlemen,—are scarcely less smitten with the mania of creating 'an eldest son' to the exclusion and degradation of their younger children; and by the individuals thus defrauded by their nearest and dearest, is the idolatry of Mammon pursued without the least regard to self-respect, or the rights of their fellow-creatures. Injured, they injure in their turn. Their days are devoted to a campaign for the recovery of their birthright. Interested marriages, shabby bargains, and political jobbery, may be traced to the vile system of things which converts the elder son into a Dives, and makes a Lazarus of his brother."

But democrats have quite as great a love for riches as aristocrats; and many austere republicans are eager to be millionaires. Forms of government do not influence the desire for wealth. The elder Cato was a usurer. One of his means of making money was by buying young half-fed slaves at a low price; then, by fattening them up, and training them to work, he sold them at an enhanced price. Brutus, when in the Isle of Cyprus, lent his money at forty-eight per cent. interest,[4] and no one thought the worse of him for his Usury. Washington, the hero of American freedom, bequeathed his slaves to his wife. It did not occur to him to give them their liberty. Municipal jobbery is not unknown in New York; and its influential citizens are said to be steeped to the lips in political corruption. Mr. Mills says, that the people of the North-Eastern States have apparently got rid of all social injustices and inequalities; that the proportion of population to capital and land is such as to ensure abundance for every able-bodied man; that they enjoy the six points of the Charter, and need never complain of poverty. Yet "all that these advantages have done for them is, that the life of the whole of our sex is devoted to dollar-hunting; and of the other, to breeding dollar-hunters. This," Mr. Mill adds, "is not a kind of social perfection which philanthropists to come will feel any very eager desire to assist in realizing."[5]

Saladin the Great conquered Syria, Arabia, Persia, and Mesopotamia. He was the greatest warrior and conqueror of his time. His power and wealth were enormous. Yet he was fully persuaded of the utter hollowness of riches. He ordered, by his will, that considerable sums should be distributed to Mussulmans, Jews, and Christians, in order that the priests of the three religions might implore for him the mercy of God. He commanded that the shirt or tunic which he wore at the time of his death should be carried on the end of a spear throughout the whole camp and at the head of his army, and that the soldier who bore it should pause at intervals and say aloud, "Behold all that remains of the Emperor Saladin!—of all the states he had conquered; of all the provinces he had subdued; of the boundless treasures he had amassed; of the countless wealth he possessed, he retained, in dying, nothing but this shroud!"

Don Jose de Salamanca, the great railway contractor of Spain, was, in the early part of his life, a student at the University of Granada. He there wore, as he himself says, the oldest and most worn of cassocks. He was a diligent student; and after leaving college he became a member of the Spanish press. From thence he was translated to the Cabinet of Queen Christina, of which he became Finance Minister. This brought out his commercial capacities, and induced him to enter on commercial

---

4. Cicero's Letters
5. Principles of Political Economy, Book iv., ch. vi.

speculations. He constructed railways in Spain and Italy, and took the principal share in establishing several steam-shipping companies. But while pursuing commerce, he did not forget literature. Once a week he kept an open table, to which the foremost men in literature and the press were invited. They returned his hospitality by inviting him to a dinner on the most economic scale. Busts of Shakespeare, Cervantes, Dante, Schiller, and other literary men, adorned the room.

In returning thanks for his health, Salamanca referred to his university experience, and to his labours in connection with the press. "Then," he went on to say, "the love of gold took possession of my soul, and it was at Madrid that I found the object of my adoration; but not, alas! without the loss of my juvenile illusions. Believe me, gentlemen, the man who can satisfy all his wishes has no more enjoyment. Keep to the course you have entered on, I advise you. Rothschild's celebrity will expire on the day of his death. Immortality can be earned, not bought. Here are before us the effigies of men who have gloriously cultivated liberal arts; their busts I have met with in every part of Europe; but nowhere have I found a statue erected to the honour of a man who has devoted his life to making money."

Riches and happiness have no necessary connection with each other. In some cases it might be said that happiness is in the inverse proportion to riches. The happiest part of most men's lives is while they are battling with poverty, and gradually raising themselves above it. It is then that they deny themselves for the sake of others,—that they save from their earnings to secure a future independence,—that they cultivate their minds while labouring for their daily bread,—that they endeavour to render themselves wiser and better—happier in their homes and more useful to society at large. William Chambers, the Edinburgh publisher, speaking of the labours of his early years, says, "I look back to those times with great pleasure, and I am almost sorry that I have not to go through the same experience again; for I reaped more pleasure when I had not a sixpence in my pocket, studying in a garret in Edinburgh, than I now find when sitting amidst all the elegancies and comforts of a parlour."

There are compensations in every condition of life. The difference in the lot of the rich and the poor is not so great as is generally imagined. The rich man has often to pay a heavy price for his privileges. He is anxious about his possessions. He may be the victim of extortion. He is apt to be cheated. He is the mark for every man's shaft. He is surrounded

Riches and Charity

by a host of clients, till his purse bleeds at every pore. As they say in Yorkshire when people become rich, the money soon "broddles through." Or, if engaged in speculation, the rich man's wealth may fly away at any moment. He may try again, and then wear his heart out in speculating on the "chances of the market." Insomnia is a rich man's disease. The thought of his winnings and losings keeps him sleepless. He is awake by day, and awake by night. "Riches on the brain" is full of restlessness and agony.

The rich man over-eats or over-drinks; and he has gout. Imagine a man with a vice fitted to his toe. Let the vice descend upon the joint, and be firmly screwed down. Screw it again. He is in agony. Then suddenly turn the screw tighter—down, down! That is gout! Gout—of which Sydenham has said, that "unlike any other disease, it kills more rich men than poor, more wise than simple. Great kings, emperors, generals, admirals, and philosophers, have died of gout. Hereby nature shows her impartiality, since those whom she favours in one way, she afflicts in another Or, the rich man may become satiated with food, and lose his appetite; while the poor man relishes and digests anything. A beggar asked alms of a rich man "because he was hungry." "Hungry?" said the millionaire; "how I envy you!" Abernethy's prescription to the rich man was, "Live upon a shilling a day, and earn it!" When the Duke of York consulted him about his health, Abernethy's answer was, "Cut off the supplies, and the enemy will soon leave the citadel." The labourer who feels little and thinks less, has the digestion of an ostrich; while the non-worker is never allowed to forget that he has a stomach, and is obliged to watch every mouthful that he eats. Industry and indigestion are two things seldom found united.

Many people envy the possessions of the rich, but will not pass through the risks, the fatigues, or the dangers of acquiring them. It is related of the Duke of Dantzic that an old comrade, whom he had not seen for many years, called upon him at his hotel in Paris, and seemed amazed at the luxury of his apartments, the richness of his furniture, and the magnificence of his gardens. The Duke, supposing that he saw in his old comrade's face a feeling of jealousy, said to him bluntly, "You may have all that you see before you, on one condition." "What is that?" said his friend. "It is that you will place yourself twenty paces off, and let me fire at you with a musket a hundred times." "I will certainly not accept your offer at that price." "Well," replied the Marshal, "to gain all that you see before you, I have faced more than a thousand gunshots, fired at not move than ten paces off."

Riches and Charity

The Duke of Marlborough often faced death. He became rich, and left a million and a half to his descendants to squander. The Duke was a penurious man. He is said to have scolded his servant for lighting four candles in his tent, when Prince Eugene called upon him to hold a conference before the battle of Blenheim. Swift said of the Duke, "I dare hold a wager that in all his compaigns he was never known to lose his baggage." But this merely showed his consummate generalship. When ill and feeble at Bath, he is said to have walked home from the rooms to his lodgings, to save sixpence. And yet this may be excused, for he may have walked home for exercise. He is certainly known to have given a thousand pounds to a young and deserving soldier who wished to purchase a commission. When Bolingbroke was reminded of one of the weaknesses of Marlborough, he observed, "He was so great a man, that I forgot that he had that defect."

It is no disgrace to be poor. The praise of honest poverty has often been sung. When a man will not stoop to do wrong, when he will not sell himself for money, when he will not do a dishonest act, then his poverty is most honourable. But the man is not poor who can pay his way, and save something besides. He who pays cash for all that he purchases, is not poor but well off. He is in a happier condition than the idle gentleman who runs into debt, and is clothed, shod, and fed at the expense of his tailor, shoemaker, and butcher. Montesquieu says, that a man is not poor because he has nothing, but he is poor when he will not or cannot work. The man who is able and willing to work, is better off than the man who possesses a thousand crowns without the necessity for working.

Nothing sharpens a man's wits like poverty. Hence many of the greatest men have originally been poor men. Poverty often purifies and braces a man's morals. To spirited people, difficult tasks are usually the most delightful ones. If we may rely upon the testimony of history, men are brave, truthful, and magnanimous, not in proportion to their wealth, but in proportion to their smallness of means. And the best are often the poorest,—always supposing that they have sufficient to meet their temporal wants. A divine has said that God has created poverty, but He has not created misery. And there is certainly a great difference between the two. While honest poverty is honourable, misery is humiliating; inasmuch as the latter is for the most part the result of misconduct, and often of idleness and drunkenness. Poverty is no disgrace to him who can put up with it; but he who finds the beggar's staff once get warm in his hand, never does any good, but a great amount of evil.

Riches and Charity

The poor are often the happiest of people—far more so than the rich; but though they may be envied, no one will be found willing to take their place. Moore has told the story of the over-fed, over-satisfied eastern despot, who sent a messenger to travel through the world, in order to find out the happiest man. When discovered, the messenger was immediately to seize him, take his shirt off his back, and bring it to the Caliph. The messenger found the happiest man in an Irishman,—happy, dancing, and flourishing his shillelagh. But when the ambassador proceeded to seize him, and undress him, he found that the Irishman had got no shirt to his back!

The portion of Agur is unquestionably the best: "Remove far from me vanity and lies; give me neither poverty nor riches; feed me with food convenient for me." The unequal distribution of the disposition to be happy, is of far greater importance than the unequal distribution of wealth. The disposition to be content and satisfied, said David Hume, is at least equal to an income of a thousand a year. Montaigne has observed that Fortune confers but little. Human good or ill does not depend upon it. It is but the seed of good, which the soul, infinitely stronger than wealth, changes and applies as it pleases, and is thus the only cause of a happy or unhappy disposition.

England is celebrated for its charities. M. Guizot declares that there is nothing in this land that so fills the mind of the stranger with amazement at our resources, and admiration at our use of them, as the noble free-gift monuments raised on every side for the relief of multiform suffering. The home philanthropist, who looks a little deeper than the foreign visitor, may be disposed to take another view of the effects of money-giving. That charity produces unmixed good, is very much questioned. Charity, like man, is sometimes blind, and frequently misguided. Unless money is wisely distributed, it will frequently do more harm than good. If charity could help or elevate the poor, London would now be the happiest city in the world; for about three millions of money are spent on charity, and about one in every three of the London population are relieved by charitable institutions.

It is very easy to raise money for charity. Subscription lists constantly attest the fact. A rich man is asked by some influential person for money. It is very easy to give it. It saves time to give it. It is considered a religious duty to give it. Yet to give money unthinkingly, to give it without considering how it is to be used,—instead of being for the good of our fellow-creatures,—may often prove the greatest injury we could inflict upon them. True benevolence does not consist in giving money. Nor can charitable donations, given indiscriminately to the poor, have any other effect than to sap the foundations of self-respect, and break down the very outworks of virtue itself. There are many forms of benevolence which create the very evils they are intended to cure, and encourage the poorer classes in the habit of dependence upon the charity of others,—to the neglect of those far healthier means of social well-being which lie within their own reach.

One would think that three million a year were sufficient to relieve all the actual distress that exists in London. Yet the distress, notwithstanding all the money spent upon it, goes on increasing. May not the money spent in charity, create the distress it relieves,—besides creating other distress which it fails to relieve? Uneducated and idle people will not exert themselves for a living, when they have the hope of obtaining the living without exertion. Who will be frugal and provident, when charity offers all that frugality and providence can confer? Does not the gift of the advantages, comforts, and rewards of industry, without the necessity of labouring for them, tend to sap the very foundations of energy and self-reliance? Is not the circumstance that poverty is the only requisite qualification on the part of the applicant for charity, calculated to tempt the people to self-indulgence, to dissipation, and to those courses of life which keep them poor?

Men who will not struggle and exert themselves, are those who are helped first. The worst sort of persons are made comfortable: whilst the hard-working, self-supporting man, who disdains to throw himself upon charity, is compelled to pay rates for the maintenance of the idle. Charity stretches forth its hand to the rottenest parts of society; it rarely seeks out, or helps, the struggling and the honest. As Carlyle has said, "O my astonishing benevolent friends! that never think of meddling with the material while it continues sound; that stress and strain it with new rates and assessments, till even it has given way and declared itself rotten; whereupon you greedily snatch at it, and say, 'Now let us try to do some good upon it!'"

The charity which merely consists in giving, is an idle indulgence—often an idle vice. The mere giving of money will never do the work of philanthropy. As a recent writer has said, "The crimes of the virtuous, the blasphemies of the pious, and the follies of the wise, would scarcely fill a larger volume than the cruelties of the humane. In this world a large part of the occupation of the wise has been to neutralize the efforts of the good."

"Public charities," said the late Lord Lytton, "are too often merely a bonus to public indolence and vice. What a dark lesson of the fallacy of human wisdom does this knowledge strike into the heart! What a waste of the materials of kindly sympathies! What a perversion individual mistakes can cause, even in the virtues of a nation! Charity is a feeling dear to the pride of the human heart—it is an aristocratic emotion! Mahomet testified his deep knowledge of his kind when he allowed the vice hardest to control,—sexual licentiousness; and encouraged the virtue easiest to practise,—charity."[6]

There are clergymen in London who say that charity acts against the extension of religion amongst the people. The Rev. Mr. Stone says, "He is an unwelcome visitor to the poor who brings the Bible in one hand, without a loaf, a blanket, or a shilling in the other. And no wonder. By the prevailing system of charitable relief they have been nursed in this carnal spirit; they have been justified in those selfish expectations. Instead of being allowed to learn the great and salutary lesson of providence, that there is a necessary connection between their conduct and their condition, they have, by this artificial system, been taught that indigence is of itself sufficient to constitute a claim to relief. They have been thus encouraged in improvidence, immorality, fraud, and hypocrisy."

The truest philanthropists are those who endeavour to prevent misery, dependence, and destitution; and especially those who diligently help the poor to help themselves. This is the great advantage of the "Parochial Mission-Women Association."[7] They bring themselves into close communication with the people in the several parishes of London, and endeavour to assist them in many ways. But they avoid giving indiscriminate alms. Their objects are "to help the poor to help themselves, and to raise them by making them feel that they can help themselves." There is abundant room for philanthropy amongst all classes; and it is most gratifying to find ladies of high distinction taking part in this noble work.

There are numerous other societies established of late years, which afford gratifying instances of the higher and more rational, as well as really more Christian, forms of charity. The societies for improving the dwellings of the industrial classes,—for building baths and washhouses,—for establishing workmen's, seamen's, and servants' homes,—for cultivating habits of providence and frugality amongst the working-classes,—and

---

6. Lord Lytton—England and the English, p. 124.
7. See East and West, edited by the Countess Spencer.

for extending the advantages of knowledge amongst the people,—are important agencies of this kind. These, instead of sapping the foundations of self-reliance, are really and truly helping the people to help themselves, and are deserving of every approbation and encouragement. They tend to elevate the condition of the mass; they are embodiments of philanthropy in its highest form; and are calculated to bear good fruit through all time.

Rich men, with the prospect of death before them, are often very much concerned about their money affairs. If unmarried and without successors, they find a considerable difficulty in knowing what to do with the pile of gold they have gathered together during their lifetime. They must make a will, and leave it to somebody. In olden times, rich people left money to pay for masses for their souls. Perhaps many do so still. Some founded almshouses; others hospitals. Money was left for the purpose of distributing doles to poor persons, or to persons of the same name and trade as the deceased.

"These doles," said the wife of a clergyman in the neighbourhood of London, "are doing an infinite deal of mischief: they are rapidly pauperising the parish." Not long since, the town of Bedford was corrupted and demoralized by the doles and benefactions which rich men had left to the poorer classes. Give a man money without working for it, and he will soon claim it as a right. It practically forbids him to exercise forethought, or to provide against the vicissitudes of trade, or the accidents of life. It not only breaks down the bulwarks of independence, but the outposts of virtue itself.

Large sums of money are left by rich men to found "Charities." They wish to do good, but in many cases they do much moral injury. Their "Charities" are anything but charitable. They destroy the self-respect of the working-classes, and also of the classes above them. "We can get this charity for nothing. We can get medical assistance for nothing. We can get our children educated for nothing. Why should we work? Why should we save?" Such is the idea which charity, so-called, inculcates. The "Charitable Institution" becomes a genteel poor-house; and the lesson is extensively taught that we can do better by begging than by working.

The bequeathment of Stephen Girard, the wealthy American merchant, was of a different character. Girard was a native of Bordeaux. An orphan at an early age, he was put on board a ship as a cabin boy. He made his first voyage to North America when about ten or twelve years old. He had little education, and only a limited acquaintance with reading and writing. He worked hard. He gradually improved in means so that he was able to set up a store. Whilst living in Water Street, New York, he fell in love with Polly Luna, the daughter of a caulker. The father forbade the marriage. But Girard persevered, and at length he won and married Polly Lum. It proved a most unfortunate marriage. His wife had no sympathy with him; and he became cross, snappish, morose. He took to sea again; and at forty he commanded his own sloop, and was engaged in the coasting trade between New York, Philadelphia, and New Orleans.

Then he settled in Philadelphia, and became a merchant. He devoted his whole soul to his business; for he had determined to become rich. He practised the most rigid economy. He performed any work by which money could be made. He shut his heart against the blandishments of life. The desire for wealth seems to have possessed his soul. His life was one of unceasing labour. Remember, that Girard was unhappy at home. His nature might have been softened, had he been blessed with a happy wife. He led ten miserable years with her; and then she became insane. She lay for about twenty years in the Pennsylvania hospital, and died there.

Yet there was something more than hardness and harshness in Girard. There was a deep under-current of humanity in him. When the yellow fever broke out in Philadelphia, in 1793, his better nature showed itself. The people were smitten to death by thousands. Nurses could not be found to attend the patients in the hospital. It was regarded as certain death to nurse the sick.

"Wealth had no power to bribe, nor beauty to charm, the oppressor; But all perished alike beneath the scourge of his anger; Only, alas I the poor, who had neither friends nor attendants, Crept away to die in the almshouse, home of the homeless."

It was at this time, when many were stricken with fever, that Girard abandoned his business, and offered his services as superintendent of the public hospital. He had Peter Helm for his associate. Girard's business faculty immediately displayed itself. His powers of organization were immense, and the results of his work were soon observed. Order began to reign where everything had before been in confusion. Dirt was conquered by cleanliness. Where there had been wastefulness, there was now thriftiness. Where there had been neglect, there was unremitting attention. Girard saw that every case was properly attended to. He himself attended to the patients afflicted by the loathsome disease, ministered to the dying, and performed the last kind offices for the dead. At last the plague was stayed; and Girard and Helm returned to their ordinary occupations.

The visitors of the poor in Philadelphia placed the following minute on their books: "Stephen Girard and Peter Helm, members of the committee, commiserating the calamitous state to which the sick may probably be reduced for want of suitable persons to superintend the hospital, voluntarily offered their services for that benevolent employment, and excited a surprise and satisfaction that can be better conceived than expressed."

The results of Stephen Girard's industry and economy may be seen in Philadelphia—in the beautiful dwelling houses, row after row,—but more than all, in the magnificent marble edifice of Girard College. He left the greater part of his fortune for public purposes,—principally to erect and maintain a public library and a large orphanage. It might have been in regard to his own desolate condition, when cast an orphan amongst strangers and foreigners, that he devised his splendid charity for poor, forlorn, and fatherless children. One of the rooms in the college is singularly furnished. "Girard had directed that a suitable room was to be set apart for the preservation of his books and papers; but from excess of pious care, or dread of the next-of kin, all the plain homely man's effects were shovelled into this room. Here are his boxes and his bookcase, his gig and his gaiters, his pictures and his pottery; and in a bookcase, hanging with careless grace, are his braces—old homely knitted braces, telling their tale of simplicity and carefulness."[8]

One of the finest hospitals in London is that founded by Thomas Guy, the bookseller. He is said to have been a miser. At all events he must have been a thrifty and saving man. No foundation such as that of Guy's can be accomplished without thrift. Men who accomplish such things must deny themselves for the benefit of others. Thomas Guy appears early to have projected schemes of benevolence. He first built and endowed almshouses at Tamworth for fourteen poor men and women, with pensions for each occupant; and with a thoughtfulness becoming his vocation, he furnished them with a library. He had himself been educated at Tamworth, where he had doubtless seen hungry and homeless persons suffering from cleanness of teeth and the winter's rage; and the almshouses were his contribution for their relief. He was a bookseller in London at that time. Guy prospered, not so much by bookselling, as by buying and selling South Sea Stock. When the bubble burst, he did not hold a share: but he had realized a profit of several hundred thousand

---

8. Gentleman's Magazine, April. 1875. George Dawson on "Niagara and Elsewhere."

pounds. This sum he principally employed in building and endowing the hospital which bears his name. The building was roofed in before his death, in 1724.

Scotch benefactors for the most part leave their savings for the purpose of founding hospitals for educational purposes. There was first the Heriot's Hospital, founded in Edinburgh by George Heriot, the goldsmith of James I., for maintaining and educating a hundred and eighty boys. But the property of the hospital having increased in value—the New Town of Edinburgh being for the most part built on George Heriot's land—the operations of the charity have been greatly extended; as many as four thousand boys and girls being now educated free of expense, in different parts of the city. There are also the George Watson's Hospital, the John Watson's Hospital, the Orphan Hospital, two Maiden Hospitals, the Cauven's Hospital, the Donaldson's Hospital, the Stewart's Hospital, and the splendid Fettes College (recently opened),—all founded by Scottish benefactors for the ordinary education of boys and girls, and also for their higher education. Edinburgh may well be called the City of Educational Endowments. There is also the Madras College, at St. Andrews, founded by the late Andrew Bell, D.D.; the Dollar Institution, founded by John Macrat; and the Dick Bequest, for elevating the character and position of the parochial schools and schoolmasters, in the counties of Aberdeen, Banff, and Moray. The effects of this last bequest have been most salutary. It has raised the character of the education given in the public schools, and the results have been frequently observed at Cambridge, where men from the northern counties have taken high honours in all departments of learning.

English benefactors have recently been following in the same direction. The Owen's College at Manchester; the Brown Library and Museum at Liverpool; the Whitworth Benefaction, by which thirty scholarships of the annual value of £100 each have been founded for the promotion of technical instruction; and the Scientific College at Birmingham, founded by Sir Josiah Mason, for the purpose of educating the rising generation in "sound, extensive, and practical scientific knowledge,"—form a series of excellent institutions which will, we hope, be followed by many similar benefactions. A man need not moulder with the green grass over his grave, before his means are applied to noble purposes. He can make his benefactions while living, and assist at the outset in carrying out his liberal intentions.

Among the great benefactors of London, the name of Mr. Peabody, the American banker, cannot be forgotten. It would take a volume to discuss his merits, though we must dismiss him in a paragraph. He was one of the first to see, or at all events to make amends for, the houseless condition of the working classes of London. In the formation of railways under and above ground, in opening out and widening new streets, in erecting new public buildings,—the dwellings of the poor were destroyed, and their occupants swarmed away, no one knew whither. Perhaps they crowded closer together, and bred disease in many forms. Societies and companies were formed to remedy the evil to a certain extent. Sir Sydney Waterlow was one of the first to lead the way, and he was followed by others. But it was not until Mr. Peabody had left his splendid benefaction to the poor of London, that any steps could be taken to deal with the evil on a large and comprehensive scale. His trustees have already erected ranges of workmen's dwellings in many parts of the metropolis,—which will from time to time be extended to other parts. The Peabody dwellings furnish an example of what working men's dwellings ought to be. They are clean, tidy, and comfortable homes. They have diminished drunkenness; they have promoted morality. Mr. Peabody intended that his bounty should "directly ameliorate the condition and augment the comforts of the poor," and he hoped that the results would "be appreciated, not only by the present, but by future generations of the people of London." From all that the trustees have done, it is clear that they are faithfully and nobly carrying out his intentions.

All these benefactors of the poor were originally men of moderate means. Some of them were at one time poor men. Sir Joseph Whitworth was a journeyman engineer with Mr. Clement, in Southwark, the inventor of the planing machine. Sir Josiah Mason was by turns a costermonger, journeyman baker, shoemaker, carpet weaver, jeweller, split-steel ring maker (here he made his first thousand pounds), steel-pen maker, copper-smelter, and electro-plater, in which last trade he made his fortune. Mr. Peabody worked his way up by small degrees, from a clerk in America to a banker in London. Their benefactions have been the result of self-denial, industry, sobriety, and thrift.

Benevolence throws out blossoms which do not always ripen into fruit. It is easy enough to project a benevolent undertaking, but more difficult to carry it out. The author was once induced to take an interest in a proposed Navvy's Home; but cold water was thrown upon the project, and it failed. The navvy workmen, who have made the railways and docks of England, are a hard-working but a rather thriftless set. They are good-hearted fellows, but sometimes drunken. In carrying out their operations, they often run great dangers. They are sometimes so seriously injured by wounds and fractures as to be disabled for life. For instance, in carrying out the works of the Manchester, Sheffield, and Lincolnshire Railway, there were twenty-two cases of compound fractures seventy-four simple fractures, besides burns from blasts, severe contusions, lacerations, and dislocations. One man lost both his eyes by a blast, another had his arm broken by a blast. Many lost their fingers, feet, legs, and arms; which disabled them for further work. Knowing the perils to which railway labourers were exposed, it occurred to a late eminent contractor to adopt some method for helping and comforting them in their declining years. The subject was brought under the author's notice by his friend the late Mr. Eborall, in the following words: "I have just been visiting a large contractor—a man of great wealth; and he requests your assistance in establishing a 'Navvy's Home.' You know that many of the contractors and engineers, who have been engaged in the construction of railways, are men who have accumulated immense fortunes: the savings of some of them amount to millions. Well, my friend the contractor not long since found a miserable, worn-out old man in a ditch by the roadside. 'What,' said he, 'is that you?' naming the man in the ditch by his name. 'Ay,' replied the man, "deed it is!' 'What are you doing there?' 'I have come here to die. I can work no more.' 'Why don't you go to the workhouse? they will attend to your wants there.' 'No! no workhouse for me! If I am to die, I will die in the open air.' The contractor recognized in the man one of his former navvies. He had worked for him and for other contractors many years; and while they had been making their fortunes, the navvy who had worked for them had fallen so low as to be found dying in a ditch. The contractor was much affected. He thought of the numerous other navvies who must be wanting similar help. Shortly after, he took ill, and during his illness, thinking of what he might do for the navvies, the idea occurred to him of founding a 'Navvy's Home;' and he has desired me to ask you to assist him in bringing out the institution."

It seemed to the author an admirable project, and he consented to do all that he could for it. But when the persons who were the most likely to contribute to such an institution were applied to, they threw such floods of cold water upon it,[9] that it became evident, in the face of their opposition, that "The Navvy's Home" could not be established.

---

9. With one admirable exception. A noble-hearted man, still living volunteered a very large subscription towards the establishment of "the Navvy's Home."

Of course, excuses were abundant. "Navvies were the most extravagant workmen. They threw away everything that they earned. They spent their money on beer, whisky, tally-women, and champagne. If they died in ditches, it was their own fault. They might have established themselves in comfort, if they wished to do so. Why should other people provide for them in old age, more than for any other class of labourers? There was the workhouse: let them go there." And so on. It is easy to find a stick to beat a sick dog. As for the original projector, he recovered his health, he forgot to subscribe for "The Navvy's Home," and the scheme fell to the ground.

"The devil was sick, the devil a saint would be: The devil grew well, the devil a saint was he.'

Chapter 15

Healthy Homes

"The best security for civilization is the dwelling. "—B. Disraeli.

"Cleanliness is the elegance of the poor."—English Proverb.

"Sanitas sanitatum, et omnia sanitas."["Cleanliness of cleanliness, and all is cleanliness."]—Julius Menochius.

"Virtue never dwelt long with filth and nastiness."—Count Rumford.

"More servants wait on man than he'll take notice of: in every path he treads down that which doth befriend him when sickness makes him pale and wan."—George Herbert.

 Health is said to be wealth. Indeed, all wealth is valueless without health. Every man who lives by labour, whether of mind or body, regards health as one of the most valuable of possessions. Without it, life would be unenjoyable. The human system has been so framed as to render enjoyment one of the principal ends of physical life. The whole arrangement, structure, and functions of the human system are beautifully adapted for that purpose.

 The exercise of every sense is pleasurable,—the exercise of sight, hearing, taste, touch, and muscular effort. What can be more pleasurable, for instance, than the feeling of entire health,—health, which is the sum-total of the functions of life, duly performed? "Enjoyment," says Dr. Southwood Smith, "is not only the end of life, but it is the only condition of life which is compatible with a protracted term of existence. The happier a human being is, the longer he lives; the more he suffers, the sooner he dies. To add to enjoyment, is to lengthen life; to inflict pain, is to shorten its duration."

Happiness is the rule of healthy existence; pain and misery are its exceptional conditions. Nor is pain altogether an evil; it is rather a salutary warning. It tells us that we have transgressed some rule, violated some law, disobeyed some physical obligation. It is a monitor which warns us to amend our state of living. It virtually says,—Return to nature, observe her laws, and be restored to happiness. Thus, paradoxical though it may seem, pain is one of the conditions of the physical well-being of man; as death, according to Dr. Thomas Brown, is one of the conditions of the enjoyment of life.

To enjoy physical happiness, therefore, the natural laws must be complied with. To discover and observe these laws, man has been endowed with the gift of reason. Does he fail to exercise this gift,—does he neglect to comply with the law of his being,—then pain and disease are the necessary consequence.

Man violates the laws of nature in his own person, and he suffers accordingly. He is idle and overfeeds himself: he is punished by gout, indigestion, or apoplexy. He drinks too much: he becomes bloated, trembling, and weak; his appetite falls off, his strength declines, his constitution decays; and he falls a victim to the numerous diseases which haunt the steps of the drunkard.

Society suffers in the same way. It leaves districts undrained, and streets uncleaned. Masses of the population are allowed to live crowded together in unwholesome dens, half poisoned by the mephitic air of the neighbourhood. Then a fever breaks out,—or a cholera, or a plague. Disease spreads from the miserable abodes of the poor into the comfortable homes of the rich, carrying death and devastation before it. The misery and suffering incurred in such cases, are nothing less than wilful, inasmuch as the knowledge necessary to avert them is within the reach of all.

Wherever any number of persons live together, the atmosphere becomes poisoned, unless means be provided for its constant change and renovation. If there be not sufficient ventilation, the air becomes charged with carbonic acid, principally the product of respiration. Whatever the body discharges, becomes poison to the body if introduced again through the lungs. Hence the immense importance of pure air. A deficiency of food may be considerably less injurious than a deficiency of pure air. Every person above fourteen years of age requires about six hundred cubic feet of shut-up space to breathe in during the twenty-four hours.[1] If he sleeps in a room of smaller dimensions, he will suffer more or less, and gradually approach the condition of being smothered.

Shut up a mouse in a glass receiver, and it will gradually die by rebreathing its own breath. Shut up a man in a confined space, and he will die in the same way. The English soldiers expired in the Black Hole of Calcutta because they wanted pure air. Thus about half the children born in some manufacturing towns die, before they are five years old, principally because they want pure air. Humboldt tells of a sailor who was dying of fever in the close hold of a ship. His comrades brought him out of his hold to die in the open air. Instead of dying, he revived, and eventually got well. He was cured by the pure air.

The most common result of breathing impure air, amongst adults, is fever. The heaviest municipal tax, said Dr. Southwood Smith, is the fever tax. It is estimated that in Liverpool some seven thousand persons are yearly attacked by fever, of whom about five hundred die. Fever usually attacks persons of between twenty and thirty, or those who generally have small families depending on them for support. Hence deaths from fever, by causing widowhood and orphanage, impose a very heavy tax upon the inhabitants of all the large manufacturing towns. Dr. Playfair, after carefully considering the question, is of opinion that the total pecuniary loss inflicted on the county of Lancashire from preventible disease, sickness, and death, amounts to not less than five millions sterling annually. But this is only the physical and pecuniary loss. The moral loss is infinitely greater.

Where are now the "happy humble swains" and the "gentle shepherds" of the old English poets? At the present time, they are nowhere to be found. The modern Strephon and Phyllis are a very humble pair, living in a clay-floored cottage, and maintaining a family on from twelve to fifteen shillings a week. And so far from Strephon spending his time in sitting by a purling stream playing "roundelays" upon a pipe,—poor fellow! he

---

1. Where six hundred cubic feet of space is allowed, the air requires to be changed, by ventilation, five times in the hour, in order to keep it pure. The best amount of space to be allowed for a healthy adult is about eight hundred cubic feet. The air which is breathed becomes so rapidly impure, that a constant supply of fresh air must be kept up to make the air of the shut-up space fit for breathing. The following are some amounts of space per head which are met with in practice:—

Artizan rooms 200 cubic feet. Metropolitan Lodging Houses 240 cubic feet. Poor Law Board Dormitories 300 cubic feet. Barrack Regulation 60 cubic feet. The best Hospitals 1,500 to 2,000 cubic feet.

can scarcely afford to smoke one, his hours of labour are so long, and his wages are so small. As for Daphnis, he is a lout, and can neither read nor write; nor is his Chloe any better.

Phineas Fletcher thus sang of "The Shepherd's Home:"—

"Thrice, oh, thrice happie shepherd's life and state!
When courts are happinesse, unhappie pawns!
His cottage low, and safely humble gate
Shuts out proud Fortune, with her scorns and fawns:
No feared treason breaks his quiet sleep:
Singing all day, his flocks he learns to keep:
Himself as innocent as are his simple sheep.
His certain life, that never can deceive him,
Is full of thousand sweets and rich content:
The smooth-leaved beeches in the field receive him
With coolest shades, till noontide's rage is spent:
His life is neither tost in boist'rous seas
Of troublous world, nor lost in slothful ease;
Pleased and full blest he lives, when he his God can please."

Where, oh where, has this gentle shepherd gone? Have spinning-jennies swallowed him up? Alas! as was observed of Mrs. Harris, "there's no such a person." Did he ever exist? We have a strong suspicion that he never did, save in the imaginations of poets.

Before the age of railroads and sanitary reformers, the pastoral life of the Arcadians was a beautiful myth, The Blue Book men have exploded it for ever. The agricultural labourers have not decent houses,—only miserable huts, to live in. They have but few provisions for cleanliness or decency. Two rooms for sleeping and living in, are all that the largest family can afford. Sometimes they have only one. The day-room, in addition to the family, contains the cooking utensils, the washing apparatus, agricultural implements, and dirty clothes. In the sleeping apartment, the parents and their children, boys and girls, are indiscriminately mixed, and frequently a lodger sleeps in the same and only room, which has generally no window,—the openings in the half-thatched roof admitting light, and exposing the family to every vicissitude of the weather. The husband, having no comfort at home, seeks it in the beershop. The children grow up without decency or self-restraint. As for the half-hearted wives and daughters, their lot is very miserable.

It is not often that village affairs are made the subject of discussion in newspapers, for the power of the press has not yet reached remote country places. But we do hear occasionally of whole villages being pulled down and razed, in order to prevent them "becoming nests of beggars' brats." A member of Parliament did not hesitate to confess before a Parliamentary Committee, that he "had pulled down between twenty-six and thirty cottages, which, had they been left standing, would have been inhabited by young married couples." And what becomes of the dispossessed? They crowd together in the cottages which are left standing, if their owners will allow it; or they crowd into the workhouses; or, more generally, they crowd into the towns, where there is at least some hope of employment for themselves and their children.

Our manufacturing towns are not at all what they ought to be; not sufficiently pure, wholesome, or well-regulated. But the rural labourers regard even the misery of towns as preferable to the worse misery of the rural districts; and year by year they crowd into the seats of manufacturing industry in search of homes and employment. This speaks volumes as to the actual state of our "boasted peasantry, their country's pride."

The intellectual condition of the country labourers seems to be on a par with their physical state. Those in the western counties are as little civilized as the poor people in the east of London. A report of the Diocesan Board of the county of Hereford states that "a great deal of the superstition of past ages lingers in our parishes. The observation of lucky and unlucky days and seasons is by no means unusual; the phases of the moon are regarded with great respect,—in one, medicine may be taken, in another it is advisable to kill a pig; over the doors of many houses may be found twigs placed crosswise, and never suffered to lose their cruciform position; and the horseshoe preserves its old station on many a stable-door. Charms are devoutly believed in; a ring made from a shilling, offered at the communion, is an undoubted cure for fits; hair plucked from the crop on an ass's shoulder, and woven into a chain, to be put round a child's neck, is powerful for the same purpose; and the hand of a corpse applied to the neck is believed to disperse a wen. The 'evil eye,' so long dreaded in uneducated countries, has its terrors among us; and if a person of ill life be suddenly called away, there are generally some who hear his 'tokens,' or see his ghost. There exists, besides, the custom of communicating deaths to hives of bees, in the belief that they invariably abandon their owners if the intelligence be withheld."

Sydney Smith has said, with more truth than elegance, that in the infancy of all nations, even the most civilized, men lived the life of pigs; and if sanitary reporters had existed in times past as they do now, we should doubtless have received an account of the actual existence and domestic accommodation of the old English "swains" and "shepherds," very different from that given by Phineas Fletcher. Even the mechanics of this day are more comfortably lodged than the great landed gentry of the Saxon and Norman periods: and if the truth could be got at, it would be found that, bad as is the state of our agricultural labourers now, the condition of their forefathers was no better.

The first method of raising a man above the life of an animal is to provide him with a healthy home. The Home is after all the best school for the world. Children grow up into men and women there; they imbibe their best and their worst morality there; and their morals and intelligence are in a great measure well or ill trained there. Men can only be really and truly humanized and civilized through the institution of the Home. There is domestic purity and moral life in the good home; and individual defilement and moral death in the bad one. The schoolmaster has really very little to do with the formation of the characters of children. These are formed in the home, by the father and mother,—by brothers, sisters, and companions. It does not matter how complete may be the education given in schools. It may include the whole range of knowledge: yet if the scholar is under the necessity of daily returning to a home which is indecent, vicious, and miserable, all this learning will prove of comparatively little value. Character and disposition are the result of home training; and if these are, through bad physical and moral conditions, deteriorated and destroyed, the intellectual culture acquired in the school may prove an instrumentality for evil rather than for good.

The home should not be considered merely as an eating and sleeping place; but as a place where self-respect may be preserved, and comfort secured, and domestic pleasures enjoyed. Three-fourths of the petty vices which degrade society, and swell into crimes which disgrace it, would shrink before the influence of self-respect. To be a place of happiness, exercising beneficial influences upon its members,—and especially upon the children growing up within it,—the home must be pervaded by the spirit of comfort, cleanliness, affection, and intelligence. And in order to secure this, the presence of a well-ordered, industrious, and educated woman is indispensable. So much depends upon the woman, that we might almost pronounce the happiness or unhappiness of the home to be woman's work. No nation can advance except through the improvement of the nation's homes; and these can only be improved through the instrumentality of women. They must know how to make homes comfortable; and before they can know, they must have been taught.

Women must, therefore, have sufficient training to fit them for their duties in real life. Their education should be conducted throughout, with a view to their future position as wives, mothers, and housewives. But amongst all classes, even the highest, the education of girls is rarely conducted with this object. Amongst the working people, the girls are sent out to work; amongst the higher classes, they are sent out to learn a few flashy accomplishments; and men are left to pick from them, very often with little judgment, the future wives and mothers of England.

Men themselves attach little or no importance to the intelligence or industrial skill of women; and they only discover their value when they find their homes stupid and cheerless. Men are caught by the glance of a bright eye, by a pair of cherry cheeks, by a handsome figure; and when they "fall in love," as the phrase goes, they never bethink them of whether the "loved one" can mend a shirt or cook a pudding. And yet the most sentimental of husbands must come down from his "ecstatics" so soon as the knot is tied; and then he soon enough finds out that the clever hands of a woman are worth far more than her bright glances; and if the shirt and pudding qualifications be absent, then woe to the unhappy man, and woe also to the unhappy woman! If the substantial element of physical comfort be absent from the home, it soon becomes hateful; the wife, notwithstanding all her good looks, is neglected; and the public-house separates those whom the law and the Church have joined together.

Men are really desperately ignorant respecting the home department. If they thought for a moment of its importance, they would not be so ready to rush into premature housekeeping. Ignorant men select equally ignorant women for their wives; and these introduce into the world families of children, whom they are utterly incompetent to train as rational or domestic beings. The home is no home, but a mere lodging, and often a very comfortless one.

We speak not merely of the poorest labourers, but of the best-paid workmen in the large manufacturing towns. Men earning from two to three pounds a week,—or more than the average pay of curates and bankers' clerks,—though spending considerable amounts on beer, will

Healthy Homes

often grudge so small a part of their income as half-a-crown a week to provide decent homes for themselves and their children. What is the consequence? They degrade themselves and their families. They crowd together, in foul neighbourhoods, into dwellings possessing no element of health or decency; where even the small rental which they pay is in excess of the accommodation they receive. The results are inevitable,—loss of self-respect, degradation of intelligence, failure of physical health, and premature death. Even the highest-minded philosopher, placed in such a situation, would gradually gravitate towards brutality.

But the amount thus saved, or rather not expended on house-rent, is not economy; it is reckless waste. The sickness caused by the bad dwelling involves frequent interruptions of work, and drains upon the Savings Bank or the Benefit Society; and a final and rapid descent to the poor-rates. Though the loss to the middle and upper classes is great, the loss is not for a moment to be compared with that which falls upon the working classes themselves, through their neglect in providing wholesome and comfortable dwellings for their families. It is, perhaps, not saying too much to aver, that one-half the money expended by benefit societies in large towns, may be set down as pecuniary loss arising from bad and unhealthy homes.

But there is a worse consequence still. The low tone of physical health thereby produced is one of the chief causes of drunkenness. Mr. Chadwick once remonstrated with an apparently sensible workman on the expenditure of half his income on whisky. His reply was, "Do you, sir, come and live here, and you will drink whisky too." Mr. Leigh says, "I would not be understood that habits of intoxication are wholly due to a defective sanitary condition; but no person can have the experience I have had without coming to the conclusion that unhealthy and unhappy homes,—loss of vital and consequently of industrial energy, and a consciousness of inability to control external circumstances,—induce thousands to escape from miserable depression in the temporary excitement of noxious drugs and intoxicating liquors. They are like the seamen who struggle for awhile against the evils by which they are surrounded, but at last, seeing no hope, stupefy themselves with drink, and perish."

It may be said, in excuse, that working people must necessarily occupy such houses as are to be had, and pay the rental asked for them, bad and unwholesome though they be. But there is such a thing as supply and demand; and the dwellings now supplied are really those which are most in demand, because of their lowness of rental. Were the working classes to shun unwholesome districts, and low-priced dwellings, and rent only such tenements as were calculated to fulfil the requirements of a wholesome and cleanly home, the owners of property would be compelled to improve the character of their houses, and raise them to the required standard of comfort and accommodation. The real remedy must lie with the working classes themselves. Let them determine to raise their standard of rental, and the reform is in a great measure accomplished.

We have already shown how masters have done a great deal for the better accommodation of their work-people—how the benefactors of the poor, such as Mr. Peabody and Lady Burdett Coutts, have promoted the building of healthy homes. Yet the result must depend upon the individual action of the working classes themselves. When they have the choice of living in a dwelling situated in a healthy locality, and of another situated in an unhealthy locality, they ought to choose the former. But very often they do not. There is perhaps a difference of sixpence a week in the rental, and, not knowing the advantages of health, they take the unhealthy dwelling because it is the cheapest. But the money that sickly people have to pay for physic, doctors' bills, and loss of wages, far more than exceeds the amount saved by cheaper rental,—not to speak of the loss of comfort, the want of cleanliness, and the depression of spirits, which is inevitable where foul air is breathed.

To build a wholesome dwelling costs little more than to build an unwholesome one. What is wanted on the part of the builder is, a knowledge of sanitary conditions, and a willingness to provide the proper accommodation. The space of ground covered by the dwelling is the same in both cases; the quantity of bricks and mortar need be no greater; and pure air is of the same price as foul air. Light costs nothing.

A healthy home, presided over by a thrifty, cleanly woman, may be the abode of comfort, of virtue, and of happiness. It may be the scene of every ennobling relation in family life. It may be endeared to a man by many delightful memories, by the affectionate voices of his wife, his children, and his neighbours. Such a Home will be regarded, not as a mere nest of common instinct, but as a training-ground for young immortals, a sanctuary for the heart, a refuge from storms, a sweet resting-place after labour, a consolation in sorrow, a pride in success, and a joy at all times.

Much has been done to spread the doctrines of Sanitary Science. There is no mystery attached to it, otherwise we should have had professors teaching it in colleges (as we have now), and graduates practising it amongst the people. It is only of recent years that it has received general recognition; and we owe it, not to the medical faculty, but to a barrister, that it has become embodied in many important Acts of Parliament.

Edwin Chadwick has not yet received ordinary justice from his contemporaries. Though he has been one of the most indefatigable and successful workers of the age, and has greatly influenced the legislation of his time, he is probably less known than many a fourth-rate parliamentary talker.

Mr. Chadwick belongs to a Lancashire family, and was born near Manchester. He received his education chiefly in London. Having chosen the law for his profession, he was enrolled a student of the Inner Temple in his twenty-sixth year. There he "ate his way" to the Bar; maintaining himself by reporting and writing for the daily press. He was not a man of an extraordinary amount of learning. But he was a sagacious and persevering man. He was ready to confront any amount of labour in prosecuting an object, no matter how remote its attainment might at first sight appear to be.

At an early period in his career, Edwin Chadwick became possessed by an idea. It is a great thing to be thoroughly possessed by an idea, provided its aim and end be beneficent. It gives a colour and bias to the whole of a man's life. The idea was not a new one; but being taken up by an earnest, energetic, and hard-working man, there was some hope for the practical working out of his idea in the actual life of humanity. It was neither more nor less than the Sanitary Idea,—the germ of the sanitary movement.

We must now briefly state how he worked his way to its practical realization. It appears that Mr. Morgan, the Government actuary, had stated before a parliamentary committee, that though the circumstances of the middle classes had improved, their "expectation of life" had not lengthened. This being diametrically opposed to our student's idea, he endeavoured to demonstrate the fallacy of the actuary's opinion. He read up and sifted numerous statistical documents,—Blue Books, life-tables, and population-tables. He bored his way through the cumbrous pile, and brought an accumulation of facts from the most unlooked-for quarters, for the purpose of illustrating his idea, and elucidating his master-thought.

The result was published in the Westminster Review for April, 1828. Mr. Chadwick demonstrated, by an immense array of facts and arguments, that the circumstances which surround human beings must have an influence upon their health; that health must improve with an improvement of these circumstances; that many of the diseases and conditions unfavourable to human life were under man's control, and capable of being removed; that the practice of vaccination, the diminution of hard drinking amongst the middle and upper classes, the increase of habits of cleanliness, the improvements in medical science, and the better construction of streets and houses, must, according to all medical and popular experience, have contributed, à priori, to lengthen life; and these he proved by a citation of facts from numerous authentic sources. In short, Mr. Morgan was wrong. The "expectancy of life," as is now universally admitted, has improved and is rapidly improving amongst the better classes; but it was never thoroughly demonstrated until Edwin Chadwick undertook the discussion of the question.

Another article, which Mr. Chadwick published in the London Review, in 1829, on "Preventive Police," was read by Jeremy Bentham, then in his eighty-second year, who so much admired it, that he craved an introduction to the writer. The consequence was the formation of a friendship that lasted without interruption until the death of the philosopher in 1832. Mr. Bentham wished to engage the whole of his young friend's time in assisting him with the preparation of his Administrative Code, and he offered to place him in independent circumstances if he would devote himself exclusively to the advancement of his views. The offer was, however, declined.

Mr. Chadwick completed his law studies, and was called to the bar in November, 1830. He was preparing to enter upon the practice of common law, occasionally contributing articles to the Westminster, when he was, in 1832, appointed a commissioner, in conjunction with Dr. Southwood Smith and Mr. Tooke, to investigate the question of Factory Labour, which Lord Ashley and Mr. Sadler were at that time strongly pressing upon public attention. The sanitary idea again found opportunity for expression in the report of the commission, which referred to "defective drainage, ventilation, water supply, and the like, as causes of disease,— acting, concurrently with excessive toil, to depress the health and shorten the lives of the factory population."

In the same year (1832) an important Commission of Inquiry was appointed by Lord Grey's Government, in reference to the operation of the Poor Laws in England and Wales. Mr. Chadwick was appointed one of the assistant commissioners, for the purpose of taking evidence on the subject; and the districts of London and Berkshire were allotted to him. His report, published in the following year, was a model of what a report should be. It was full of information, admirably classified and arranged, and was so racy,—by virtue of the facts brought to light, and the care taken to preserve the very words of the witnesses as they were spoken,—that the report may be read with interest by the most inveterate enemy of blue-books.

Mr. Chadwick showed himself so thoroughly a master of the subject,—his suggestions were so full of practical value,—that he was, shortly after the publication of the report, advanced from the post of assistant commissioner to that of chief commissioner: and he largely shared, with Mr. Senior, in the labours and honours of the commissioners' report submitted to the House of Commons in 1834, and also in the famous Poor-Law Amendment Act passed in the same year, in which the recommendations of the commissioners were substantially adopted and formalized.

One may venture to say now, without fear of contradiction, that that law was one of the most valuable that has been placed on the statute-book in modern times. And yet no law proved more unpopular than this was, for years after it had been enacted. But Mr. Chadwick never ceased to have perfect faith in the soundness of the principles on which it was based, and he was indefatigable in defending and establishing it. It has been well said, that "to become popular is an easy thing; but to do unpopular justice,—that requires a Man." And Edwin Chadwick is the man who has never failed in courage to do the right thing, even though it should prove to be the unpopular thing.

Whilst burrowing amidst the voluminous evidence on the Poor Laws, Mr. Chadwick never lost sight of his sanitary idea. All his reports were strongly imbued with it. One-fourth of the then existing pauperism was traced by him to the preventible causes of disease. His minute investigations into the condition of the labouring population and of the poorer classes generally, gave him a thorough acquaintance with the physical evils that were preying upon the community, carrying them off by fevers, consumption, and cholera; and the sanitary idea took still firmer possession of his mind.

One day, in 1838, while engaged in his official vocation of Secretary to the Poor-Law Commission, an officer of the Whitechapel Union hastily entered the Board-room of the Poor-Law Commission, and, with a troubled countenance, informed the secretary that a terrible fever had broken out round a stagnant pool in Whitechapel; that the people were dying by scores; and that the extreme malignity of the cases gave reason to apprehend that the disease was allied to Asiatic cholera. On hearing

Healthy Homes

this, the Board, at Mr. Chadwick's instance, immediately appointed Drs. Arnott, Kay, and Southwood Smith to investigate the causes of this alarming mortality, and to report generally upon the sanitary condition of London. This inquiry at length ripened into the sanitary inquiry.

In the meantime, Mr. Chadwick had been engaged as a member of the Commission, to inquire as to the best means of establishing an efficient constabulary force in England and Wales. The evidence was embodied in a report, as interesting as a novel of Dickens, which afforded a curious insight into the modes of living, the customs and habits, of the lowest classes of the population. When this question had been dismissed, Mr. Chadwick proceeded to devote himself almost exclusively to the great work of his life,—the Sanitary Movement.

The Bishop of London, in 1839, moved in the Lords, that the inquiry which had been made at Mr. Chadwick's instance by Drs. Southwood Smith, Arnott, and Kay, into the sanitary state of the metropolis, should be extended to the whole population, city, rural, and manufacturing, of England and Wales. Some residents in Edinburgh also petitioned that Scotland might be included; and accordingly, in August, 1839, Lord John Russell addressed a letter to the Poor-Law Board, authorizing them by royal command to extend to the whole of Great Britain the inquiry into preventible disease, which had already been begun with regard to the metropolis. The onerous task of setting on foot and superintending the inquiry throughout,—of sifting the evidence, and classifying and condensing it for the purposes of publication,—devolved upon Mr. Chadwick.

The first Report on the Health of Towns was ready for publication in 1842. It ought to have appeared as the Official Report of the Poor-Law Board; but as the commissioners (some of whom were at variance with Mr. Chadwick with respect to the New Poor-Law) refused to assume the responsibility of a document that contained much that must necessarily offend many influential public bodies, Mr. Chadwick took the responsibility upon himself, and it was published as hisreport,—which indeed it was,—and accepted from him as such by the commissioners.

The amount of dry, hard work encountered by Mr. Chadwick in the preparation of this and his other reports can scarcely be estimated, except by those who know anything of the labour involved in extracting from masses of evidence, written and printed, sent in from all parts of the empire, only the most striking results bearing upon the question in hand, and such as are deemed worthy of publication. The mountains of paper which Mr. Chadwick has thus bored through in his lifetime must have been immense; and could they now be presented before him in one pile, they would appal even his stout heart!

The sensation excited throughout the country by the publication of Mr. Chadwick's Sanitary Report was immense. Such a revelation of the horrors lying concealed beneath the fair surface of our modern civilization, had never before been published. But Mr. Chadwick had no idea of merely creating a sensation. He had an object in view, which he persistently pursued. The report was nothing, unless its recommendations were speedily carried into effect. A sanitary party was formed; and the ministers for the time being, aided by members of both sides in politics, became its influential leaders.

A Sanitary Commission was appointed in 1844, to consider the whole question in its practical bearings. The Commission published two reports, with a view to legislation, but the Free-Trade struggle interfered, and little was done for several years. Meanwhile our sanitary reformer was occupied as a Commissioner in inquiring into the condition of the metropolis. The Commission published three reports, in which the defective drainage, sewage, and water-supply of London were discussed in detail; and these have recently been followed by important acts of legislation.

The sanitary idea at length had its triumph in the enactment of the Public Health Act of 1848, and the appointment of a General Board of Health (of which Mr. Chadwick was a member) to superintend its administration. Numerous supplemental measures have since been enacted, with the view of carrying into practical effect the sanitary principles adopted by the Board. Reports continued to be published, from time to time, full of valuable information: for instance, in reference to the application of Sewage water to agricultural purposes; on Epidemic Cholera; on Quarantine; on Drainage; on Public Lodging-houses; and the like. The sanitary movement, in short, became a "great fact;" and that it is so, we have mainly to thank Edwin Chadwick—the missionary of the Sanitary idea. It is true he was eventually dismissed from his position of influence at the Board of Health,—partly through spleen, but chiefly because of his own unaccommodating nature,—unaccommodating especially to petty local authorities and individual interests opposed to the public good. But with all thinking and impartial men, his character stands as high as it ever did. At all events, his works remain.

We do not know a more striking instance than that presented by this gentleman's career, of the large amount of good which a man strongly possessed by a beneficent idea can accomplish, provided he have only the force of purpose and perseverance to follow it up. Though Mr. Chadwick has not been an actual legislator, he has nevertheless been the mover of more wise measures than any legislator of our time. He created a public opinion in favour of sanitary reform. He has also impressed the minds of benevolent individuals with the necessity for providing improved dwellings for the people; and has thus been the indirect means of establishing the Peabody Dwellings, the Baroness Coutts' Dwellings, and the various Societies for erecting improved dwellings for the industrial classes.

Edwin Chadwick has thus proved himself to be one of the most useful and practical of public benefactors. He deserves to be ranked with Clarkson or Howard. His labours have been equally salutary; some will say that they have been much more so in their results.

Sanitary science may be summed up in the one word—Cleanliness. Pure water and pure air are its essentials. Wherever there is impurity, it must be washed away and got rid of. Thus sanitary science is one of the simplest and most intelligible of all the branches of human knowledge. Perhaps it is because of this, that, like most common things, it has continued to receive so little attention. Many still think that it requires no science at all to ventilate a chamber, to clean out a drain, and to keep house and person free from uncleanness.

Sanitary science may be regarded as an unsavoury subject. It deals with dirt and its expulsion—from the skin, from the house, from the street, from the city. It is comprised in the words—wherever there is dirt, get rid of it instantly; and with cleanliness let there be a copious supply of pure water and of pure air for the purposes of human health.

Take, for instance, an unhealthy street, or block of streets, in a large town. There you find typhus fever constantly present. Cleanse and sewer the street; supply it with pure air and pure water, and fever is forthwith banished. Is not this a much more satisfactory result than the application of drugs? Fifty thousand persons, says Mr. Lee, annually fall victims to typhus fever in Great Britain, originated by causes which are preventible. The result is the same as if these fifty thousand persons were annually taken out of their wretched dwellings, and put to death! We are shocked by the news of a murder—by the loss of a single life by physical causes! And yet we hear, almost without a shudder, the reiterated statement of the loss of tens of thousands of lives yearly from physical causes in daily operation. The annual slaughter from preventible causes of typhus fever is double the amount of what was suffered by the allied armies at the battle of Waterloo! By neglect of the ascertained conditions of healthful living, the great mass of the people lose nearly half the natural period of their lives. "Typhus," says a medical officer, "is a curse which man inflicts upon himself by the neglect of sanitary arrangements."

Mr. Chadwick affirmed that in the cellars of Liverpool, Manchester, and Leeds, he had seen amongst the operatives more vice, misery, and degradation than those which, when detailed by Howard, had excited the sympathy of the world. The Irish poor sink into the unhealthy closes, lanes, and back streets of large towns; and so frequent are the attacks of typhus among them, that in some parts of the country the disease is known as "the Irish fever." It is not merely the loss of life that is so frightful; there is also the moral death that is still more appalling in these unhealthy localities. Vice and crime consort with foul living. In these places, demoralization is the normal state. There is an absence of cleanliness, of decency, of decorum; the language used is polluting, and scenes of profligacy are of almost hourly occurrence,—all tending to foster idleness, drunkenness, and vicious abandonment. Imagine such a moral atmosphere for women and children!

The connection is close and intimate between physical and moral health, between domestic well-being and public happiness. The destructive influence of an unwholesome dwelling propagates a moral typhus worse than the plague itself. Where the body is enfeebled by the depressing influences of vitiated air and bodily defilement, the mind, almost of necessity, takes the same low, unhealthy tone. Self-respect is lost; a stupid, inert, languid feeling overpowers the system; the character becomes depraved; and too often—eager to snatch even a momentary enjoyment, to feel the blood bounding in the veins,—the miserable victim flies to the demon of strong drink for relief; hence misery, infamy, shame, crime, and wretchedness.

This neglect of the conditions of daily health is a frightfully costly thing. It costs the rich a great deal of money in the shape of poor-rates, for the support of widows made husbandless, and children made fatherless, by typhus. It costs them also a great deal in disease; for the fever often spreads from the dwellings of the poor into the homes of the rich, and carries away father, mother, or children. It costs a great deal in subscriptions to maintain dispensaries, infirmaries, houses of recovery, and asylums for the destitute. It costs the poor still more; it costs them their health, which is their only capital. In this is invested their all: if they

Healthy Homes

lose it, their docket is struck, and they are bankrupt. How frightful is the neglect, whether it be on the part of society or of individuals, which robs the poor man of his health, and makes his life a daily death!

Why, then, is not sanitary science universally adopted and enforced? We fear it is mainly through indifference and laziness. The local authorities—municipalities and boards of guardians—are so many Mrs. Maclartys in their way. Like that dirty matron, they "canna be fashed." To remove the materials of disease requires industry, constant attention, and—what is far more serious—increased rates. The foul interests hold their ground, and bid defiance to the attacks made upon them. Things did very well, they say, in "the good old times,"—why should they not do so now? When typhus or cholera breaks out, they tell us that Nobody is to blame.

That terrible Nobody! How much he has to answer for. More mischief is done by Nobody than by all the world besides. Nobody adulterates our food. Nobody poisons us with bad drink. Nobody supplies us with foul water. Nobody spreads fever in blind alleys and unswept lanes. Nobody leaves towns undrained. Nobody fills gaols, penitentiaries, and convict stations. Nobody makes poachers, thieves, and drunkards.

Nobody has a theory too—a dreadful theory. It is embodied in two words—Laissez faire—Let alone. When people are poisoned by plaster of Paris mixed with flour, "Let alone" is the remedy. When Cocculus indicus is used instead of hops, and men die prematurely, it is easy to say, "Nobody did it." Let those who can, find out when they are cheated: Caveat emptor. When people live in foul dwellings, let them alone. Let wretchedness do its work; do not interfere with death.

"It matters nothing to me," said a rich man who heard of a poor woman and her sick child being driven forth from a town for begging. The workhouse authorities would have nothing to do with her, and sent her away. But the poor woman went and sat down with her child at the rich man's door; the child died there; the contagion of typhus was wafted into the gilded saloon and the luxurious bed-chamber and the rich man's child fell a victim to the disease.

But Nobody has considerably less power in society than he once had: and our hope is, that he may ultimately follow in the wake of Old Bogie, and disappear altogether. Wherever there is suffering and social depression, we may depend upon it that Somebody is to blame. The responsibility rests somewhere; and if we allow it to remain, it rests with us. We may not be able to cope with the evil as individuals, single-handed; but it becomes us to unite, and bring to bear upon the evil the joint moral power of society in the form of a law. A Law is but the expression of a combined will; and it does that for society, which society, in its individual and separate action, cannot so well or efficiently do for itself. Laws may do too much; they may meddle with things which ought to be "let alone;" but the abuse of a thing is no proper argument against its use, in cases where its employment is urgently called for.

Mere improvement of towns, however,—as respects drainage, sewerage, paving, water supply, and abolition of cellar dwellings,—will effect comparatively little, unless we can succeed in carrying the improvement further,—namely, into the Homes of the people themselves. A well-devised system of sanitary measures may ensure external cleanliness,—may provide that the soil on which the streets of houses are built shall be relieved of all superfluous moisture, and that all animal and vegetable refuse shall be promptly removed,—so that the air circulating through the streets, and floating from them into the houses of the inhabitants, shall not be laden with poisonous miasmata, the source of disease, suffering, and untimely death. Cellar dwellings may be prohibited, and certain regulations as to the buildings hereafter to be erected may also be enforced. But here municipal or parochial authority stops: it can go no further; it cannot penetrate into the Home, and it is not necessary that it should do so.

The individual efforts of the community themselves are therefore needed; and any legislative enactments which dispensed with these would probably be an evil. The Government does not build the houses in which the people dwell. These are provided by employers and by capitalists, small and large. It is necessary, therefore, to enlist these interests in the cause of sanitary improvement, in order to ensure success.

Individual capitalists have already done much to provide wholesome houses for their working people, and have found their account in so doing, by their increased health, as well as in their moral improvement in all ways. Capitalists imbued with a benevolent and philanthropic spirit can thus spread blessings far and wide. And were a few enterprising builders in every town to take up this question practically, and provide a class of houses for workpeople, with suitable accommodation; provided with arrangements for ventilation, cleanliness, and separation of the sexes, such as health and comfort require; they would really be conferring an amount of benefit on the community at large, and, at the same time, we believe, upon themselves, which it would not be easy to overestimate.

But there also needs the active co-operation of the dwellers in poor men's homes themselves. They, too, must join cordially in the sanitary movement; otherwise comparatively little good can be effected. You may provide an efficient water supply, yet, if the housewife will not use the water as it ought to be used,—if she be lazy and dirty,—the house will be foul and comfortless still. You may provide for ventilation, yet, if offensive matters be not removed, and doors and windows are kept closed, the pure outer air will be excluded, and the house will still smell fusty and unwholesome. In any case, there must be a cleanly woman to superintend the affairs of the house; and she cannot be made so by Act of Parliament! The Sanitary Commissioners cannot, by any "Notification," convert the slatternly shrew into a tidy housewife, nor the disorderly drunkard into an industrious, home-loving husband. There must, therefore, be individual effort on the part of the housewife in every working man's Home. As a recent writer on Home Reform observes,—

"We must begin by insisting that, however much of the physical and moral evils of the working classes may be justly attributable to their dwellings, it is too often the case that more ought, in truth, to be attributed to themselves. For, surely, the inmate depends less on the house, than the house on the inmate; as mind has more power over matter than matter over mind. Let a dwelling be ever so poor and incommodious, yet a family with decent and cleanly habits will contrive to make the best of it, and will take care that there shall be nothing offensive in it which they have power to remove. Whereas a model house, fitted up with every convenience and comfort which modern science can supply, will, if occupied by persons of intemperate and uncleanly habits, speedily become a disgrace and a nuisance. A sober, industrious, and cleanly couple will impart an air of decency and respectability to the poorest dwelling; while the spendthrift, the drunkard, or the gambler will convert a palace into a scene of discomfort and disgust. Since, therefore, so much depends on the character and conduct of the parties themselves, it is right that they should feel their responsibility in this matter, and that they should know and attend to the various points connected with the improvement of their own Homes."

While this important truth should be kept steadily in view, every possible exertion ought, at the same time, to be made to provide a greater abundance of comfortable, decent, and comely dwellings for the working classes; for it is to be lamented that, in many districts, they are, as it were, forced by the necessities of their condition to gravitate into localities, and to inhabit dwellings where decency is rendered almost impossible, where life becomes a slow dying, and where the influences operating on the entire human energies, physical and moral, are of the most deleterious character.

Homes are the manufactories of men, and as the Homes are, so will the men be. Mind will be degraded by the physical influences around it,—decency will be destroyed by constant contact with impurity and defilement,—and coarseness of manners, habits, and tastes, will become inevitable. You cannot rear a kindly nature, sensitive against evil, careful of proprieties, and desirous of moral and intellectual improvement, amidst the darkness, dampness, disorder, and discomfort which unhappily characterize so large a portion of the dwellings of the poor in our large towns; and until we can, by some means or other, improve their domestic accommodation, their low moral and social condition must be regarded as inevitable.

We want not only a better class of dwellings, but we require the people to be so educated as to appreciate them. An Irish landlord took his tenantry out of their mud huts, and removed them into comfortable dwellings which he had built for their accommodation. When he returned to his estate, he was greatly disappointed. The houses were as untidy and uncomfortable as before. The pig was still under the bed, and the hens over it. The concrete floor was as dirty as the mud one had been. The panes of the windows were broken, and the garden was full of weeds. The landlord wrote to a friend in despair. The friend replied, "You have begun at the wrong end. You ought to have taught them the value of cleanliness, thriftiness, and comfort." To begin at the beginning, therefore, we must teach the people the necessity of cleanliness, its virtues and its wholesomeness; for which purpose it is requisite that they should be intelligent, capable of understanding ideas conveyed in words, able to discern, able to read, able to think. In short, the people, as children, must first have been to school, and properly taught there; whereas we have allowed the majority of the working people to grow up untaught, nearly half of them unable to read and write; and then we expect them to display the virtues, prudence, judgment, and forethought of well-educated beings!

It is of the first importance to teach people cleanly habits. This can be done without teaching them either reading or writing. Cleanliness is more than wholesomeness. It furnishes an atmosphere of self-respect, and influences the moral condition of the entire household. It is the best exponent of the spirit of Thrift. It is to the economy of the household, what hygiene is to the human body. It should preside at every detail of domestic service. It indicates comfort and well-being. It is among the distinctive attributes of civilisation, and marks the progress of nations.

Dr. Paley was accustomed to direct the particular attention of travellers in foreign countries to the condition of the people as respects cleanliness, and the local provisions for the prevention of pollution. He was of opinion that a greater insight might thus be obtained into their habits of decency, self-respect, and industry, and into their moral and social condition generally, than from facts of any other description. People are cleanly in proportion as they are decent, industrious, and self-respecting. Unclean people are uncivilized. The dirty classes of great towns are invariably the "dangerous classes" of those towns. And if we would civilize the classes yet uncivilized, we must banish dirt from amongst them.

Yet dirt forms no part of our nature. It is a parasite, feeding upon human life, and destroying it. It is hideous and disgusting. There can be no beauty where it is. The prettiest woman is made repulsive by it. Children are made fretful, impatient, and bad-tempered by it. Men are degraded and made reckless by it. There is little modesty where dirt is,—for dirty is indecency. There can be little purity of mind where the person is impure; for the body is the temple of the soul, and must be cleansed and purified to be worthy of the shrine within. Dirt has an affinity with self-indulgence and drunkenness. The sanitary inquirers have clearly made out that the dirty classes are the drunken classes; and that they are prone to seek, in the stupefaction of beer, gin, and opium, a refuge from the miserable depression caused by the foul conditions in which they live.

We need scarcely refer to the moral as well as the physical beauty of cleanliness—cleanliness which indicates self-respect, and is the root of many fine virtues—and especially of purity, delicacy, and decency. We might even go farther, and say that purity of thought and feeling result from habitual purity of body. For the mind and heart of man are, to a very great extent, influenced by external conditions and circumstances; and habit and custom, as regards outward things, stamp themselves deeply on the whole character,—alike upon the moral feelings and the intellectual powers.

Moses was the most practical of sanitary reformers. Among the eastern nations generally, cleanliness is a part of religion. They esteem it not only as next to godliness, but as a part of godliness itself. They connect the idea of internal sanctity with that of external purification. They feel that it would be an insult to the Maker they worship to come into His presence covered with impurity. Hence the Mahommedans devote almost as much care to the erection of baths, as to that of mosques; and alongside the place of worship is usually found the place of cleansing, so that the faithful may have the ready means of purification previous to their act of worship.

"What worship," says a great writer, "is there not in mere washing! perhaps one of the most moral things a man, in common cases, has it in his power to do. Strip thyself, go into the bath, or were it into the limpid pool of a running brook, and there wash and be clean; thou wilt step out again a purer and a better man. This consciousness of perfect outer pureness—that to thy skin there now adheres no foreign speck of imperfection—how it radiates on thee, with cunning symbolic influences to thy very soul! thou hast an increased tendency towards all good things whatsoever. The oldest eastern sages, with joy and holy gratitude, had felt it to be so, and that it was the Maker's gift and will."

The common well-being of men, women, and children depends upon attention to what at first sight may appear comparatively trivial matters. And unless these small matters be attended to, comfort in person, mind, and feeling is absolutely impossible. The physical satisfaction of a child, for example, depends upon attention to its feeding, clothing, and washing. These are the commonest of common things, and yet they are of the most essential importance. If the child is not properly fed and clothed, it will grow up feeble and ill-conditioned. And as the child is, so will the man be.

Grown people cannot be comfortable without regular attention to these common matters. Every one needs, and ought to have, comfort at home; and comfort is the united product of cleanliness, thrift, regularity, industry,—in short, a continuous performance of duties, each in itself apparently trivial. The cooking of a potato, the baking of a loaf, the mending of a shirt, the darning of a pair of stockings, the making of a bed, the scrubbing of a floor, the washing and dressing of a baby, are all matters of no great moment; but a woman ought to know how to do these, before the management of a household, however poor, is entrusted to her.

"Why," asked Lord Ashburton in a lecture to the students of the Wolvesey training-schools, "why was one mother of a family a better economist than another? Why could one live in abundance where another starved? Why, in similar dwellings, were the children of one parent healthy, of another puny and ailing? Why could this labourer do with ease a task that would kill his fellow? It was not luck nor chance that decided those differences; it was the patient observation of nature that suggested to some gifted minds rules for their guidance which had escaped the heedlessness of others."

It is not so much, however, the patient observation of nature, as good training in the home and in the school, that enables some women to accomplish so much more than others, in the development of human beings, and the promotion of human comfort. And to do this efficiently, women as well as men require to be instructed as to the nature of the objects upon which they work.

Take one branch of science as an illustration—the physiological. In this science we hold that every woman should receive some instruction. And why? Because, if the laws of physiology were understood by women, children would grow up into better, healthier, happier, and probably wiser, men and women. Children are subject to certain physiological laws, the observance of which is necessary for their health and comfort. Is it not reasonable, therefore, to expect that women should know something of those laws, and of their operation? If they are ignorant of them they will be liable to commit all sorts of blunders, productive of suffering, disease, and death. To what are we to attribute the frightful mortality of children in most of our large towns—where one-half of all that are born perish before they reach their fifth year? If women, as well as men, knew something of the laws of healthy living, about the nature of the atmosphere, how its free action upon the blood is necessary to health—of the laws of ventilation, cleanliness, and nutrition,—we cannot but think that the moral, not less than the physical condition of the human beings committed to their charge, would be greatly improved and promoted.

Were anything like a proper attention given to common things, there would not be such an amount of discomfort, disease, and mortality amongst the young. But we accustom people to act as if there were no such provisions as natural laws. If we violate them, we do not escape the consequences because we have been ignorant of their mode of operation. We have been provided with intelligence that we might knowthem; and if society keep its members blind and ignorant, the evil consequences are inevitably reaped. Thus tens of thousands perish for lack of knowledge of even the smallest, and yet most necessary conditions of right living.

Women have also need to be taught the important art of domestic economy. If they do not earn the family income, at least they have to spend the money earned; and their instruction ought to have a view to the spending of that money wisely. For this purpose, a knowledge of arithmetic is absolutely necessary. Some may say, "What use can a woman have for arithmetic?" But when men marry, they soon find this out. If the woman who has a household to manage be innocent of addition and multiplication; and if she fail to keep a record of her income or expenditure, she will, before long, find herself in great trouble. She will find that she cannot make the ends meet, and then run into debt. If she spend too much on dress, she will have too little for food or education. She will commit extravagances in one direction or another, and thus subject her household to great discomfort. She may also bring her husband into trouble through the debts she has contracted, and make a beginning of his misfortunes and sometimes of his ruin.

Much might be said in favour of household management, and especially in favour of improved cookery. Ill-cooked meals is a source of discomfort in many families. Bad cooking is waste,—waste of money and loss of comfort. Whom God has joined in matrimony, ill-cooked joints and ill-boiled potatoes have very often put asunder. Among the "common things" which educators should teach the rising generation, this ought certainly not to be overlooked. It is the commonest and yet most neglected of the branches of female education.

The greater part of human labour is occupied in the direct production of the materials for human food. The farming classes and their labourers devote themselves to the planting, rearing, and reaping of oats and other cereals; and the grazing farmer to the production of cattle and sheep, for the maintenance of the population at large. All these articles—corn, beef, mutton, and such-like—are handed over to the female half of the human species to be converted into food, for the sustenance of themselves, their husbands, and their families. How do they use their power? Can they cook? Have they been taught to cook? Is it not a fact that, in this country, cooking is one of the lost or undiscovered arts?

Thousands of artizans and labourers are deprived of half the actual nutriment of their food, and continue half-starved, because their wives are utterly ignorant of the art of cooking. They are yet in entire darkness as to the economizing of food, and the means of rendering it palatable and digestible.

Even the middle classes are badly served in this respect. "If we could see," says a public writer, "by the help of an Asmodeus, what is going on at the dinner hour of the humbler of the middle class,—what a spectacle of discomfort, waste, ill-temper, and consequent ill-conduct it would be!

The man quarrels with his wife because there is nothing he can eat, and he generally makes up in drink for the deficiencies in the article of food. There is thus not only the direct waste of food and detriment to health, but the further consequent waste of the use of spirits, with its injury to the habits and the health."

On the other hand, people who eat well, drink moderately; the satisfaction of the appetite dispensing with the necessity for resorting to stimulants. Good humour too, and good health, follow a good meal; and by a good meal we mean anything, however simple, well dressed in its way. A rich man may live very expensively and very ill; and a poor man may live frugally and very well, if it be his good fortune to have a good cook in his wife or in his servant.

The most worthless unit in a family is an ill-managing wife, or an indolent woman of any sort. The fair sex are sometimes very acute in what concerns themselves. They keep a tight hand over their dressmakers and milliners. They can tell to a thread when a flounce is too narrow or a tuck too deep. But if their knowledge only extends to their own dress, they are not help-meets, but incumbrances. If they know nothing of their kitchen, and are at the mercy of the cook, their table will soon become intolerable. Bad soup, soft and flabby fish, meat burnt outside and raw within. The husband will soon fly from the Barmecide feast, and take refuge in his club, where he will not only find food that he can digest, but at the same time fly from the domestic discord that usually accompanies ill-cooked victuals at home.

Mr. Smee says that "diseases of the digestive organs greatly exceed in England the relative number found in other countries." The reason is, that in no other country do men eat so much ill-cooked food. The least observant of travellers must have been struck with admiration at the readiness with which a dinner of eight or ten dishes of various eatables makes its appearance in foreign inns; particularly when he remembers the perpetual mutton chop and mashed potatoes of the English road. The author remembers arriving at a roadside inn, in a remote part of Dauphiny, immediately under the foot of the Pic du Midi. On looking at the clay floor, and the worn state of the furniture, he remarked to his friend, "Surely we can get no dinner here." "Wait till you see," was his answer. In about half-an-hour, the table (though propped up) was spread with a clean table-cloth; and successive dishes of soup, fowl, "ros-bif," pomme-de-terre frite, French beans, with wholesome bread and butter, made their appearance. In the principal inns of most provincial towns in England, it would not have been possible to obtain such a dinner.

Great would be the gain to the community if cookery were made an ordinary branch of female education. To the poor, the gain would be incalculable. "Among the prizes which the Bountifuls of both sexes are fond of bestowing in the country, we should like to see some offered for the best boiled potato, the best grilled mutton chop, and the best seasoned hotch-potch, soup, or broth. In writing of a well-boiled potato, we are aware that we shall incur the contempt of many for attaching importance to a thing they suppose to be so common. But the fact is, that their contempt arises, as is often the origin of contempt, from their ignorance—there being not one person in a hundred who has ever seen and tasted that great rarity—a well-boiled potato."[2]

In short, we want common sense in cookery, as in most other things. Food should be used, and not abused. Much of it is now absolutely wasted, wasted for want of a little art in cooking it. Food is not only wasted by bad cooking; but much of it is thrown away which French women would convert into something savoury and digestible. Health, morals, and family enjoyments, are all connected with the question of cookery. Above all, it is the handmaid of Thrift. It makes the most and the best of the bounties of God. It wastes nothing, but turns everything to account. Every Englishwoman, whether gentle or simple, ought to be accomplished in an art which confers so much comfort, health, and wealth upon the members of her household.

"It appears to me," said Mrs. Margaretta Grey, "that with an increase of wealth unequally distributed, and a pressure of population, there has sprung up amongst us a spurious refinement, that cramps the energy and circumscribes the usefulness of women in the upper class of society. A lady, to be such, must be a lady, and nothing else. . . . Ladies dismissed from the dairy, the confectionery, the store-room, the still-room, the poultry-yard, the kitchen-garden, and the orchard" [she might have added, the spinning-wheel], "have hardly yet found for themselves a sphere equally useful and important in the pursuits of trade and art, to which to apply their too abundant leisure.

"When, at any time, has society presented, on the one hand, so large an array of respectably educated individuals, embarrassed for want of a proper calling, and, on the other, so ponderous a multitude of untrained, neglected poor, who cannot, without help, rise out of their misery and degradation? What an obstruction to usefulness and all eminence of

---

2. Examiner.

character is that of being too rich, or too genteelly connected, to work at anything!"[3]

Many intelligent, high-minded ladies, who have felt disgusted at the idleness to which "society" condemns them, have of late years undertaken the work of visiting the poor and of nursing—a noble work. But there is another school of usefulness which stands open to them. Let them study the art of common cookery, and diffuse the knowledge of it amongst the people. They will thus do an immense amount of good; and bring down the blessings of many a half-hungered husband upon their benevolent heads. Women of the poorer classes require much help from those who are better educated, or who have been placed in better circumstances than themselves. The greater number of them marry young, and suddenly enter upon a life for which they have not received the slightest preparation. They know nothing of cookery, of sewing or clothes mending, or of economical ways of spending their husbands' money. Hence slatternly and untidy habits, and uncomfortable homes, from which the husband is often glad to seek refuge in the nearest public-house. The following story, told by Joseph Corbett, a Birmingham operative, before a Parliamentary Committee, holds true of many working people in the manufacturing districts.

"My mother," he said, "worked in a manufactory from a very early age. She was clever and industrious, and, moreover, she had the reputation of being virtuous. She was regarded as an excellent match for a working man. She was married early. She became the mother of eleven children: I am the eldest. To the best of her ability she performed the important duties of a wife and mother. But she was lamentably deficient in domestic knowledge. In that most important of all human instruction—how to make the home and the fireside to possess a charm for her husband and children—she had never received one single lesson. She had children apace. As she recovered from her lying-in, so she went to work, the babe being brought to her at stated times to receive nourishment. As the family increased, so everything like comfort disappeared altogether. The power to make home cheerful and comfortable was never given to her. She knew not the value of cherishing in my father's mind a love of domestic objects. Not one moment's happiness did I ever see under my father's roof. All this dismal state of things I can distinctly trace to the entire and perfect absence of all training and instruction to my mother.

---

3. Memoir of John Grey, of Dalston. p. 290.

He became intemperate; and his intemperance made her necessitous. She made many efforts to abstain from shop-work; but her pecuniary necessities forced her back into the shop. The family was large; and every moment was required at home. I have known her, after the close of a hard day's work, sit up nearly all night for several nights together washing and mending clothes. My father could have no comfort there. These domestic obligations, which in a well-regulated house (even in that of a working man, where there are prudence and good management) would be done so as not to annoy the husband, were to my father a sort of annoyance; and he, from an ignorant and mistaken notion, sought comfort in an alehouse. My mother's ignorance of household duties; my father's consequent irritability and intemperance; the frightful poverty; the constant quarrelling; the pernicious example to my brothers and sisters; the bad effect upon the future conduct of my brothers,—one and all of us being forced out to work so young that our feeble earnings would produce only 1s. a week,—cold and hunger, and the innumerable sufferings of my childhood, crowd upon my mind and overpower me. They keep alive a deep anxiety for the emancipation of thousands of families in this great town (Birmingham) and neighbourhood, who are in a similar state of horrible misery. My own experience tells me that the instruction of the females in the work of a house, in teaching them to produce cheerfulness and comfort at the fireside, would prevent a great amount of misery and crime. There would be fewer drunken husbands and disobedient children. As a working man, within my own observation, female education is disgracefully neglected. I attach more importance to it than to anything else; for woman imparts the first impressions to the young susceptible mind; she models the child from which is formed the future man."

Chapter 16

The Art of Living

"Deem no man, in any age, gentle for his lineage. Though he be not highly born, he is gentle if he doth what 'longeth to a gentleman."—Chaucer.

"Every one is the son of his own work."—Cervantes.

"Serve a noble disposition, though poor; the time comes that he will repay thee."—George Herbert.

"Although men are accused for not knowing their own weakness, yet perhaps as few know their own strength. It is in men as in soils, where sometimes there is a vein of gold, which the owner knows not of."—Swift.

"Let not what I cannot have my cheer of mind destroy."—Cibber.

The Art of Living deserves a place among the Fine Arts. Like Literature, it may be ranked with the Humanities. It is the art of turning the means of living to the best account,—of making the best of everything. It is the art of extracting from life its highest enjoyment, and, through it, of reaching its highest results.

To live happily, the exercise of no small degree of art is required. Like poetry and painting, the art of living comes chiefly by nature; but all can cultivate and develop it. It can be fostered by parents and teachers, and perfected by self-culture. Without intelligence, it cannot exist.

Happiness is not, like a large and beautiful gem, so uncommon and rare, that all search for it is vain, all efforts to obtain it hopeless; but it consists of a series of smaller and commoner gems, grouped and set together, forming a pleasing and graceful whole. Happiness consists in the enjoyment of little pleasures scattered along the common path of life, which, in the eager search for some great and exciting joy, we are apt to overlook. It finds delight in the performance of common duties, faithfully and honourably fulfilled.

The art of living is abundantly exemplified in actual life. Take two men of equal means,—one of whom knows the art of living, and the other not. The one has the seeing-eye and the intelligent mind. Nature is ever new to him, and full of beauty. He can live in the present, rehearse the past, or anticipate the glory of the future. With him, life has a deep meaning, and requires the performance of duties which are satisfactory to his conscience, and are therefore pleasurable. He improves himself, acts upon his age, helps to elevate the depressed classes, and is active in every good work. His hand is never tired, his mind is never weary. He goes through life joyfully, helping others to its enjoyment. Intelligence, ever expanding, gives him every day fresh insight into men and things. He lays down his life full of honour and blessing, and his greatest monument is the good deeds he has done, and the beneficent example he has set before his fellow-creatures.

The other has comparatively little pleasure in life. He has scarcely reached manhood, ere he has exhausted its enjoyments. Money has done everything that it could for him. Yet he feels life to be vacant and cheerless. Travelling does him no good; for, for him history has no meaning. He is only alive to the impositions of innkeepers and couriers, and the disagreeableness of travelling for days amidst great mountains, among peasants and sheep, cramped up in a carriage. Picture galleries he feels to be a bore, and he looks into them because other people do. These "pleasures" soon tire him, and he becomes blasé. When he grows old, and has run the round of fashionable dissipations, and there is nothing left which he can relish, life becomes a masquerade, in which he recognizes only knaves, hypocrites, and flatterers. Though he does not enjoy life, yet he is terrified to leave it. Then the curtain falls. With all his wealth, life has been to him a failure, for he has not known the Art of Living, without which life cannot be enjoyed.

It is not wealth that gives the true zest to life,—but reflection, appreciation, taste, culture. Above all, the seeing eye and the feeling heart are indispensable. With these, the humblest lot may be made blest. Labour and toil may be associated with the highest thoughts and the purest tastes. The lot of labour may thus become elevated and ennobled. Montaigne observes that "all moral philosophy is as applicable to a vulgar and private life as to the most splendid. Every man carries the entire form of the human condition within him."

Even in material comfort, good taste is a real economist, as well as an enhancer of joy. Scarcely have you passed the doorstep of your friend's house, when you can detect whether taste presides within it or not. There is an air of neatness, order, arrangement, grace, and refinement, that gives a thrill of pleasure, though you cannot define it, or explain how it is. There is a flower in the window, or a picture against the wall, that marks the home of taste. A bird sings at the window-sill; books lie about; and the furniture, though common, is tidy, suitable, and, it may be, even elegant.

The art of living extends to all the economies of the household. It selects wholesome food, and serves it with taste. There is no profusion; the fare may be very humble, but it has a savour about it; everything is so clean and neat, the water so sparkles in the glass, that you do not desire richer viands, or a more exciting beverage. Look into another house, and you will see profusion enough, without either taste or order. The expenditure is larger, and yet you do not feel "at home" there. The atmosphere seems to be full of discomfort. Books, hats, shawls, and stockings in course of repair, are strewn about. Two or three chairs are loaded with goods. The rooms are hugger-mugger. No matter how much money is spent, it does not mend matters. Taste is wanting, for the manager of the household has not yet learnt the Art of Living.

You see the same contrast in cottage life. The lot of poverty is sweetened by taste. It selects the healthiest, openest neighbourhood, where the air is pure and the streets are clean. You see, at a glance, by the sanded doorstep, and the window-panes without a speck,—perhaps blooming roses or geraniums shining through them,—that the tenant within, however poor, knows the art of making the best of his lot. How different from the foul cottage-dwellings you see elsewhere; with the dirty children playing in the gutters; the slattern-like women lounging by the door-cheek; and the air of sullen poverty that seems to pervade the place. And yet the weekly income in the former home may be no greater, perhaps even less, than in that of the other.

How is it, that of two men, working in the same field or in the same shop, one is merry as a lark,—always cheerful, well-clad, and as clean as his work will allow him to be,—comes out on Sunday mornings in his best suit, to go to church with his family,—is never without a penny in his purse, and has something besides in the savings bank,—is a reader of books and a subscriber to a newspaper, besides taking in some literary journal for family reading; whilst the other man, with equal or even superior weekly wages, comes to work in the mornings sour and sad,—is always full of grumbling,—is badly clad and badly shod,—is never seen out of his house on Sundays till about midday, when he appears in his shirt-sleeves, his face unwashed, his hair unkempt, his eyes bleared and bloodshot,—his children left to run about the gutters, with no one apparently to care for them,—is always at his last coin, except on Saturday night, and then he has a long score of borrowings to repay,—belongs to no club, has nothing saved, but lives literally from hand to mouth,—reads none, thinks none, but only toils, eats, drinks, and sleeps;—why is it that there is so remarkable a difference between these two men?

Simply for this reason,—that the one has the intelligence and the art to extract joy and happiness from life,—to be happy himself, and to make those about him happy; whereas the other has not cultivated his intelligence, and knows nothing whatever of the art of either making himself or his family happy. With the one, life is a scene of loving, helping, and sympathizing,—of carefulness, forethought, and calculation—of reflection, action, and duty;—with the other, it is only a rough scramble for meat and drink; duty is not thought of, reflection is banished, prudent forethought is never for a moment entertained.

But look to the result; the former is respected by his fellow-workmen and beloved by his family,—he is an example of well-being and well-doing to all who are within reach of his influence; whereas the other is as unreflective and miserable, as nature will allow him to be,—he is shunned by good men,—his family are afraid at the sound of his footsteps, his wife perhaps trembling at his approach,—he dies without leaving any regrets behind him, except, it may be, on the part of his family, who are left to be maintained by the charity of the public, or by the pittance doled out by the overseers.

For these reasons, it is worth every man's while to study the important Art of living happily. Even the poorest man may by this means extract an increased amount of joy and blessing from life. The world need not be "a vale of tears," unless we ourselves will it to be so. We have the command, to a great extent, over our own lot. At all events, our mind is our own possession; we can cherish happy thoughts there; we can regulate and control our tempers and dispositions to a considerable extent; we can educate ourselves, and bring out the better part of our nature, which in most men is allowed to sleep a deep sleep; we can read good books, cherish pure thoughts, and lead lives of peace, temperance, and virtue, so as to secure the respect of good men, and transmit the blessing of a faithful example to our successors.

The Art of Living is best exhibited in the Home. The first condition of a happy home, where good influences prevail over bad ones, is Comfort. Where there are carking cares, querulousness, untidiness, slovenliness, and dirt, there can be little comfort either for man or woman. The husband who has been working all day, expects to have something as a compensation for his toil. The least that his wife can do for him, is to make his house snug, clean, and tidy, against his home-coming at eve. That is the truest economy—the best housekeeping—the worthiest domestic management—which makes the home so pleasant and agreeable, that a man feels when approaching it, that he is about to enter a sanctuary; and that, when there, there is no alehouse attraction that can draw him away from it.

Some say that we worship Comfort too much. The word is essentially English, and is said to be untranslateable, in its full meaning, into any foreign language. It is intimately connected with the Fireside. In warmer climes, people contrive to live out of doors. They sun themselves in the streets. Half their life is in public. The genial air woos them forth, and keeps them abroad. They enter their houses merely to eat and sleep. They can scarcely be said to live there.

How different is it with us! The raw air without, during so many months of the year, drives us within doors. Hence we cultivate all manner of home pleasures. Hence the host of delightful associations which rise up in the mind at the mention of the word Home. Hence our household god, Comfort.

We are not satisfied merely with a home. It must be comfortable. The most wretched, indeed, are those who have no homes—the homeless! But not less wretched are those whose homes are without comfort—those of whom Charles Lamb once said, "The homes of the very poor are no homes." It is Comfort, then, that is the soul of the home—its essential principle—its vital element.

Comfort does not mean merely warmth, good furniture, good eating and drinking. It means something higher than this. It means cleanliness, pure air, order, frugality,—in a word, house-thrift and domestic government. Comfort is the soil in which the human being grows,—not only physically, but morally. Comfort lies, indeed, at the root of many virtues.

Wealth is not necessary for comfort. Luxury requires wealth, but not comfort. A poor man's home, moderately supplied with the necessaries of life, presided over by a cleanly, frugal housewife, may contain all the elements of comfortable living. Comfortlessness is for the most part caused, not so much by the absence of sufficient means, as by the absence of the requisite knowledge of domestic management.

Comfort, it must be admitted, is in a great measure relative. What is comfort to one man, would be misery to another. Even the commonest mechanic of this day would consider it miserable to live after the style of the nobles a few centuries ago; to sleep on straw beds, and live in rooms littered with rushes. William the Conqueror had neither a shirt to his back, nor a pane of glass to his windows. Queen Elizabeth was one of the first to wear silk stockings. The Queens before her were stockingless.

Comfort depends as much on persons as on "things." It is out of the character and temper of those who govern homes, that the feeling of comfort arises, much more than out of handsome furniture, heated rooms, or household luxuries and conveniences.

Comfortable people are kindly-tempered. Good temper may be set down as an invariable condition of comfort. There must be peace, mutual forbearance, mutual help, and a disposition to make the best of everything. "Better is a dinner of herbs where love is, than a stalled ox and hatred therewith."

Comfortable people are persons of common sense, discretion, prudence, and economy. They have a natural affinity for honesty and justice, goodness and truth. They do not run into debt,—for that is a species of dishonesty. They live within their means, and lay by something for a rainy day. They provide for the things of their own household,—yet they are not wanting in hospitality and benevolence on fitting occasions. And what they do, is done without ostentation.

Comfortable people do everything in order. They are systematic, steady, sober, industrious. They dress comfortably. They adapt themselves to the season,—neither shivering in winter, nor perspiring in summer. They do not toil after a "fashionable appearance." They expend more on warm stockings than on gold rings; and prefer healthy, good bedding, to gaudy window-curtains. Their chairs are solid, not gimcrack. They will bear sitting upon, though they may not be ornamental.

The organization of the home depends for the most part upon woman. She is necessarily the manager of every family and household. How much, therefore, must depend upon her intelligent co-operation! Man's life revolves round woman. She is the sun of his social system. She is the queen of domestic life. The comfort of every home mainly depends upon her,—upon her character, her temper, her power of organization, and her business management. A man may be economical; but unless there be economy at home, his frugality will be comparatively useless. "A man cannot thrive," the proverb says, "unless his wife let him."

House-thrift is homely, but beneficent. Though unseen of the world, it makes many people happy. It works upon individuals; and by elevating them, it elevates society itself. It is in fact a receipt of infallible efficacy, for conferring the greatest possible happiness upon the greatest possible number. Without it legislation, benevolence, and philanthropy are mere palliatives, sometimes worse than useless, because they hold out hopes which are for the most part disappointed.

How happy does a man go forth to his labour or his business, and how doubly happy does he return from it, when he knows that his means are carefully husbanded and wisely applied by a judicious and well-managing wife. Such a woman is not only a power in her own house, but her example goes forth amongst her neighbours, and she stands before them as a model and a pattern. The habits of her children are formed after her habits: her actual life becomes the model after which they unconsciously mould themselves; for example always speaks more eloquently than words: it is instruction in action—wisdom at work.

First amongst woman's qualities is the intelligent use of her hands and fingers. Every one knows how useful, how indispensable to the comfort of a household, is the tidy, managing, handy woman. Pestalozzi, with his usual sagacity, has observed, that half the education of a woman comes through her fingers. There are wisdom and virtue at her finger-ends. But intellect must also accompany thrift: they must go hand in hand. A woman must not only be clever with her fingers, but possessed of the power of organizing household work.

There must be Method. The late Sir Arthur Helps observed, that "as women are at present educated, they are for the most part thoroughly deficient in method. But this surely might be remedied by training. To take a very humble and simple instance. Why is it that a man-cook is always better than a woman-cook? Simply because a man is more methodical in his arrangements, and relies more upon his weights and measures. An eminent physician told me that he thought women were absolutely deficient in the appreciation of time. But this I hold to be merely one instance of their general want of accuracy, for which there are easy remedies: that is, easy if begun early enough."

Accordingly, to manage a household efficiently, there must be Method. Without this, work cannot be got through satisfactorily either in offices, workshops, or households. By arranging work properly, by doing everything at the right time, with a view to the economy of labour, a large amount of business can be accomplished. Muddle flies before method; and hugger-mugger disappears. There is also a method in spending—in laying out money,—which is as valuable to the housewife, as method is in accomplishing her work. Money slips through the fingers of some people like quicksilver. We have already seen that many men are spendthrifts. But many women are the same. At least they do not know how to expend their husband's earnings to the best advantage. You observe things very much out of place—frills and ruffles and ill-darned stockings—fine bonnets and clouted shoes—silk gowns and dirty petticoats; while the husband goes about ragged and torn, with scarcely a clean thing about him.

Industry is of course essential. This is the soul of business; but, without method, industry will be less productive. Industry may sometimes look like confusion. But the methodical and industrious woman gets through her work in a quiet, steady style,—without fuss, or noise, or dust-clouds.

Prudence is another important household qualification. Prudence comes from cultivated judgment: it means practical wisdom. It has reference to fitness, to propriety; it judges of the right thing to be done, and of the right way of doing it. It calculates the means, order, time, and method of doing. Prudence learns much from experience, quickened by knowledge.

Punctuality is another eminently household qualification. How many grumblings would be avoided in domestic life, by a little more attention being paid to this virtue. Late breakfasts and late dinners,—"too late" for church and market,—"cleanings" out of time, and "washings" protracted till midnight,—bills put off with a "call again tomorrow,"—engagements and promises unfulfilled,—what a host of little nuisances spring to mind, at thought of the unpunctual housewife! The unpunctual woman, like the unpunctual man, becomes disliked, because she consumes our time, interferes with our plans, causes uneasy feelings, and virtually tells us that we are not of sufficient importance to cause her to be more punctual. To the business man, time is money, and to the business woman it is more,—it is peace, comfort, and domestic prosperity.

Perseverance is another good household habit. Lay down a good plan, and adhere to it. Do not be turned from it without a sufficient reason. Follow it diligently and faithfully, and it will yield fruits in good season. If the plan be a prudent one, based on practical wisdom, a ll things will gravitate towards it, and a mutual dependence will gradually be established among all the parts of the domestic system.

We might furnish numerous practical illustrations of the truth of these remarks, but our space is nearly filled up, and we must leave the reader to supply them from his or her own experience.

There are many other illustrations which might be adduced, of the art of making life happy. The management of the temper is an art full of beneficent results. By kindness, cheerfulness, and forbearance, we can be happy almost at will; and at the same time spread happiness about us on every side. We can encourage happy thoughts in ourselves and others. We can be sober in habit. What can a wife and her children think of an intemperate husband and father? We can be sober in language, and shun cursing and swearing—the most useless, unmeaning, and brutal of vulgarities. Nothing can be so silly and unmeaning—not to say shocking, repulsive, and sinful—as the oaths so common in the mouths of vulgar swearers. They are profanation without purpose—impiety without provocation—blasphemy without excuse.

This leads us to remark, in passing, that in this country we are not sufficiently instructed in the Art of Good Manners. We are rather gruff, and sometimes unapproachable. Manners do not make the man, as the proverb alleges; but manners make the man much more agreeable. A man may be noble in his heart, true in his dealings, virtuous in his conduct, and yet unmannerly. Suavity of disposition and gentleness of manners give the finish to the true gentleman.

By Good Manners we do not mean Etiquette. This is only a conventional set of rules adopted by what is called "good society;" and many of the rules of etiquette are of the essence of rudeness. Etiquette does not permit genteel people to recognize in the streets a man with a shabby coat though he be their brother. Etiquette is a liar in its "not at home,"—ordered to be told by servants to callers at inconvenient seasons.

Good manners include many requisites; but they chiefly consist in politeness, courtesy, and kindness. They cannot be taught by rule, but they may be taught by example. It has been said that politeness is the art of showing men, by external signs, the internal regard we have for them. But a man may be perfectly polite to another, without necessarily having any regard for him. Good manners are neither more nor less than beautiful behaviour. It has been well said that "a beautiful form is better than a beautiful face, and a beautiful behaviour is better than a beautiful form; it gives a higher pleasure than statues or pictures; it is the finest of the fine arts."

Manner is the ornament of action; indeed a good action, without a good manner of doing it, is stripped of half its value. A poor fellow gets into difficulties, and solicits help of a friend. He obtains it, but it is with a "There-take that; but I don't like lending." The help is given with a kind of kick, and is scarcely accepted as a favour. The manner of the giving long rankles in the mind of the acceptor. Thus good manners mean kind manners,—benevolence being the preponderating element in all kinds of pleasant intercourse between human beings.

A story is told of a poor soldier having one day called at the shop of a hairdresser, who was busy with his customers, and asked relief,—stating that he had stayed beyond his leave of absence, and unless he could get a lift on the coach, fatigue and severe punishment awaited him. The hairdresser listened to his story respectfully, and gave him a guinea. "God bless you, sir!" exclaimed the soldier, astonished at the amount. "How can I repay you? I have nothing in the world but this"—pulling out a dirty piece of paper from his pocket; "it is a receipt for making blacking; it is the best that was ever seen; many a half-guinea I have had for it from the officers, and many bottles I have sold; may you be able to get something for it to repay you for your kindness to the poor soldier." Oddly enough, that dirty piece of paper proved worth half a million of money to the hairdresser. It was no less than the receipt for the famous Day and Martin's blacking; the hairdresser being the late wealthy Mr. Day, whose manufactory is one of the notabilities of the metropolis.

Good manners have been supposed to be a peculiar mark of gentility, and that the individual exhibiting them has been born in some upper class of society. But the poorest classes may exhibit good manners towards each other, as well as the richest. One may be polite and kind towards others, without a penny in the purse. Politeness goes very far; yet it costs nothing. It is the cheapest of commodities. But we want to be taught good manners, as well as other things. Some happy natures are "to the manner born." But the bulk of men need to be taught manners, and this can only be efficiently done in youth.

We have said that working men might study good manners with advantage. Why should they not respect themselves and each other? It is by their demeanour towards each other—in other words, by their manners—that self-respect and mutual respect are indicated. We have been struck by the habitual politeness of even the poorest classes on the Continent. The workman lifts his cap and respectfully salutes his fellow-workman in passing. There is no sacrifice of manliness in this, but rather grace and dignity. The working man, in respecting his fellow, respects himself and his order. There is kindness in the act of recognition, as well as in the manner in which it is denoted.

We might learn much from the French people in this matter. They are not only polite to each other, but they have a greater respect for property. Some may be disposed to doubt this, after the recent destruction of buildings in Paris. But the Communists must be regarded as altogether exceptional people; and to understand the French character, we must look to the body of the population scattered throughout France. There we find property much more respected by the people than amongst ourselves. Even the beggar respects the fruit by the roadside, although there is nobody to protect it. The reason of this is, that France is a nation of small proprietors,—that property is much more generally diffused and exposed,—and parents of even the lowest class educate their children in carefulness of and fidelity to the property of others.

This respect for property is also accompanied with that respect for the feelings of others, which constitutes what is called Good Manners. This is carefully inculcated in the children of all ranks in France. They are very rarely rude. They are civil to strangers. They are civil to each other. Mr. Laing, in his "Notes of a Traveller," makes these remarks: "This deference to the feelings of others in all that we do is a moral habit of great value when it is generally diffused, and enters into the home training of every family. It is an education both of the parent and child in morals, carried on through the medium of external manners. . . . It is a fine distinction of the French national character, and of social economy, that practical morality is more generally taught through manners, among and by the people themselves, than in any country in Europe."[1]

The same kindly feeling might be observed throughout the entire social intercourse of working men with each other. There is not a moment in their lives in which the opportunity does not occur for exhibiting good manners—in the workshop, in the street, and at home. Provided there be a wish to please others by kind looks and ways, the habit of combining good manners with every action will soon be formed. It is not merely the pleasure a man gives to others by being kind to them: he receives tenfold more pleasure himself. The man who gets up and offers his chair to a woman, or to an old man—trivial though the act may seem,—is

---

1. Samuel Laing—Notes of Traveller, on the Social and Political State of France, Prussia, Switzerland, Italy, and other Parts of Europe, p. 55.

rewarded by his own heart, and a thrill of pleasure runs through him the moment he has performed the kindness.

Workpeople need to practise good manners towards each other the more, because they are under the necessity of constantly living with each other and amongst each other. They are in constant contact with their fellow-workmen, whereas the richer classes need not mix with men unless they choose, and then they can select whom they like. The working man's happiness depends much more upon the kind looks, words, and acts of those immediately about him, than the rich man's does. It is so in the workshop, and it is the same at home. There the workman cannot retire into his study, but must sit amongst his family, by the side of his wife, with his children about him. And he must either live kindly with them—performing kind and obliging acts towards his family,—or he must see, suffer, and endure the intolerable misery of reciprocal unkindness.

Admitted that there are difficulties in the way of working men cultivating the art of good manners—that their circumstances are often very limited, and their position unfavourable, yet no man is so poor but that he can be civil and kind, if he choose; and to be civil and kind is the very essence of good manners. Even in the most adverse circumstances a man may try to do his best. If he do—if he speak and act courteously and kindly to all,—the result will be so satisfactory, so self-rewarding, that he cannot but be stimulated to persevere in the same course. He will diffuse pleasure about him in the home, make friends of his work-fellows, and be regarded with increased kindness and respect by every right-minded employer. The civil workman will exercise increased power amongst his class, and gradually induce them to imitate him by his persistent steadiness, civility, and kindness. Thus Benjamin Franklin, when a workman, reformed the habits of an entire workshop.

Then, besides the general pleasure arising from the exercise of Good Manners, there is a great deal of healthful and innocent pleasure to be derived from amusements of various kinds. One cannot be always working, eating, and sleeping. There must be time for relaxation—time for mental pleasures—time for bodily exercise.

There is a profound meaning in the word Amusement; much more than most people are disposed to admit. In fact, amusement is an important part of education. It is a mistake to suppose that the boy or the man who plays at some outdoor game is wasting his time. Amusement of any kind is not wasting time, but economizing life.

Relax and exercise frequently, if you would enjoy good health. If you do not relax, and take no exercise, the results will soon appear in bodily ailments, which always accompany sedentary occupations. "The students," says Lord Derby, "who think they have not time for bodily exercise, will sooner or later find time for illness."

There are people in the world who would, if they had the power, hang the heavens about with crape; throw a shroud over the beautiful and life-giving bosom of the planet; pick the bright stars from the sky; veil the sun with clouds; pluck the silver moon from her place in the firmament; shut up our gardens and fields, and all the flowers with which they are bedecked; and doom the world to an atmosphere of gloom and cheerlessness. There is no reason nor morality in this, and there is still less religion.

A benevolent Creator has endowed man with an eminent capacity for enjoyment,—has set him in a fair and lovely world, surrounded him with things good and beautiful,—and given him the disposition to love, to sympathize, to help, to produce, to enjoy; and thus to become an honourable and a happy being, bringing God's work to perfection, and enjoying the divine creation in the midst of which he lives.

Make a man happy, and his actions will be happy too; doom him to dismal thoughts and miserable circumstances, and you will make him gloomy, discontented, morose, and probably vicious. Hence coarseness and crime are almost invariably found amongst those who have never been accustomed to be cheerful, whose hearts have been shut against the purifying influences of a happy communion with nature, or an enlightened and cheerful intercourse with man.

Man has a strong natural appetite for relaxation and amusement, and, like all other natural appetites, it has been implanted for a wise purpose. It cannot be repressed, but will break out in one form or another. Any well-directed attempt to promote an innocent amusement, is worth a dozen sermons against pernicious ones. If we do not provide the opportunity for enjoying wholesome pleasures, men will certainly find out vicious ones for themselves. Sydney Smith truly said, "In order to attack vice with effect, we must set up something better in its place."

Temperance reformers have not sufficiently considered how much the drinking habits of the country are the consequences of gross tastes, and of the too limited opportunities which exist in this country for obtaining access to amusements of an innocent and improving tendency. The workman's tastes have been allowed to remain uncultivated; present wants engross his thoughts; the gratification of his appetites is his highest pleasure; and when he relaxes, it is to indulge immoderately in beer or whisky. The Germans were at one time the drunkenest of nations; they are now amongst the soberest. "As drunken as a German boor," was a common proverb. How have they been weaned from drink? Principally by Education and Music.

Music has a most humanizing effect. The cultivation of the art has a most favourable influence upon public morals. It furnishes a source of pleasure in every family. It gives home a new attraction. It makes social intercourse more cheerful. Father Mathew followed up his Temperance movement by a Singing movement. He promoted the establishment of musical clubs all over Ireland: for he felt that, as he had taken the people's whisky from them, he must give them some wholesome stimulus in its stead. He gave them Music. Singing classes were established, to refine the taste, soften the manners, and humanize the mass of the Irish people. But we fear that the example set by Father Mathew has already been forgotten.

"What a fulness of enjoyment," says Channing, "has our Creator placed within our reach, by surrounding us with an atmosphere which may be shaped into sweet sounds! And yet this goodness is almost lost upon us, through want of culture of the organ by which this provision is to be enjoyed."

How much would the general cultivation of the gift of music improve us as a people! Children ought to learn it in schools, as they do in Germany. The voice of music would then be heard in every household. Our old English glees would no longer be forgotten. Men and women might sing in the intervals of their work,—as the Germans do in going to and coming from their wars. The work would not be worse done, because it was done amidst music and cheerfulness. The breath of society would be sweetened, and pleasure would be linked with labour.

Why not have some elegance in even the humblest home? We must of course have cleanliness, which is the special elegance of the poor. But why not have pleasant and delightful things to look upon? There is no reason why the humbler classes should not surround themselves with the evidences of beauty and comfort in all their shapes, and thus do homage alike to the gifts of God and the labours of man. The taste for the beautiful is one of the best and most useful endowments. It is one of the handmaids of civilization. Beauty and elegance do not necessarily belong to the homes of the rich. They are, or ought to be, all-pervading. Beauty in all things,—in nature, in art, in science, in literature, in social and domestic life.

How beautiful and yet how cheap are flowers. Not exotics,—but what are called common flowers. A rose, for instance, is among the most beautiful of the smiles of nature. The "laughing flowers," exclaims the poet! But there is more than gaiety in blooming flowers, though it takes a wise man to see the beauty, the love, and the adaptation, of which they are full.

What should we think of one who had invented flowers; supposing that, before him, flowers were unknown? Would he not be regarded as the opener-up of a paradise of new delight? should we not hail the inventor as a genius, as a god? And yet these lovely offsprings of the earth have been speaking to man from the first dawn of his existence until now, telling him of the goodness and wisdom of the Creative Power, which bade the earth bring forth, not only that which was useful as food,—but also flowers, the bright consummate flowers, to clothe it in beauty and joy!

Bring one of the commonest field-flowers into a room, place it on a table or chimneypiece, and you seem to have brought a ray of sunshine into the place. There is a cheerfulness about flowers. What a delight are they to the drooping invalid! They are like a sweet draught of enjoyment, coming as messengers from the country, and seeming to say, "Come and see the place where we grow, and let your heart be glad in our presence."

What can be more innocent than flowers! They are like children undimmed by sin. They are emblems of purity and truth, a source of fresh delight to the pure and innocent. The heart that does not love flowers, or the voice of a playful child, cannot be genial. It was a beautiful conceit that invented a language of flowers, by which lovers were enabled to express the feelings that they dared not openly speak. But flowers have a voice for all,—old and young, rich and poor. "To me," says Wordsworth,

"The meanest flower that blows can give Thoughts that do often lie too deep for tears."

Have a flower in the room, by all means! It will cost only a penny, if your ambition is moderate; and the gratification it gives will be beyond price. If you can have a flower for your window so much the better. What can be more delicious than the sun's light streaming through flowers— through the midst of crimson fuchsias or scarlet geraniums? To look out into the light through flowers—is not that poetry? And to break the force of the sunbeams by the tender resistance of green leaves? If you can train a nasturtium round the window, or some sweet peas, then you will have the most beautiful frame you can invent for the picture without, whether it be the busy crowd, or a distant landscape, or trees with their lights and shades, or the changes of the passing clouds. Any one may thus look through flowers for the price of an old song. And what pure taste and refinement does it not indicate on the part of the cultivator! A flower in the window sweetens the air, makes the room look graceful, gives the sun's light a new charm, rejoices the eye, and links nature with beauty. The flower is a companion that will never say a cross thing to any one, but will always look beautiful and smiling. Do not despise it because it is cheap, and because everybody may have the luxury as well as yourself. Common things are cheap, but common things are invariably the most valuable. Could we only have fresh air or sunshine by purchase, what luxuries they would be considered; but they are free to all, and we think little of their blessings.

There is, indeed, much in nature that we do not yet half enjoy, because we shut our avenues of sensation and feeling. We are satisfied with the matter of fact, and look not for the spirit of fact, which is above it. If we opened our minds to enjoyment, we might find tranquil pleasures spread about us on every side. We might live with the angels that visit us on every sunbeam, and sit with the fairies who wait on every flower. We want more loving knowledge to enable us to enjoy life, and we require to cultivate the art of making the most of the common means and appliances for enjoyment, which lie about us on every side.

A snug and a clean home, no matter how tiny it be, so that it be wholesome; windows into which the sun can shine cheerily; a few good books (and who need be without a few good books in these days of universal cheapness?)—no duns at the door, and the cupboard well supplied, and with a flower in your room! There is none so poor as not to have about him these elements of pleasure.

But why not, besides the beauty of Nature, have a taste for the beauty of Art? Why not hang up a picture in the room? Ingenious methods have been discovered—some of them quite recently—for almost infinitely multiplying works of art, by means of wood engravings, lithographs, photographs, and autotypes, which render it possible for every person to furnish his rooms with beautiful pictures. Skill and science have thus brought Art within reach of the poorest.

Any picture, print, or engraving, that represents a noble thought, that depicts a heroic act, or that brings a bit of nature from the fields or the streets into our room, is a teacher, a means of education, and a help to self-culture. It serves to make the home more pleasant and attractive. It sweetens domestic life, and sheds a grace and beauty about it. It draws the gazer away from mere considerations of self, and increases his store of delightful associations with the world without, as well as with the world within.

The portrait of a great man, for instance, helps us to read his life. It invests him with a personal interest. Looking at his features, we feel as if we knew him better, and were more closely related to him. Such a portrait, hung up before us daily, at our meals and during our leisure hours, unconsciously serves to lift us up and sustain us. It is a link that in some way binds us to a higher and nobler nature.

It is said of a Catholic money-lender that when about to cheat, he was wont to draw a veil over the face of his favourite saint. Thus the portraiture of a great and virtuous man is in some measure a companionship of something better than ourselves; and though we may not reach the standard of the hero, we may to a certain extent be influenced by his likeness on our walls.

It is not necessary that a picture should be high-priced in order to be beautiful and good. We have seen things for which hundreds of guineas have been paid, that have not one-hundredth part of the meaning or beauty that is to be found in Linton's woodcut of Rafaelle's Madonna, which may be had for twopence. The head reminds one of the observation made by Hazlitt upon a picture, that it seems as if an unhandsome act would be impossible in its presence. It embodies the ideas of mother's love, womanly beauty, and earnest piety. As some one said of the picture: "It looks as if a bit of Heaven were in the room."

Picture-fanciers pay not so much for the merit, as for the age and the rarity of their works. The poorest may have the seeing eye for beauty, while the rich man may be blind to it. The cheapest engraving may communicate the sense of beauty to the artizan, while the thousand-guinea picture may fail to communicate to the millionaire anything,— excepting perhaps the notion that he has got possession of a work which the means of other people cannot compass.

Does the picture give you pleasure on looking at it? That is one good test of its worth. You may grow tired of it; your taste may outgrow it, and demand something better, just as the reader may grow out of Montgomery's poetry into Milton's. Then you will take down the daub, and put up a picture with a higher idea in its place. There may thus be a steady progress of art made upon the room walls. If the pictures can be put in frames, so much the better; but if they cannot, no matter; up with them! We know that Owen Jones says it is not good taste to hang prints upon walls—he would merely hang room papers there. But Owen Jones may not be infallible; and here we think he is wrong. To our eyes, a room always looks unfurnished, no matter how costly and numerous the tables, chairs, and ottomans, unless there be pictures upon the walls.

It ought to be, and no doubt it is, a great stimulus to artists to know that their works are now distributed in prints and engravings, to decorate and beautify the homes of the people. The wood-cutter, the lithographer, and the engraver, are the popular interpreters of the great artist. Thus Turner's pictures are not confined to the wealthy possessors of the original works, but may be diffused through all homes by the Millars, and Brandards, and Wilmotts, who have engraved them. Thus Landseer finds entrance, through woodcuts and mezzotints, into every dwelling. Thus Cruikshank preaches temperance, and Ary Scheffer purity and piety. The engraver is the medium by which art in the palace is conveyed into the humblest homes in the kingdom.

The Art of Living may be displayed in many ways. It may be summed up in the words,—Make the best of everything. Nothing is beneath its care; even common and little things it turns to account. It gives a brightness and grace to the home, and invests Nature with new charms. Through it, we enjoy the rich man's parks and woods, as if they were our own. We inhale the common air, and bask under the universal sunshine. We glory in the grass, the passing clouds, and the flowers. We love the common earth, and hear joyful voices through all Nature. It extends to every kind of social intercourse. It engenders cheerful goodwill and loving sincerity. By its help we make others happy, and ourselves blest. We elevate our being and ennoble our lot. We rise above the grovelling creatures of earth, and aspire to the Infinite. And thus we link time to eternity; where the true Art of Living has its final consummation.

www.ingramcontent.com/pod-product-compliance
Lightning Source LLC
Chambersburg PA
CBHW032102090426
42743CB00007B/209